Evolving Towards Rule of Law in China: Changes Over the Past 10 Years

Yun Changzhi

Published by
ACA Publishing Ltd.
University House
11-13 Lower Grosvenor Place,
London SW1W 0EX, UK
Tel: +44 (0)20 7834 7676
Fax: +44 (0)20 7973 0076
E-mail: info@alaincharlesasia.com
Web:www.alaincharlesasia.com
Beijing Office
Tel: +86(0)10 8472 1250
Fax: +86(0)10 5885 0639
Author:
Yun Changzhi, Vice President & General Counsel,
Beyondsoft Corporation
Visiting Professor, School of Law, Central University of
Finance and Economics
Editors:
David Lammie, Martin Savery and Zhao Daxin
Publisher:
ACA Publishing in association with China National
Publications Import and Export (Group) Corporation (CNPIEC)
and Beijing T-Win Consulting Co Ltd

Published by ACA Publishing Ltd in April 2015

ALL RIGHTS RESERVED. NO PART OF THIS
PUBLICATION MAY BE REPRODUCED IN MATERIAL FORM,
BY ANY MEANS, WHETHER GRAPHIC,
ELECTRONIC, MECHANICAL OR OTHER, INCLUDING
PHOTOCOPYING OR INFORMATION STORAGE, WHOLE OR IN PART, AND
MAY NOT BE USED TO PREPARE
OTHER PUBLICATIONS WITHOUT WRITTEN
PERMISSION FROM THE PUBLISHER.

The greatest care has been taken to ensure accuracy but the
publisher can accept no responsibility for errors or omissions, or
for any liability occasioned by relying on its content.

ISBN 978-0-9927625-9-9

A catalogue record for Evolving Towards Rule of Law in China:
Changes over the Past 10 Years is available from the National
Bibliographic Service of the British Library.

Contents

Author's note and acknowledgements..5

Foreword..7

Chapter 1 – Towards an era of respect for rights and balance of power

Horizontal allocation of state power...12

Vertical allocation of state power..15

Handling and coordinating horizontal relations between different regions and those between local governments...17

Respecting and safeguarding constitutional rights, especially human rights.....19

Conclusion..28

Chapter 2 – Between economic rights and market regulation

Overview...30

Civil law..30

Commercial law...53

Chapter 3 – China's criminal law in the last decade

Introduction...75

Progress and development of China's criminal law in the last decade........78

Conclusion..109

Chapter 4 – Procedural democracy and visible justice

Overview...111

The criminal procedural law..111

The civil procedural law...130

Chapter 5 – From the mechanism of planned economy to the mechanism of market and regulation

Trade law..141

Competition laws..148

Banking law..154

Tax law..159

Product quality law...167

Law of the PRC on protection of consumer rights and interests.........................168

Chapter 6 – A balance between "administrative efficiency" and "administration power control"

Overview...171

Administrative licence law of the PRC in 2003..172

Civil servant law of the PRC in 2005..179

Regulation of the PRC on the disclosure of government information in 2007...184

State compensation law of the PRC, revised in 2010 and in 2012 188

The law of the PRC on administrative supervision (revised in 2010).................193

Administrative compulsion law of the PRC in 2011..197

The regulation on the expropriation of buildings on state-owned land and compensation in 2011..201

Conclusion..204

Chapter 7 – Towards a security system of human rights and social rights

China's labour law system...206

China's social security law..220

Chapter 8 – New perspectives on the rule of law

System improvement...229

Internal judicial mechanism...231

Judicial independence..233

Democracy...234

Publicity...235

Demonstrate the national attributes of judicial discretionary power...................236

Subject and integrity..237

Author's note and acknowledgements

This book was begun in 2004, two years after I completed the first of my overseas comparative studies at the University of Pennsylvania. The original intention was to write a single book on China's legal system, spanning the period between the country's accession to the WTO and the present day. It soon became clear, however, that the topic was too broad for just one book. Moreover, the upcoming legal reforms in China after its entry into the WTO needed time to become established. So the writing of this book was stalled for a few years. For 10 years after that, we witnessed remarkably rapid marketisation and urbanisation and a host of accompanying legislation. During these years, I wrote and published articles on various aspects of the Chinese legal system that were most important to the lives of the common people, as well as the private sector in the economy.

As David Kennedy wrote in his well-known article, "The mystery of Global Governance", that "it can feel like a project of the utmost seriousness and urgency to interpret the world in constitutional terms". We were very much struck by the extent to which mainstream Chinese legal thinking has internalised Western modernism and become used to Western legal terminologies centering on the core value of the Western legal system, such as rule by law, constitutionalism and freedom of trade. In line with the profound reforms in legal thinking, we can also see that the legal framework governing civil and economic transactions has long been incomplete and extremely difficult to handle. More comprehensive structures have been put in place in recent years and a relatively complete system of laws and regulations governing almost every aspect of modern society in the 21st century has been built up. However, problems arising out of inconsistencies, unclear rules and legislative gaps continue to exist, as will be shown in the chapters of this book.

The specific topics covered in this book centering on China's ongoing market oriented legal reform are very far from making up a complete picture of China's legal system. The latter remains a rapidly expanding and changing story as the economy, political system and society become ever more complex and multifaceted. This book provides a structured and up-to-date introduction to the

Chinese legal system and investigates how the current governments has used the law, and other forms of regulation, to govern or address the topics, issues and disputes. It should be noted that the book focuses mainly on legal system in mainland China; areas including Hong Kong, Macau and Taiwan are part of China, but they have a different legal system, and so they are not covered in the book.

I am extremely grateful to my supervisor, Mr Sheng Jiemin (盛杰民), for his consistent encouragement and guidance during my studies at Peking University Law School. I am also indebted to Ms Jiang XinRan (姜欣然), whose academic thinking and advice have deeply affected my own thinking about Chinese tax and other economic law regimes. During my writing, I also received valuable comments, inspiration and help from Mr Zhao Daxin (赵大新), Ms Zhou Si (周思), Mr. Zhao Cheng (赵承), Ms Yang Fan (杨帆), Mr. Fan Dongyi (范东煜), Mr Huangkun (黄琨), Mr Yang Lu (杨路), Ms Jiang Miao (姜淼), Professor Wu Tao (吴韬) and Professor Wang Qian (王迁), I appreciate their kindness, generosity, rigour and help. Most of my work was undertaken in the library of Peking University. I thank the library for all the facilities and for providing a place where I was able to work efficiently and energetically.

Last, but not least, I want to express my special gratitude to my family. It is their unconditional understanding and support that has impelled me forward to where I am now and surely further in future. My father, Yun Fengguan (云逢冠), my mother, Wu Yuexia (吴月霞) and my sister, Yun Nuannuan (云暖暖) have all done everything they can for me. I hope that I can in some way repay their love with this book.

Foreword

It is my great pleasure and honour to be asked to introduce this book, written by Yun Changzhi, a talented young scholar and practitioner. I have worked very closely with Mr Yun as a supervisor while he studied at Peking University Law School for his LL.M. and LL.D. degrees. During this time I have been very impressed by the dedicated manner with which he carried out his work assignments and pursued his academic coursework. Mr Yun has displayed high maturity, motivation and seriousness of purpose, which I have rarely encountered during my extensive interactions with young legal scholars in China. He is very bright and industrious and has demonstrated an eagerness to focus on his academic interest in various topics of China's current legal systems, especially the fast-developing competition laws and enforcement system and international trade-related law system in China. This book reflects the result of research and thinking on legal reforms in China conducted by Mr Yun in recent years, during which we witnessed a golden age of China's robust economic growth and huge social transformations.

The immense changes China's economy over the last 37 years has generated complex social, political and institutional challenges that would test even the most robust system of government, let alone one emerging from many years of chaos. After years of intensive discussions, the social consensuses in current China is that all such problems incurred with the transformation and fast development of China's economy could only be solved by adopting "rule by law" as the super principle in governing such a big country. This book is written for readers seeking to understand the latest development in political, commercial and civil legal environment in China. What laws and regulations have been legislated in the past decade? What is the background or arguments for such new legislation? How are the rights and benefits they bestow enforced? It is written for those who are interested in business, complex commercial transactions, civil and criminal procedures, worker rights or those who just want to know more about China's recent developments. This book will give them a solid introduction to the laws and regulations in contemporary China. Some readers will notice the areas of China's law that still needing reform, and others will be surprised how well-developed and sophisticated many Chinese laws are.

I believe this book will add insight and understanding into the area of China's legal system and provide a benchmark of comprehensive examination of the area for future research.

Sheng Jiemin, Professor of Law, Peking University

Chapter 1

Towards an era of respect for rights and balance of power

— An overview of new developments in China's constitutional system since 2000

In 2012, China overtook the US to become the world's largest trading nation.[1] Since joining the World Trade Organisation (WTO) more than a decade ago, China has witnessed a rapid expansion of its trade with the outside world and a distinct increase in its material wealth, both of which have led to calls for a higher standard of legal construction at home. Traditionally, China has been viewed with suspicion by the West due to its perceived backwardness in implementing the rule of law. However, many scholars have pointed out that the progress made by China in promoting the rule of law is similar to the reconstruction of its legal system more than three decades ago after the chaos of the 1970s. Indeed, in order to adapt itself to the post-WTO-accession trading environment in the era of economic globalisation, China has introduced much new revolutionary economic and commercial legislation, or made amendments to existing economic and commercial laws and administrative regulations, including supplements made to the Anti-dumping Regulations (enacted in 2002 and amended in 2004) and the Regulations on Anti-dumping Subsidies (enacted in 2002 and amended in 2004), the Company Law (2005), the Securities Law (2004), the Patent Law (2008) and the Copyright Law (2010). This wave of legislation or amendments to existing laws after China's entry into the WTO, which is directly connected to the functioning of a market economy and macroeconomic regulation, is based on the fundamental principle under WTO legislation that international laws shall take precedence over domestic legislation and is aimed at implementing WTO legislation through making domestic laws.

In addition, with growing exchanges between China and other countries and regions of the world, the increasingly open mentality of its citizens and the rising

---

[1] Please refer to http://www.bxqw.com/userlist/hbpd/newshow-24653.html. According to trade figures released by the US Department of Commerce on 8 February 2013, the trade volume of the US in 2012 was US$3,863bn, up by 3.5% on the previous year. According to figures released by Chinese customs authorities in January of the same year, the total trade volume of China in 2012 stood at US$3,866.7bn, slightly higher than that of the US in the same year.

awareness of democracy among its citizens after it joined the WTO, China is paying ever more attention to improving the system of rights and obligations under its most fundamental legislation, namely, the Constitution. In 2013, heralded by an article in Caijing magazine, a stirring debate on constitutional government almost engulfed legal scholars and practitioners in China, after which three schools of views have emerged: socialist constitutionalism, anti-constitutionalism and pan-constitutionalism.[2] The involvement of online new media in the debate enhanced the enlightening effects of the discussions and resulted in a more in-depth exploration of constitutionalism. However, paying close attention to the Constitution and acknowledging its fundamental importance to the social governance of the country, and realising constitutionalism in a steady and progressive way in light of China's actual conditions, had already been a mainstream belief of both the intelligentsia and Chinese society in general. That a country must have a constitution and that it must protect the rights and interests of its citizens and ensure the normal and compliant operation of its political system on the basis of the Constitution, are at the very core of a constitution.

The US, which was the first country in the world to adopt modern constitutionalism, created a power structure featuring the checks and balances between the three branches of power. Abraham Lincoln, one of the best-known US presidents, pointed out the very nature of governmental power in his famous Gettysburg Address of 1863, i.e., the government must be "of the people, by the people and for the people". The 1789 French Declaration of the Rights of Man and of the Citizen asserted that: "A society in which the observance of the law is not assured, nor the separation of powers defined, has no constitution at all." Therefore, it can be seen that restraining public power, creating a "limited government" and improving the regime for the protection of citizens' rights are the essential elements of modern constitutionalism. On this basis, China is currently far from the ideal constitutional government, whether in terms of institutions or the reality, given its unique history and the twists and turns that the country has gone through since the founding of the People's Republic in 1949. However, it cannot be denied that, since it joined the WTO, China has made notable progress in its Constitution and legislation in related fields, and has not stalled its drive to protect human rights and restrain governmental powers.

In terms of China's approach to constitutional amendment, the Constitution of China stipulates three different procedures -Constitutional amendment, Constit-

---

[2] Please refer to the article by Xu Qianchuan, Six Questions to "The Three Sides in the Debate over Constitutionalism", carried by Caijing in the 31 July2013 issue of the magazine. Representative figures of the three schools are Tong Zhiwei, Wang Tingyou and He Weifang. The full article is available at http://www.glocal.org.hk/articles/23818

utional interpretation and Constitutional mandate - in response to the need for upgrading and improving social governance required by the times. Before the current Constitution (generally known as the "1982 Constitution" among scholars) was even born, the Constitution Amendment Committee and the then Standing Committee of the National People's Congress (NPC), China's national legislature, had already decided to treat the upcoming constitution as being half-finished and permitted to advance with the times. Peng Zhen, then Chairperson of the NPC Standing Committee, emphasised that the draft of the 1982 Constitution put to vote was the outcome of an institutional selection and elimination process and therefore could not be expected to be fully inclusive. "Some opinions, though reasonable, are not included into the Constitution, the most fundamental piece of legislation of the country, either because the necessary conditions or expertise are not available, or because it would be more appropriate to include them in other legislations and regulatory documents." In other words, the original version of the current Constitution included only the consensus that could be reached and feasible rules and institutions under the prevailing circumstances. Therefore, practicality for practical reasons, feasibility and importance were chosen as the standards for deciding whether a specific rule was included or not, rather than institutional expectations. The subsequent series of constitutional amendments and mandates of China embodied such a standard, i.e. practical need.

In China, an amendment to the Constitution is proposed by the NPC Standing Committee or the NPC, and is voted on by NPC deputies. Through constitutional amendments, the meaning and content of provisions in the Constitution may be altered, supplemented or expanded. Since the current constitution came into force, it has undergone four rounds of amendments, which involve a total of 31 provisions. Constitutional amendments play a dominant role in the evolution of the Constitution.

Constitutional interpretation is another feasible approach to improving the Constitution. Article 67 of China's current Constitution endows the NPC Standing Committee with the power to make constitutional interpretations. However, it falls short of providing any necessary and feasible institutional details regarding constitutional interpretations, and it does not specify who is responsible for proposing such interpretations, how and by what procedure they are made or how effective they are.

The Constitution includes a considerable number of articles on legislative mandates, effectively empowering the NPC and NPC Standing Committee to refine and expand relevant rules and systems enshrined in the Constitution. "The organisational and operational procedures of the NPC and its Standing Committee shall be specified by laws"; the organisation of the State Council, or cabinet, is subject to relevant laws and administrative regulations. All such stipulations show that the NPC and NPC Standing Committee have the power to create and improve relevant and adjacent laws, regulations and institutions, and further specify and expand the contents of relevant institutions provided under the Constitution.

In order to ensure the stability and authoritativeness of the Constitution, China has avoided making frequent constitutional amendments. Even in the case of China's entry into the WTO, a highly important event in the country's history, China responded by merely adopting the Fourth Amendment to the Constitution at the Second Session of the 10th NPC in 2004. As for constitutional rights and fundamental principles in the Constitution, as well as constitutional institutions, China tends to create, confirm or improve such rights, principles or institutions through legislation, especially those made by the NPC and NPC Standing Committee, instead of resorting to constitutional amendments. Such legislation not only provides clearer principles and rules for coordinating inter-departmental and intra-departmental relations in the government as well as relations between local governmental authorities, but also enriches China's constitutional system, providing a relatively strong legal guarantee for the rights and freedoms of citizens in an era when China is faced with economic globalisation and new social problems brought about by economic changes in the country.

Horizontal allocation of state power

The horizontal allocation of state power in China is mainly realised under the people's congress system. According to the Constitution, national and local people's congresses, as legislatures, are at the centre of the state power system. The State Council, the Supreme People's Court (the highest court in China) and the Supreme People's Procuratorates (the highest prosecution body in China) are elected, approved and supervised by, and accountable to the National People's Congress. Similarly, local governments and provincial supreme courts and procuratorates are elected, approved and supervised by, and accountable to local people's congresses. Viewed from the perspective of power allocation, this arrangement is based on a one-way model and hence different from the tripartite system featuring a separation of the legislative, executive and judicial powers. The Constitution itself does not include any specific provision concerning how state organs are supervised or the extent of such supervision. In this respect, some legislative improvements have been made in recent years.

Improving the administrative litigation system and enhancing supervision by judicial organs over governmental bodies

The draft amendment to the Administrative Procedural Law was submitted to the sixth session of the 12th NPC for deliberation on 23 December 2013, marking the start of the first major revision made to the law since it came into force 23 years ago. Xin Chunying, Deputy Chairperson of the Legislative Affairs Commission under the NPC Standing Committee, noted that the proposed revision was made in response to some prominent problems in judicial practice and was aimed at restraining administrative power and ensuring that people's courts would be able to exercise their adjudication power independently. More specifically, the amendment mainly involves: improving rules concerning case filing, and rules concerning evidence, so as to enhance the guarantee of citizens' right to sue governmental bodies; eliminating practices such as replacing litigation with mediation and non-local jurisdiction, so More specifically, the amendment mainly involves: improving rules concerning case filing, and rules concerning evidence, so as to enhance the guarantee of citizens' right to sue governmental bodies; eliminating practices such as replacing litigation with mediation and non-local jurisdiction, so as to reduce interference by administrative bodies and free grassroots courts from the restraints of local interests.

The Administrative Procedural Law is a lever that regulates relations between citizens' rights and public power. Through improving ways in which private citizens and entities can sue governmental agencies, the draft amendment is expected to create a better balance between the exercise of executive power on the one hand and the protection of the rights of citizens, legal persons and other entities on the other. It is also intended to restrain public power and reduce infringement on the rights and freedoms of citizens.

Clarifying and consolidating the principle of the independence of adjudication

The current Constitution of China guarantees the independence of people's courts in adjudication and emphasises that they are free from "interference by governmental agencies, social organisations and individuals". However, judging by the wording of the Constitution, people's procuratorates, as judicial supervisory bodies, and people's congresses and their standing committees as state power organs, have the right to supervise the operation of people's courts through statutory procedures. On the one hand, people's procuratorates are expected to "counterbalance" people's courts in the trial of "criminal cases", so as to "ensure that they will correctly and effectively implement laws". On the other hand, people's congresses and their standing committees are empowered to appoint and dismiss the staff of people's courts on the same hierarchical level as themselves, and supervise their work. In practice, the ruling party also intervenes in the work of people's courts. All such involvements and intervention *are de facto* violations of the principle of adjudication independence.

The Law on Lawyers actually sets an isolation wall between the standing committees of people's congresses and the people's courts, so as to prevent members of the standing committees from interfering in the operation of judicial organs. While Article 13 of the 1996 version of the law provided that "current employees of state organs may not work concurrently as practising lawyers", and that "lawyers cannot practise law during their tenure as members of the standing committee of any people's congress", those provisions were deleted in the 2007 amendment of that law and a new provision was added in their place: "A lawyer who serves as an employee of the standing committee of any people's congress may not work as agent ad litem or defender during their tenure as such", which effectively narrows the restriction on employees of the people's congresses from practising as lawyers to serving as attorneys of law or defenders for clients in litigation. Although it is not clear whether deputies to the people's congresses can work as non-litigation lawyers and whether and how they interfere in judicial affairs, such an easing of restriction is nonetheless a backward step in the drive to improve the Constitution.

The main contribution made by the Law on the Supervision by the Standing Committees of People's Congresses is that it negates in principle the supervision over individual cases. Starting from the 1980s, local people's congresses and the NPC both enhanced their supervision over individual cases handled by people's courts. This was tantamount to "usurping juridical power" and was therefore against Constitutional provisions on the division of power between state and judicial organisations. This state of affairs changed when the NPC Standing Committee moved to exclude the supervision of the hearing of individual cases from the Supervision Law. This law, which came into force in 2007, provides that the supervision by standing committees of people's congresses over the operation of people's courts and people's procuratorates is primarily realised through hearing and deliberating on special work reports submitted by such judicial organs, carrying out inspections into the work of such organs, and causing judicial organs to optimise their internal supervisory institutions, instead of directly intervening in litigation issues. Thus, the handling by the Law of the issue of supervision over specific cases has further clarified relations between the people's congresses and the courts of law and shored up the principle of judicial independence.

According to the Decision of the Central Committee of the Communist Party of China on Some Major Issues Concerning Comprehensively Deepening the Reform adopted at the Third Plenary Session of the 18th National Congress of the Communist Party of China, judicial reform will be mainly focused on two areas: the independent and fair exercise of prosecution and adjudication powers, and optimising the operation regime of judicial power. The Decision calls for promoting the centralised and unified management of personnel and assets of local courts and procuratorates below the provincial level, exploring a judicial jurisdiction system featuring appropriate separation between judicial organs and administrative geographic divisions, so as to ensure the proper implementation of national laws. As a result, the personnel and assets of intermediate courts in China will be placed under the direct administration of provincial higher courts. This will mark the most substantial reform affecting intermediate people's courts in three decades, signifying an end to the current state of affairs in which courts, which are wrongly perceived as "administrative bodies" under local governments, depend on local government for funding. The courts will therefore be freed from control by local government leadership. The reform is viewed as the first step towards decoupling courts from local governments and achieving adjudication independence. Core to judicial reform is judicial independence, which determines the success or failure of judicial reform and aims at ultimately achieving judicial fairness and realising substantive justice to the greatest extent possible on the basis of ensuring procedural justice. However, judging by the current state of affairs, severing the economic and administrative relations between intermediate courts and local governments cannot be completed overnight, and judicial independence cannot be realised in a short period of time, which means that judicial reform in China may be a long process.

Vertical allocation of state power

China's current constitution sets out a series of principles and rules in connection with the handling of relations between central and local authorities and the relations between different levels of government. For example, Paragraph 4 of Article 3 stipulates that: "Powers are allocated among central and local state organs according to the principle of giving full play to the initiative and motivation of local authorities under the unified leadership of the central authorities". This principle is the most fundamental one for handling relations between central and local authorities. However, in some crucial areas, the boundary between the power allocated to the central government and that allocated to local governments remains unclear.

Allocation of the power to make laws: reservation of law and local affairs

The Constitution creates a fundamental hierarchical system regarding the force of laws and administrative regulations. According to the Constitution, the NPC and NPC Standing Committee exercise national legislative power. The former is vested with the power to amend the Constitution, and to formulate and amend fundamental laws. The latter is empowered to interpret the Constitution and laws and formulate other laws, and to amend certain aspects of the country's fundamental laws. The State Council has the right to formulate administrative regulations in accordance with the Constitution and applicable laws. Provincial-level people's congresses and their standing committees are empowered to formulate local laws and administrative regulations provided they do not go against the Constitution, as well as national laws and administrative regulations; people's congresses in autonomous regions of minority ethnic groups are empowered to formulate administrative regulations on regional autonomy and special administrative regulations on specific issues.

The Law on Legislation, which was promulgated in 2000, demarcates the boundaries between the power to make laws and the power to make local administrative regulations through establishing the law reservation regime and introducing the concept of "local affairs". However, the boundaries of the 10 categories of law reservations are still in need of further clarification, and the concept of "local affairs" also lacks the denotation and connotation necessary for it to guide local legislatures. In particular, the Legislative Affairs Committee of the NPC Standing Committee has often extended the boundary of the law reservations in interpreting the notion while narrowing the interpretation of "local affairs". Following China's entry into the WTO, the improvement of China's market economy has increased demand for new laws, requiring greater order in China's legislation. Therefore, the amendment of the Law on Legislation has been designated as a top priority of the legislative agenda of the 12th NPC Standing Committee. In the amendment, making changes to the legislative power is expected to be a focal point. In local legislative practices, malpractices such as making law in excess of empowerment or redundant legislation are prevalent. For instance, some regions have promulgated regulations on financial administration, financial and fiscal supervision and management of non-tax revenues at town or township level. It remains an unanswered question whether such local administrative regulations involve the fundamental fiscal or taxation systems of the country. To answer that question, the expected amendment to the Law on Legislation must further clarify the scope and restrictions of local law-making.

Allocation of fiscal power: the tax revenue division regime

China's current Constitution does not include any detailed provision on the respective fiscal powers and duties of central and local governments. There is a de facto absence of necessary specification as to the division of power to levy taxes among different levels of government and the sharing of fiscal burdens among them. The launch of the 1993 reform of China's tax revenue system, since when tax revenues have been divided between central and local governments, has not only enhanced the Chinese government's macroeconomic regulation capabilities, but also played a positive role in facilitating the formation of a national, unified market. However, the fiscal arrangement under the Constitution has remained unchanged in the past decade or so, even though local governments in China are facing increasing fiscal burdens, which has resulted in their over-dependence on revenues generated by the sale or rental of state-owned land.

Handling and coordinating horizontal relations between different regions and those between local governments

China's current constitution fails to include necessary and clear-cut rules regarding horizontal local relations in government - in other words, relations between different regions and those between local governments. In addition, the amendments made to the Constitution have so far failed to adopt the existing principles according to which such horizontal local relations are managed. Therefore, similar rules are mostly manifested in legislation promulgated by the NPC and NPC Standing Committee.

Coordinating jurisdiction over litigations

The first rules dealing with horizontal local relations in China emerged in the procedural laws. The Civil Procedural Law, the Criminal Procedural Law and the Administrative Procedural Law all include provisions concerning jurisdiction over legal proceedings, namely, territorial jurisdiction, jurisdiction by referral and jurisdiction by designation. The rules concerning the jurisdiction over legal proceedings have managed to maintain their consistency in spite of the major rounds of amendments that the procedural laws have gone through, which is helpful to local courts in overcoming regional barriers and providing solid rules for the courts to decide whether to place cases on dockets.

Handling regional trade disputes

In centralised and federal countries alike, local governments tend to set up trade barriers against each other so as to maximise their respective interests. The task of minimising the tendency of local governments to pursue self-interest, and form a win-win or win-for-all pattern of interest distribution, is one that the Constitution and the Constitutional system must face and solve. However, China's current Constitution does not include any clear rules in this aspect.

In 2007, the NPC Standing Committee, through the Anti-monopoly Law, further prohibited administrative bodies and organisations under their authority from hindering the free cross-region flow of goods, or seeking to exclude or restrict non-local businesses from participating in local bidding. It does this by setting discriminative qualification requirements and review and approval standards or failing to disclose information according to law, or exclude or restrict non-local businesses from making local investments or setting up local branches by subjecting such non-local businesses to unfair treatment. Although it does not conform to international norms to contain administrative-power-based monopolies through the Anti-monopoly Law, such an approach is nonetheless suitable to the conditions that prevail in China. The above-mentioned provisions of the law undoubtedly enhance legislation in market rules, and are therefore conducive to breaking local barriers, blockades and monopolies. Ultimately, therefore, they are favourable for promoting and protecting fair competition.

The promulgation of China's 2008 Anti-monopoly Law was also aimed at meeting the need for institutional responses to worldwide market consolidation and allocation of resources on a global scale. While this law does not stipulate any extraterritorial enforcement powers similar to those provided under legislations by the US or the EU, it is nonetheless a measure for promoting economic integration.

In 2013, anti-monopoly law enforcement authorities in China meted out a large number of fines in accordance with the law. For example, the National Development and Reform Commission imposed fines on five foreign milk power producers -- Mead Johnson, Dumex, Abbott, Friesland and Fonterra -- that totalled Rmb670m, a record sum in the five years since the law came into effect. This case, viewed in combination with price-fixing cases involving some crystal display panel producers, the case of Moutai-Wuliangye Group and the case of Shanghai gold and platinum jewellery companies, is interpreted as a strong signal by the Chinese government to maintain a fair market environment and promote fair market competition. With China increasingly bringing itself into line with international standards in anti-monopoly law enforcement, it is likely that the country will pay greater attention to anti-monopoly tools and strictly enforce anti-trust legislation so as to create a better market economy environment. The Anti-monopoly Law, which is sometimes known as "the Constitution for the Economy", has become fundamental to China's market economy and a legal guarantee for free competition in the domestic market.

As a newly promulgated law, the Anti-monopoly Law is more in need of improvement than the much more mature legislation in the EU and the US, both of which have a long tradition in anti-trust legislation. A notable drawback of China's Anti-monopoly Law, for instance, are the highly ambiguous relations between the functions of the three anti-monopoly enforcement agencies. Though enforcing the anti-trust law does protect market competition and consumer rights, it is nonetheless hoped that the law enforcement agencies will comply with the inherent rules of the market and refrain from abusing their powers.

Respecting and safeguarding constitutional rights, especially human rights

The Constitutional culture of a country is generally rooted in a market economic system, political democracy and civic society, all of which are co-dependent and indispensable. In recent times, the global constitutional movements share a common feature in that they are paying ever greater attention to the protection of "constitutional rights" while containing the excesses of public power represented by the executive power of government. In the legal system of the US, for example, constitutional rights refer to the rights guaranteed by the Federal Constitution and interpreted by federal courts. In Germany, the basic rights enshrined in the Basic Law of that country are known as "the basic rights", another name for constitutional rights. In Japan, constitutional rights are called "basic human rights", and are considered as "rights that are indispensable for a person's survival and permanently inviolable in essence", which are confirmed and protected by the Constitution of the country.[3] In China, constitutional rights are known as "the basic rights of citizens", at the core of which are the respect for and guarantee of the human rights of citizens. Only when protecting and guaranteeing human rights are enshrined as the paramount value pursued by the Constitution can constitutionalism be said to have been truly realised. With the improvement of living standards in China brought about by deepening reform and an opening up of the economy, it is all the more important to enhance the protection of human rights and ensure the participation of citizens in democracy and politics.

Inclusion of human rights into the Constitution

In 2004, the first amendment to China's constitution in the new century was adopted at the Second Session of the 10th NPC, which is viewed as a milestone because the protection of human rights is included in the amended Article 24 of the Constitution. Behind the terse provision that "the state respects and protects human rights" is a dramatic process through which "human rights" evolved from a theoretic approach to a banner for rights protection. In 2003, the human rights issue was expanded to an unprecedented scale by a series of events, making an amendment to the Constitution all the more urgent. The first of the events involved the death of Sun Zhigang, an employee of Guangzhou Daqi Garment Company from Wuhan, capital of Hubei province in central China. He was beaten to death by eight patients at a penitentiary hospital just hours after being arrested as a vagrant for not carrying his identity card. This event inspired nation-

---

[3] Refer to A Comparative Study of Rights Not Enumerated in Constitutions, pp 168-170, Law Press of China, March 2011

wide soul-searching on the need to enhance the protection of human rights and finally prompted the State Council to abolish custody and repatriation, a practice that was suspected of violating human rights. Other events in the same year also sparked heated public debate. They included judicial organs' review of the detention of suspects beyond the statutory time limit, the abolition of the once compulsory "pre-marriage physical check-up" and an incident in Shaanxi province in which a married couple were detained by the police on the charge of watching pornographic videos in their own home. Subsequent changes brought about by such events have led to a diminution of public power and progress in the area of citizens' rights, although more progress still needs to be made.

With regard to the evolution of Constitutional jurisprudence — which is closely associated with the protection of human rights (we hope that the Chinese Constitution will demonstrate sufficient flexibility in its application to the protection of human rights) — constitutional rights in China are recognised mainly in constitutional amendment and constitutional interpretation. The former is achieved by the NPC's revision of the Constitution while the latter is mainly realised by the NPC Standing Committee's interpretation of the Constitution. Compared with constitutional amendment, according to some scholars, "constitutional interpretation is the norm and hence the preferable solution". "The extremity of constitutional interpretation is the point where constitutional amendment should start."[4] Therefore, it can be seen that constitutional interpretation, as a steadier and more progressive way of improving the Constitution, has more potential in protecting human rights and ensuring the stability and authoritativeness of the Constitution. Paragraph 1 of Article 67 of the current Constitution establishes the arrangement that the power to interpret the Constitution and supervise its implementation is granted to the NPC Standing Committee.[5] Such a provision first appeared in the 1978 Constitution of China. Earlier Constitutions, promulgated in 1954 and 1975, did not include a provision concerning the interpretation of the Constitution.

It is generally agreed that the arrangement under the current 1982 Constitution with regard to the power to interpret the Constitution are in line with China's emphasis on people's democracy and the institutional design of the people's congress. However, in practice, the constitutional interpretation regime is still in its

---

[4] Xu Xiuyi and Han Dayuan, Basic Principles of Modern Constitutional Science, Renmin University Press, 2001, pp287-299

[5] However, some scholars have pointed out that the fact that the Paragraph puts "to interpret the Constitution" and to "supervise the implementation thereof" into one and the same paragraph indicates restriction of the power of the NPC Standing Committee to "interpret the Constitution".

infancy and sometimes is effectively dormant, which is one of the key obstacles blocking the realisation of constitutional rights in China. The reason lies in the fact that, while constitutional interpretations in the US and Japan are judicial and initiated through specific cases, judicial interpretation in China is a form of legislative interpretation launched by the NPC Standing Committee in an abstract way, instead of on the basis of individual cases. The entity authorised to interpret the constitution in China is the NPC Standing Committee. In terms of the initiation of the constitutional interpretation procedure, constitutional interpretations in China are different from those in the US, EU and Japan in that they are not "made in light of and for the purpose of specific individual cases" but are "abstract interpretations separated from the application of the constitution in specific cases". In terms of the nature of constitutional interpretations, those made in the West are in essence judicial interpretations made by judicial organs while those made in China are legislative interpretations made by the legislature. Finally, in terms of timeliness, constitutional interpretation in China has always been in a state of "absence", "dormancy" or "inaction". Some scholars have complained that, "the state power organ authorised to interpret the Constitution and other laws has failed to exercise the power conferred to it, both in the past when the legal system of the country was weak as well as today, when the rule of law is promoted". They have also complained that "the constitutional interpretation procedure has never been launched", and "constitutional interpretation is yet to be resorted to for the purpose of solving the problems of the 'ageing' or 'absence' of provisions under the Constitution". It can be seen that the effectiveness of constitutional interpretation as a means to protect and guarantee constitutional rights in both a narrow and broad sense (plus the citizens' rights not listed under the Constitution) remains to be enhanced in future judicial practice. Of course, this will depend to a great extent on whether a judicial body will be authorised to interpret the Constitution on the basis of individual cases. However, given the fact that judicial bodies in China have yet to obtain independence in the real sense, it remains an open question as to when this new approach to constitutional interpretation will be adopted, since it relates directly to the reform of the country's political system.

The inclusion of the provision that "the state respects and protects human rights" not only turns "human rights" from a political concept into a legal notion in China, but also renewed the citizens' awareness of their rights and the values followed by the state. China's amended Criminal Procedural Law, which came into force on 1 January 2013, included "respect and protect human rights" in its section on the general principles of the law, and integrated the principle with more detailed articles and arrangements in the law.

In addition, the amended Criminal Procedural Law as an associated departmental law in connection with human rights protection includes under Article 50 the provision that no person may be forced to incriminate himself or herself. The law also provides under Article 54 that the confessions obtained from suspects and defendants through torture or any other illegal means, as well as testimonies and victims' statements obtained through violence or threats of violence shall be excluded. If physical or documentary evidence is obtained in violation of legal procedure and therefore may seriously impair judicial justice, necessary correction or justification must be made; otherwise, such evidence must be excluded. Such provisions provide the necessary institutional guarantee for preventing and controlling torture and other illegal collection of evidence, and serves as a bulwark safeguarding judicial justice and the legal rights of all litigation participants. The confirmation of the principle against self-incrimination, in its turn, marks a giant step forward toward more civilised criminal justice in China.

The amended Criminal Procedural Law also permits defence lawyers to get involved in their client's case earlier, i.e., during the investigation phase of a case, formally confirming the status of lawyers as "defenders" during that phase. In other words, when the police or prosecution adopts a coercive measure against a suspect or defendant, or when they interrogate the suspect or defendant for the first time, the suspect or defendant is permitted to retain an attorney of law to defend himself or herself. Furthermore, the amended Criminal Procedural Law also includes revised provisions concerning defence lawyers' access to their clients: on the day when a suspect is interrogated by investigators for the first time or when the suspect is subject to any coercive measure, the lawyer retained by the suspect may meet with the suspect, on the strength of his or her lawyer's licence, the certification issued by the law firm where he or she works and the power of attorney provided by the suspect, or as the case may be, the legal aid notice issued by the competent legal aid agency. The detention facility should make timely arrangements (up to a maximum of 48 hours after receiving the application for such a meeting) for the meeting between the suspect and his or her defence lawyer. The law also stipulates that such a meeting cannot be monitored, and the provision that "one or more investigation representatives shall be present at the meeting" is deleted. Such provisions ensure adversarial confrontation between the prosecution and the defence on an equal footing and therefore protect the defence's rights to the maximum extent legally allowed.

Another development of note is the 2009 amendment to the Law on Elections, in which the principle of "equal rights for equal votes" is embodied and former provisions that can be interpreted as "rural residents only enjoy a quarter of the suffrage of their urban counterparts" were deleted. After the amendment, provisions resulting in such disparity were deleted and deputies to the people's congresses are now elected by constituencies of the same size across the country, thus ensuring equality between citizens in voting rights.[6] The fact that such unfair provisions were kept in the Law on Elections for so many years represents a gross violation of the principle that all citizens are equal. The increase in the number of cases contending for voting rights in recent years testifies to the fact that Chinese citizens are paying more and more attention to their right to vote in elections, one of the fundamental constitutional rights of citizens. On the other hand, elections in China are still prone to considerable corruption. This is especially true in rural areas, where bribery in grassroots-level elections is prevalent since they often involve the sale or transfer of land.

Freedom of expression is an important constitutional right in many countries. For example, the first amendment made to the Constitution of the US not long after it took effect includes express provisions concerning the freedom of expression. The 1791 Constitution of France, the first written constitution on the European continent, which adopted the Declaration of Human Rights as its preamble, confirms in strong terms that it is forbidden to prohibit any person from expressing his or her thoughts and opinions. In liberal democracies, the freedom of expression is not only conducive to the freedoms and self-realisation of citizens, but also serves as a cornerstone of the democratisation process of society.

It must be pointed out that while there are provisions in the Criminal Law of China that prescribe in a negative and passive way punishments for the abuse of freedom of expression, there is no provision in the law that directly adopts the freedom of expression as its object of protection. In their approach to freedom of expression, Chinese legislatures have demonstrated a tendency against the actual exercise of this freedom, the most direct reason for which is that the central authorities are concerned that the spread of strong opinions of citizens through computer networks may have a negative impact on social order and stability. Since China was admitted into the WTO, there has been no notable step forward in the substantive protection of citizens' freedom of expression, a constitutional right. Indeed, in a judicial interpretation jointly issued by the Supreme People's Court and the Supreme People's Procuratorate in September 2013 on issues concerning the application of laws in criminal cases involving cyber-based libel and slander, it is stipulated expressly that such libel or slander may be categorised as criminal offences if they are serious enough, thus giving rise to the issue of identification of the actual degree of seriousness of such offences. This judicial interpretation has

---

[6] According to the Law on Elections before the amendment, the number of rural residents that a people's congress deputy represents is different from that of city dwellers. Indeed, a deputy elected in rural areas of the country represents four times as many voters as one elected in urban areas.

become controversial because it provides that "libel or slandering of any person through an information network shall be deemed as 'serious in circumstances'" as described under Paragraph 1 of Article 246 of the Criminal Law if the posting is clicked on or viewed for more than 5,000 times or is reposted more than 500 times. This judicial interpretation caused uproar among the public soon after its release and a middle school student who was detained after his online posting containing misinformation was reposted more than 500 times has since become the first case in which the judicial interpretation is applied. Whether the charge against the student is valid or not, the judicial interpretation, though originally intended to maintain normal social order by placing rigorous restrictions on citizens' freedom of expression, fails to take into consideration the reality of modern communications. The fact that it takes the number of views and reposts as benchmarks shows that it has been made arbitrarily and hastily, to put it mildly. In this regard, China still faces many serious challenges in properly balancing the two values of legislation, namely, to maintain social order and to protect the human rights of its citizens.

The right of information has become an integral part of human rights. Since it joined the WTO, China has been confronted with calls from both the international community and the public for transparency of the operation of its governmental bodies. As a precondition for normal bilateral trade, a country will apply to the government of its trade partner to disclose certain information.

Such duty of information disclosure means that the administrative bodies of central and local governments are obliged to disclose information in their possession, except for information involving state secrets. The Regulations on the Disclosure of Government Information of 2007 ushered China into an era in which disclosing eligible government information has become statutory and institutionalised; however, the disclosure regime in China remains imperfect and is insufficient for protecting the citizens' right of information. For one thing, relevant legislations are flawed. The Regulations on the Disclosure of Government Information are not sufficiently powerful in China and fail to cover institutions such as people's congresses, the people's political consultative conferences, courts of law and procuratorates. Besides, there is a lack of effective supervisory and assessment institutions as well as statutes for government information disclosure.

Legal possession of property

Viewed from the perspective of political theories, "the efforts to combine government-led promotion and natural evolvement is aimed at cultivating a civic society, reasonably demarcating the boundaries of state activities and creating beneficial interaction between civic society and state conducts, restraint on rights and power and the coupling of their functions, so as to ultimately combine the efforts of the state and civic society". This is the theoretical background of the emergence and development of city-dwellers as a class. As has been borne out by the reality in China since it started to implement the policy of reform and opening-up, the extent of freedoms enjoyed by the public has expanded steadily, and the circulation of resources has been stepped up. In addition, a once tightly-knit and homogenous society has been disintegrating and the pursuit for worldly needs and awareness of freedom and equality has been on the rise, all of which indicate that a fledging civic society has emerged in the country.

The 2004 amendment to the Constitution, in which the protection of the legal property of citizens is enshrined, was made in response to the reasonable need of members of civic society. The right to private property is a fundamental citizens' right, and together with the rights to life and freedom are called the three most fundamental rights of citizens. There has been a general increase in property owned by citizens since China started to implement the policy of reform and opening-up. Protection of citizens' legal private property is in essence a protection of the material foundation of other rights and freedoms of citizens. For example, the amendment has appeased the concerns of private enterprise owners who made their fortune by legal means, and therefore is conducive to encouraging and guiding the development of non-public sectors of the economy. The provision in the amendment changes the way in which property used to be categorised in China, i.e., according to the social class to which a property belongs, and will facilitate the development of civic society and ultimately promote the advance of political democracy.

In addition, through the amendment, Paragraph 3 of Article 10 of the Constitution, which used to read as "the state may, for the benefit of public interests, acquire land in accordance with law", is revised to read as "the state may, for the benefit of public interests, acquire or expropriate land in accordance with law and provide proper compensation for the acquired or expropriated land". This new provision supplies the legal basis on which relevant laws and administrative regulations can define in detail the term "public interests" and strictly controls the abuse of state power to acquire or expropriate.

The differentiation of land expropriation from land acquisition helps to clarify and distinguish the property and legal relations created by the two forms of obtaining land, and thereby makes relevant legislation in China more accurate and solid. It also provides the Constitutional basis for the Law on Land Administration and Property Right Law to further standardise and regulate land acquisition and land expropriation.

However, the term "public interest" may be interpreted in an over-broad way since the provision in the Constitution on the precondition that the acquisition and expropriation of land must be for the benefit of public interests is rather broad in nature and there is no detailed or specific provision concerning the interpretation and application of the precondition in judicial practice. As has been borne out by reality, untimely or inadequate compensation for expropriated or acquired land is not rare in practice. Therefore, it is necessary to make detailed provisions in the Law on the Administration of Land and the Property Right Law on the interpretation of "public interest", so as to define the scope of the term, increase compensation, set out a stricter procedure for land acquisition and expropriation, and carry out a more rigorous review of the purposes for which land is acquired or expropriated. Such changes are needed to properly regulate governmental acquisitions or expropriations of land, and lower the incidence of mass demonstrations and tragic events that sometimes result.

With the acceleration of urbanisation in China, disputes caused by demolition and resettlement are occurring more frequently. In such disputes, the absence of proper compensation remains a key factor, with legal rights and interests infringed upon. According to the Property Right Law adopted in 2007, proper compensation must be provided for the demolition of housing and other real estate of individuals or entities as well as the resettlement of persons necessitated by the demolition, so as to safeguard the legal rights and interests of such individuals or entities; where the personal housing of an individual is acquired, proper alternative housing conditions must be provided. No entity or individual may embezzle, divert or default on the compensation or other payments for the demolition or resettlement. This provides further protection for the private property of citizens after the Constitution was amended to include an express provision on the protection of citizens' private property. While it is true that demolition of existing housing and resettlement of those affected are for the benefit of public interest, and that individual citizens should respect this, it does not necessarily follow that demolition and resettlement must be done at the expense of the legal rights of citizens. Rather, demolition and resettlement must be subject to proper compensation in accordance with relevant laws of the state.

On 21 January 2011, the State Council promulgated the Regulations on the Acquisition of and Compensation for Housing Property on State-owned Land, to replace the Administrative Regulations on the Demolition of Urban Housing promulgated in 2001. The new document has the following characteristics:

> i. A clear distinction of the two terms "demolition and resettlement" and "acquisition". The former is defined as civil legal relations between equal entities and their rights and obligations are subject to civil legislations. When one party who intends to demolish a certain property of another party obtains the necessary licence, it may proceed to enter into a demolition and resettlement

compensation agreement with the party whose property is to be demolished. According to the agreement, the latter party assigns its property and the land on which the property is located to the demolishing party, which shall provide proper compensation to the other party. On the other hand, "expropriation" refers to the process through which the state, on the basis of public power, obtains the property of an entity, collective or individual. If the two concepts were to be mixed up, and property were expropriated in the name of demolition and resettlement, the public power would inevitably be abused to interfere in the civil legal relations between two otherwise equal parties, namely, the demolishing party and the party whose property is demolished. This distinction may be used to regulate the use of public power in the expropriation of property.

ii. Definition of public interests. Public interests are a core issue in the expropriation of housing properties. The new Regulations define the term "public interests" by use of examples: energy, transportation or other... undertakings carried out for national defence or diplomatic purposes. Such an approach clarifies to a certain extent the scope and identification standards of public interests and therefore curbs the abuse of the state power in expropriation.

iii. Fair and equitable compensation. The new Regulations include examples of items covered by the compensation, including the losses arising as a result of an interruption of business caused by the expropriation. In addition, it provides the party whose property is expropriated with the option of monetary compensation or housing property swap. It also stipulates that the compensation may not be lower than the fair market price of the housing property similar to the one expropriated at the date when the expropriation is announced, which covers compensation for the value of the housing and the land-use right, thus providing further protection for the rights and interests of the party whose property is expropriated.

iv. The shift from administrative-power-based demolition and resettlement to judicial-power-based demolition and resettlement. As the demolishing party, the government does not automatically have the right to perform forced demolition; rather, it must apply to the competent court in accordance with the law for approval. The administrative-power-based forced demolition must be abolished. In addition, forced demolition using violence or threatened violence has been banned by law, which is conducive to regulating the conducts of the demolishing party.

However, cases of unfairness on the part of the judicial authorities are not rare. Certain courts, proceeding from the need to facilitate economic development and maintain social stability, have circulated internal orders against receiving administrative litigation cases involving disputes over demolition and resettlement. In some cases, the demolishing party ignores the statutory procedure and circumvents judicial authorities to perform forced demolition. Certain procuratorates or courts even work with local governments to harm the rights and interests of the entities or individuals whose property is demolished or expropriated. There are two fundamental causes of such problems: first, the provision under the Constitution that "people's courts shall independently exercise their right of adjudication in accordance with law and shall be free from the interference by administrative organs, social organisations and individuals" fails to be implemented properly and effectively; second, the over-dependence of local governments on revenues generated through land sales. Given the unbalanced division of revenues between central and local governments, the revenues generated through land transfers account for nearly 70% of the fiscal income of local governments. These two factors can be attributed to basic issues in the Constitution: mutual check and supervision between different governmental departments, protection of citizens' rights and intra-departmental relations.

Conclusion

Looking back over the past decade or so, we cannot deny that China has been making efforts to improve its constitutional system; however, we must also admit that these efforts have amounted to only minor adjustments of the system. President Xi Jinping announced in his speech commemorating the 30th anniversary of the promulgation of China's current constitution in December 2013 that the authority of the Constitution must be upheld and that the implementation of the Constitution must be ensured. The resolution adopted at the Third Plenary Session of the 18th National Congress also called for the rule of law in China, deepening the reform of its judicial system, stepping up efforts to build a fair, efficient and authoritative socialist judicial system, safeguarding people's rights and interests, and improving the judicial institution for the protection of human rights. The Fourth Plenary Session of the 18th National Congress in October 2014 adopted "rule of law" as its theme, which has stirred expectations that constitutionalism will be realised in China. Despite these developments, we are still seeing people whose property is expropriated by force defending their legitimate rights while holding a copy of the Constitution or Property Law in their hands, or even setting themselves on fire, and we continue being informed that some people are arrested and tried on the charge of "gathering a crowd and disturbing public order". Though we are encouraged by the crop seed case of Henan province and the case of Qi Yulin, these sparks of hope have yet to be turned into flames, because attempts to create a constitutional censorship system and apply the Constitution in judicial practice have been thwarted by the authorities.

The Constitution is supposed to be the most fundamental piece of legislation in

China, yet many bodies and organs are operating in excess of the boundaries set by the Constitution. Limits are yet to be set for the powers of the government, which is the root cause for the failure of the Constitution to be effectively implemented, as well as the very reason why the abuse of power persists in spite of numerous efforts to eliminate it, and why "tigers" (high-ranking corrupt officials) and "flies" (corrupt minor officials) still prevail. For as long as the rule of people and policies, instead of the rule of law is the order of the day, the Constitution remains a set of pale, empty promises, whether viewed from the perspective of the government or that of the citizens.

Since late 2010, Arab countries in north and west Asia have been engulfed in a series of social movements around the themes of "democracy" and "economy", which have become known as the "Arab Spring". In particular, a revolution erupted in Egypt on 25 January 2011, due to the heavy concentration of power in the hands of the then president of that country. This revolution has become the largest demonstration for democracy in Egypt over the past three decades. Through the joint efforts of the opposition Muslim Brotherhood and other forces, the revolution finally toppled the government headed by former president Mubarak, and initiated a new round of constitutional amendment. Later, in 2013, the government led by the Muslim Brotherhood was overthrown by the military. One year later, riots in Kiev, capital of Ukraine, led to regime change and loss of territory in that country. From all that turbulence, China can draw lessons for itself. Following its policy of reform and opening-up, China has made spectacular economic achievements. This makes it highly unlikely that a violent revolution will ever happen in China and therefore the ruling party does not have to worry that it might be overthrown. However, worrying trends in China, such as the consolidation of privileged establishment, a widening wealth gap and decreasing social mobility area constant reminder that the ruling party and government leaders should be aware that "govern on the basis of the rule of law" is the "inevitable" path that the country must follow. Therefore, they must approach the reform of the political and judicial systems through the Constitution. An unavoidable objective of the reform is to place governmental power under genuine checks and balances, provide effective protection for citizens' rights, and achieve a deep and general consensus in society on the rule of law, so as to create a solid and flexible law-based foundation for the long-term stability and prosperity of China.

Chapter 2

Between economic rights and market regulation

— Changes in China's civil and commercial law over the last decade in response to the trend of marketisation

Overview

Civil and commercial laws are closely related to the market economy system. Friedrich Engels pointed out that: "The codes of civil law express the economic life conditions of society in legal form". The "economic life conditions of society" refer to the commodity and market economies. In a sense, civil and commercial laws aim to protect the legitimate rights and interests of the subjects of civil and commercial matters, while the commodity economy and the market economy serve as the economic basis for the survival and development of civil and commercial laws. Since the Third Plenary Session of the 11th Central Committee of the Communist Party of China, the comprehensive promotion of reform and opening up and the gradual establishment of a market economy system have contributed to the modern, scientific, standard and systematic development of civil and commercial law system closely linked with it. Since its entry to the World Trade Organization (WTO) in 2001, China has been facing an important opportunity to open its doors to the outside world on an all-round, multi-level and wide-ranging basis, which has also significantly affected the building of a legal system on civil and commercial matters. While initiating economic development, China's entry to the WTO is also "dragging" institutional reform, which is the biggest challenge that the country is facing. In constructing the legal system, the Chinese government has kept its promise to start and complete most large-scale clean-up work regarding laws and regulations, deepening the concept of rule of law in the minds of the people.

Civil law

The Civil Law involves every aspect of daily life. The implementation of General Principles of the Civil Law of the People's Republic of China in 1986, followed by the property law and the law of personal rights, has laid a foundation for China's civil law system. In terms of the property law, the implementation of the Contract Law in 1999 has filled the gap of the Economic Contract Law, the Foreign-Related Economic Contract Law and the Technology Contract Law. After seven amendments, the Property Law was finally put into effect in 2007. In addition to these two comprehensive laws, other department laws have also played an important role. They include the Land Management Law (enacted on 25 June 1986), the Urban Real Estate Administration Law (enacted on 5 July 1994 and revised in 2007), the Urban and Rural Planning Law (enacted on 1 January 2008) and the Property Law, jointly regulate the legal relations of China's real estate industry; the Guarantee Law and its judicial interpretation and supplementary-relevant provisions in the section "Security Interest" in the Property Law. In terms of personal rights, the Tort Law came into effect on 1 July 2010, in which China for the first time specified the compensation for mental damage in legal form, a development that has been long-awaited by many people. The Judicial Interpretation III of the Marriage Law, introduced on 4 July 2011, aims to solve problems that people have become highly concerned about. In terms of personal rights, the Tort Law confirms the right to privacy and provides appropriate remedies. In addition, the intellectual property law becomes a special law under the general civil law system for its unique legal status and meaning, under which the Trademark Law, the Patent Law and the Copyright Law, etc. have been appropriately amended in line with the development of the era, which not only conforms to the international trend of China's accession to the WTO, but also caters to the urgent need for China to increase its efforts to protect intellectual property. As civil legislation is advancing in all aspects and civil law academia is following the trend, some scholars are calling for a uniform civil code. Since the Standing Committee of the National People's Congress first considered the draft of the civil code on 17 December 2002, there has been no further consideration about it in the last decade. With the promulgation of the Property Law and the Tort Law, China's civil law system has been gradually improved, prompting the question of how long will it take for a unified civil code to be promulgated?

Contract law

China's contract law system began at the Third Plenary Session of the 11th Central Committee of the Communist Party. Prior to this, due to the prevalence of the planned economy, the Contract Law developed very slowly, and was basically stagnant during the Cultural Revolution period. Since the Third Plenary Session, the contract law system has undergone continuous improvement as a result of the Economic Contract Law, the Foreign-Related Economic Contract Law, the General Principles of the Civil Law, the Technology Contract Law and the unified Contract Law of the People's Republic of China.

However, with economic development, the hysteretic nature of the statute law has been gradually revealed, and the practical legal loopholes need to be filled through a variety of ways. Thus, the Supreme People's Court promulgated the Interpretation I of the Supreme People's Court on Several Issues concerning the Application of the Contract Law of the People's Republic of China, the Interpretation II of the Supreme People's Court on Several Issues concerning the Application of the Contract Law of the People's Republic of China and the Interpretation III of the Supreme People's Court on Several Issues concerning the Application of the Contract Law of the People's Republic of China in 1999, 2001 and 2012, respectively.

Judicial Interpretation I makes an additional provision on the macro aspects of the Contract Law and some specific systems, interpreting the application scope of the law, the statute of limitations, validity of the contract, right of subrogation, right of rescission, third parties in the contract transfer, concurrence concerning the right of claims and other issues, and providing a legal basis for related issues.

Judicial Interpretation II deals with the problems occurring in the practice of contract trial after the implementation of the Contract Law over the past 10 years, which is a summary and refinement in respect of the experience in solving legal issues concerning contracts. This interpretation explains the conclusion of the contract, validity of the contract, performance of the contract, termination of rights and obligations of the contract, liability for breach of contracts, supplementary provisions and other related issues, with the focus on specifying the scope of liability for fault, maintaining the effectiveness of contracts and regulating the exercise of discretion.

Judicial Interpretation III, also known as the Interpretation of the Supreme People's Court on Issues Concerning the Application of Law for the Trial of Cases of Disputes over Sales Contracts, is mainly intended to solve the issues over sales contracts, such as the establishment and validity of sales contracts, delivery of the subject matter and transfer of ownership, risk bearing of the subject matter, inspection of the subject matter and liability for breach of contracts.

Property law

The property rights system is closely related to people's lives, and the property law is also integral to a country's civil law system. Since the reform and opening up, China's property law has been unsystematic, except for being generally provided by the Constitution and being regulated by the General Principles of the Civil Law and Several Opinions on the General Principles of the Civil Law. This situation caused great difficulties to judicial practice. The Property Law was adopted by the Fifth Session of the Standing Committee of the 10th National People's Congress on 16 March 2007, and became effective on 1 October 2007. The promulgation of this law was a landmark in China's civil law system.

What significant contribution has the Property Law made to the legislation? Briefly, the progress of the Property Law is embodied in its spirit of humanism and civil rights, which is consistent with the amendments to the Constitution in 2004, and keeps pace with the mainstream thought of the international community; in addition, its unique legal rules and institutional design facilitate this Law to show significant effects in practice. The system and rules of the Property Law will now be explored.

First, Chapter II of the Property Law specifies "Creation, Change, Transfer and Elimination of Property Right", and provides, for the first time, a unified real estate registration system, making great changes to the current system. In terms of the real estate registration system, the biggest practical problem that China is facing lies in the fact that, as the real estate law has withdrawn from the civil law discipline and system for four decades, and China's legislative and legal circles are inclined to include real estate registration within the scope of administrative management, it is difficult to understand the construction of this system from the perspective of civil law, especially from the system of changes in property rights. Meanwhile, the high cost and numerous charges for real estate registration are also common in reality, and in this regard, relevant provisions have been made in the Property Law.[7]

Second, the Property Law makes a specific provision on ownership of different types of building, stating that: "An owner shall have ownership over the exclusive parts within the buildings, such as residential houses or houses used for business purposes, and shall have common ownership and the right of common management over the common parts (such as public facilities like lifts and public areas like green space) other than the exclusive parts. For the scope of "common" parts, the Property Law provides that, "roads within the building zone (or community)" and "green space" shall be commonly owned by the owners, except public roads and public green space in cities and towns. In addition, as there are increasing disputes arising from parking spaces and garages, the Property Law also specifies their own-

---

[7]Article 10 of the Property Law: "The registration of a real property shall be executed by the registration organ of the place where the real property is located. The state applies a uniform registration system over real properties. The scope, organ and measures of uniform registration shall be stipulated by the relevant laws and administrative regulations."

Article 246: Before any law or administrative regulation prescribes the scope, organ and measures for uniform registration of real properties, a local regulation may prescribe relevant matters according to the relevant provisions in this Law.

Article 22 of the Property Law: "Real property registration fees shall be collected on each piece, and may not be collected according to the size, volume, or on the basis of certain proportion of the value of the real property. The specific charging rates shall be stipulated by the relevant departments under the State Council together with the competent department of pricing."

ership: "Parking spaces and garages that are within the building area and planned for parking cars shall be used to satisfy, above all else, the needs of the owners."

Third, in the "Usufructuary Right"[8] section, the Property Law mainly provides the use of property, that is, to establish usufructuary rights for the property owned by others. In reality, the controversial issue is how to renew the term of the right to use land for construction purposes upon expiration. According to the Property Law: "The term of the right to use land for construction for dwelling houses shall be automatically renewed upon expiration. The term of the right to use land for construction not for dwelling houses shall be renewed according to legal provisions..." Thus, the basic standpoint of this provision is to distinguish residential land from non-residential land. The term of "residential land" shall be automatically extended instead of making an application for renewal, while non-residential land, especially industrial and commercial land, must submit an application for renewal. However, this provision also has some problems; for example, the Property Law makes no provision on whether the renewal shall pay the transfer fees and whether the land can be further renewed after the first renewal.

Fourth, in terms of security interest (also known as "secured property rights"), the Property Law further improves the system of real rights constructed on the basis of the Guarantee Law. In contrast to the Guarantee Law, the Property Law provides the movable property floating mortgage, allows the mortgagee and the mortgagor to conclude an agreement on the means of realising the right to mortgage, and allows fund shares and pledge of receivables and so on. Article 181 of the Property Law clearly defines the floating mortgage system, while the Guarantee Law does not recognise it.[9] Article 179 of the Property Law expressly provides that, in circumstances when "the obligor fails to pay its due debts or when the realisation of real rights for security as stipulated by the parties concerned occurs", the obligee may realise his/her or its right to mortgage according to law. Compared with the Guarantee Law, this provision establishes the circumstance for the realisation of right to mortgage as stipulated by the parties concerned. In terms of the period of exercising the right to mortgage, the judicial interpretation of the Guarantee Law defines that it shall be a period within two years after the termination of limitation of action for the principal creditor's rights, while the Property Law provides that: "A mortgagee shall exercise the right to mortgage

---

[8] Usufructuary rights include contractual right of land, the right to use land for construction, the right to use house sites and easement rights, of which the right to use land for construction is the most important.

[9] The floating mortgage system refers to the scope of properties mortgaged that are not required to be identified when entering into the mortgage contract, which contrasts it with the fixed mortgage system.

within the limitation of action for the principal creditor's rights; otherwise, such right to mortgage will not be protected by the people's court." This provision is more consistent with the attribute of security interest as an accessory right.

Fifth, the Property Law includes the protection of public property into specific systems. As a subject of ownership of public resources, the State is abstract, and its rights and obligations as well as legal liabilities are also abstract, so that a public legal person owning public assets has no real civil rights, obligations and responsibilities according to law, which is an important reason for the loss of public property. Under the premise of persisting in the basic requirements of public ownership of the means of production, the Property Law establishes effective systems for protecting public ownership and realising the requirements of public ownership from specific domination relations, and its basic manifestation is: in the Property Law, possession and domination of public assets are no longer the abstract dominance relationship between abstract subject and object, but the provisions on specific rights and obligations of the specific subjects. This is the first time that a socialist country has evolved the basic requirements of public ownership into a specific civil law system.

Subsequently, the Supreme People's Court issued the Interpretation of the Supreme People's Court on Several Issues Concerning the Specific Application of Law in the Trial of Disputes over Building Differentiation Ownership[10] and the Interpretation of the Supreme People's Court on Several Issues Concerning the Specific Application of Law in the Trial of Disputes over Realty Service[11], linking the Property Law and practice more closely.

There is no doubt that the implementation of the Property Law is a landmark in the process of legalisation in China, and its significance is reflected not only at the legal technical and institutional level, but also in legal ideas and value orientation.

In terms of legal ideas and value orientation, the Property Law has established the principle of "common acceptance and equal protection" for the first time.[12] In line with the ideology that prevailed before the reform and open-

---

[10] This judicial interpretation was adopted at the 1,464th Meeting of the Judicial Committee of the Supreme People's Court on 23 March 2009.

[11] Fa Shi (FS) [2009] No. 8; it was adopted at the 1,466th Meeting of the Judicial Committee of the Supreme People's Court on 20 April 2009.

[12] The Property Law has acknowledged the basic principle of equally protecting the properties of social members (state, collectives, individuals and other right holders), that is: "The real rights of the state, collectives, individuals or any other right holder shall be protected by law and shall not be infringed by any entities or individuals." See Article 4 of the Property Law.

ing up, socialist countries generally emphasised the differences of political status among "national, collective and individual" properties, under which circumstances legal protection was given on a differential basis. This ideology substantially harmed people's property rights, because it legally placed the people's legitimate aspirations to obtain fortune, develop and improve themselves in the position of not complying with "socialist moral standards". In this regard, the legal ownership of the people often fails to be recognised or protected by law, and may even suffer from violation of public power. Such phenomena occur frequently in China; for example, some local governments take advantage of such legislative policies to trample on the fundamental interests of the people and ignore the legitimacy of public interests in dealing with matters such as land acquisition and demolition. The "Chongqing Holdout" event is a protest against the acts infringing upon the interests of the people.[13]

Recalling the process of promulgating the Property Law, the principle of "common acceptance and equal protection" has been subject to criticism since it was proposed, and even caused a huge political storm. Some scholars and legislators believe that public power will be valid in reality no matter how it is exercised. They believe the interests between the government and the people, and between those in power and the people, are always consistent. Such an argument goes against the main ideological trend that has been advocated since the Enlightenment. In the international legislative practice of civil law, the problem that progressive thinkers have always been trying to solve is how to prevent over-strong public power harming civil rights, in which sense the "principle of equality" is proposed. The opinions of the said scholars and legislators have run against this, and unfortunately, the view that "an individual's property cannot get equal recognition and protection" has been considered to be politically rational in China.

The establishment of a market economy system and implementation of "common acceptance and equal protection" to people's individual property rights have always been an important part of China's reform. The promulgation of the Prop-

---

[13] Holdout Event: A couple named Wu Ping and Yang Wu built a two-storey brick structure covering an area of 219 square metres in 1993. In 2004, Chongqing Zhirun Real Estate joined Nanlong Company to jointly develop the project, and both had obtained a demolition permit issued by Jiulongpo District Housing Authority on 31 August 2004. On the same day, the Housing Authority posted a demolition notice on Hexing Road, and announced the assessment prices of resident houses from a local assessment company. The price caused discontent among many residents, including Wu Ping and Yang Wu. In May 2006, the developer's excavators drove into Hexing Road; after four months, Wu Ping and Yang Wu's house was still standing there; in October, water and electricity supplies to the house were cut off. In 2005, the developer applied to the District Housing Authority to require Wu Ping to move out within a definite time. But on 12 September, the Authority suspended the decision on the grounds that "the respondent argued there was not insufficient negotiation when the decision was made, and in order to defuse the demolition conflicts, the respondent posed to enter into a relocation agreement". For this decision, Wu Ping believed that District Housing Authority

erty Law has withstood the pressure and conformed to international humanism, which is a major development in China's legal civilisation. Undoubtedly, this principle will permanently exist in China's future political and economic lives.

Tort law

The construction of China's civil tort liability system has undergone a long process. A series of laws and regulations, such as the General Principles of the Civil Law in 1986 and the follow-up Opinions on the General Principles, Interpretation of the Supreme People's Court on Several Issues about the Trial of Cases Concerning the Right of Reputation issued in the form of questions and answers by the Supreme Court in 1993, the Product Quality Law and the Law on the Protection of the Rights and Interests of Consumers in 1993, have to some extent complemented the tort liability system. But the overall theoretical system remains incomplete, and judicial practice is beset with obstacles. In the 21st century, China's tort liability system has undergone major development. In 2011, the Supreme Court promulgated the Interpretation of the Supreme People's Court on Several Issues Regarding the Ascertainment of Compensation Liability for Mental Damages in Civil Torts,and enacted the Interpretation of the Supreme People's Court on Some Issues Concerning the Application of Law for the Trial of Cases on Compensation for Personal Injury in December 2003; in 2010, the Tort Law was promulgated and brought into effect by the Standing Committee of the National People's Congress, which is the comprehensive representative of China's tort laws and regulations. Since the implementation of the Tort Law, judicial practice has entered a new stage.

Compared with previous laws and regulations, the Tort Law provides the protection of civil rights more systematically and comprehensively, which can be highlighted as follows:

First, this law expressly states the "compensation for mental damage".[14] Previ-

---

and the developer had played tricks and counterfeited the records of consultation with her, and finally made the decision that infringed her interests. Her argument forced the Housing Authority to terminate the decision. Thus, the District Housing Authority filed an application to the Court for compulsory demolition. Although Wu Ping presented her views vehemently in court and cited laws skilfully like a professional lawyer, the court ultimately supported the application of the District Housing Authority. To safeguard their legitimate rights and interests, the couple commendably attempted to fight against the infringement acts through legal means. Such "nail house holdouts" are needed in China's law-based society, and only when the people have the awareness to safeguard their rights, will a law-based society be possible.

[14] Article 22 of the Tort Liability Law: "For tortuous acts that infringe on personal rights and interests and result in serious mental damage, the infringed may seek compensation for mental damage."

ously, when dealing with cases regarding the disputes over compensation for personal damage, the decision that the court pronounced the infringer to assume compensation for the victim's mental damage was based mainly on the Interpretation of the Supreme People's Court on Several Issues Regarding the Ascertainment of Compensation Liability for Mental Damages in Civil Torts.[15] It has a special significance for Tort Law in that it specifies for the first time compensation for mental damage in the legal form, but the ways to determine the amount of compensation for mental damage are not defined in this law and its other judicial interpretations; according to Article 10 of the Interpretation of the Supreme People's Court on Several Issues Regarding the Ascertainment of Compensation Liability for Mental Damages in Civil Torts, a judge can take into account certain factors[16] when deciding the amount of compensation for mental damage.

Second, the amount of compensation for death can, to a certain extent, adopt the principle of "fair compensation for the same death", as the varied calculation methods of compensation for death due to different household registers of the deceased often lead to huge difference in the compensation amounts between urban and rural residents. Such differences have occasionally aroused a debate over "unfair compensation for the same death". After the Tort Law came into force, in the event of multiple deaths caused by the same tortuous act, death compensations of equal amount may be determined by the court, rather than dependent on whether the victim's household register is urban or rural.[17] It is worth noting that the death compensations of equal amount "may" be determined. According to this provision, the judge can, in his/her discretion, decide whether to use this condition in piratical cases, that is, one case "may" apply to determining the death compensations of equal amount, while another case "may not". Thus, explicit legal reference factors need to be given by law to decide whether the judge applies the approach of "may" or "may not".

Third, the liability for causing damage to others as a result of throwing objects from high buildings. Article 87 of the Toss Liability Law provides that: "If damage to others is caused by objects thrown from buildings or by objects falling from buildings and the tortfeasor cannot be determined, users of the possible infring-

---

[15] Promulgated by the Supreme Court on 26 February 2001

[16] Seriousness of the infringer's fault, except otherwise prescribed by law; specific circumstances regarding the means, occasion and manner of the infringement; consequences of the infringement; circumstances regarding earnings gained by the infringer through the infringement; economic capability of the infringer for bearing liabilities; and the average living standard in the area where the court accepting the case is located.

[17] Article 17 of the Tort Liability Law: "In the event of multiple deaths caused by the same tortuous act, death compensations of equal amount may be determined."

ing building shall make compensation unless they can prove that they are not the tortfeasors." This is a manifestation of the doctrine of fair liability fixation of the Tort Law. Since then, controversial cases in judicial practice have clear legal provisions. Because the court has no clear basis for civil cases where damages arise from the throwing objects from high buildings, it will lead to huge controversy in the community when a court decision is made. The most typical case is the "wounding assault by an ashtray" in Zhongyu district, Chongqing city in 2000, where the victim named Hao was hit by an ashtray that fell from a building while he standing and talking to someone in the street, causing serious disability. As it could not be determined who owned the ashtray or who threw it, Hao eventually filed a lawsuit against the 22 households of the two buildings. The judge believed that the other households were likely to have thrown the ashtray, except two households where no one was home. According to the principle of presumption of fault, they must bear appropriate liabilities so long as they cannot be excluded from the possibility of throwing the ashtray through burden of proof. The court decided that all 20 households in which someone was home should compensate, totalling about Rmb8,000 per household. Public opinion was seething with indignation after the case was decided, with some people feeling sorry for those who are no doubt innocent. But in comparison, the victim is more innocent, so it may be not the worst outcome after weighing the various factors; after all, the households may be excluded from the possibility of throwing the ashtray through burden of proof, but it will be even more difficult for the victim to accuse someone to be the tortfeasor. This liability-sharing mechanism based on "collective punishment" is the manifestation of the principle of fairness and protection of a victim's rights.

Fourth, as torts are emerging via the internet, the Tort Law also makes provisions specific to them, of which the most remarkable is the "human flesh search". This search is a process to centralise the power of the majority of internet users through online communities in order to hunt for the truth or privacy of a certain thing or person, and to expose these details online. In April 2008, the "First Case Regarding Human flesh search" drew wide attention. Jiang Yan was a young woman from Beijing who committed suicide because her husband Wang Fei was having an affair. Later, Jiang Yan's sister posted an article entitled "Hello, Everyone. I am Jiang Yan's Sister" in Tianya BBS, where she revealed Jiang Yan's mental experience in the two months before her suicide, and wrote stories about Jiang Yan and Wang Fei. The name of Wang Fei and the specific name of the residential area of Jiang Yan and Wang Fei as well as other basic information were included in the article. After that, a report entitled "The Final Diary of a Girl Committing Suicide by Jumping from the 24th Floor" was published in www.daqi.com; Zhang Leyi, a classmate of Jiang Yan, registered a website at "http://orionchris.cn". Some articles published in these three websites have revealed the true identities of Wang Fei and the so-called third party, as well as information about Wang Fei's employer and residential area. After these articles were published, they immediately attracted wide attention, and many people expressed sympathy for Jiang Yan via different outlets, and some users even conducted a "human flesh search" campaign against Wang Fei. Having been severely harassed by this "human flesh search", Wang Fei filed a lawsuit against the owners of "http://orionchris.cn", "www.daqi.com" and Tianya BBS on the grounds of "disclosing personal privacy". Subsequently, Beijing Chaoyang District Court adjudicated that the owners of "http://orionchris.cn" and "www.daqi.com" had infringed upon the plaintiff's rights of reputation and privacy, and were ordered to stop infringement, make a public apology and compensate the plaintiff with Rmb3,000 and Rmb5,000 respectively for emotional distress. Hence, the first case regarding "human flesh search" came to a temporary end.

Infringement through the internet has its particularities. Taking human flesh search as an example, many parties were involved, including network providers and ordinary internet users, users initiating human flesh search, users responding to human flesh search and users harassing the victim through online information. Second, diverse objects of infringement can be involved, such as the infringement upon others' rights to privacy, reputation and property as well as a peaceful life. In the above case, Wang Fei's door was defaced by unknown internet users, with comments like "unscrupulous Wang Fei, hounding his wife to death", which has seriously infringed upon the personal dignity and property right of the owner. Third, due to internet anonymity, it is difficult to carry out investigations, and the vague boundary between personal freedom of speech and invasion of privacy has also resulted in complicated identification of liability.

According to Article 36 of the Tort Law: "A network user or network service provider who infringes upon the civil right or interest of other persons through a network shall assume the tort liability. Where a network user commits a tort through the network services, the victim of the tort shall be entitled to notify the network service provider to take such necessary measures as deletion, block or disconnection. If, after being notified, the network service provider fails to take necessary measures in a timely manner, it shall be jointly and severally liable for any additional harm to the network user. Where a network service provider knows that a network user is infringing upon a civil right or interest of other persons through its network services, and fails to take necessary measures, he/she shall be jointly and severally liable for any additional harm to the network user." Thus, this Law has intensified the liability of internet service providers. Such provision does not only facilitate the implementation of the liability mechanism to protect the rights of victims, but also purifies the network environment to some extent and encourages network service providers to perform the duties of a "gatekeeper".

Laws on intellectual property protection

Laws on intellectual property protection refer to the general term of laws and regulations regarding social relations arising from regulating the ownership, exercise, management and protection, etc. of intellectual property. Globally, intellectual property is increasingly becoming the core competitiveness of a company. Therefore, intellectual property regulations have become an important part of the fundamental laws. China's intellectual property law system includes copyright law, patent law, trademark law and other laws and regulations. After the country's accession to the WTO, these laws and regulations have been amended with reference to internationally accepted intellectual property protection agreements and conventions, and a number of important provisions are drawing closer to international standards. At the same time, content relevant to China's situation development has also been added.

1. Patent law

Patent law refers to the general term of laws and regulations regarding the inventor (or his/her successors) having the exclusive right to his/her invention and specifying the rights and obligations of the patent holder. The Patent Law of the People's Republic of China was adopted at the Fourth Session of the Standing Committee of the Sixth National People's Congress on 12 March 1984 and has undergone four amendments.

In 2001, in order to fulfil its commitments to the WTO, promote the patent system to meet international standards as soon as possible and comply with the relevant provisions of the Agreement on Trade-Related Aspects of Intellectual Property Rights (the TRIPS Agreement), China made an amendment to the Patent Law. The amendment includes: first, in order to accelerate the reform of state-owned enterprises, the Patent Law clearly states that these enterprises have the same rights and obligations as other economic sectors in terms of applying for and obtaining patents; second, in order to promote scientific and technological progress and innovation, and reflect the spirit of the government to encourage technology and other production factors to participate in income distribution, the Patent Law expressly provides that eligible inventors shall be remunerated; third, simplifying and improving the procedures of patent examination and safeguarding rights, and protecting the legitimate rights and interests of the parties concerned.

The 2008 amendment to the Patent Law was in full compliance of the TRIPS Agreement, and was primarily aimed at improving the capability of independent innovation and fostering innovation based on China's own needs, mainly including:

1) Increasing patent protection. According to the Patent Law before the amendment, an application to stop infringement can only be made upon the sale of a product, or when it is exhibited or advertised; in order to protect patent holders at an earlier stage, the revised Patent Law has increased the provision on the right of offering for sales in terms of the protection of the patent's appearance design. In addition, to further strengthen protection through legal channels, the Patent Law has added the provision on pre-trial evidence preservation and the statutory amount of compensation, and extended civil compensation liability in legal liabilities and also provided the corresponding administrative penalties so as to crack down on patent infringement more vigorously.

2) Cancelling the restriction that patent applications involving foreign interests must first apply for a Chinese patent, but the parties concerned shall receive a confidential review. In order to improve China's international competitiveness, the new Patent Law encourages units or individuals to apply for patents to foreign countries. They can also apply to foreign countries for patents regarding its or his/her invention or utility model completed in China, rather than having to apply for patents in advance in China. However, considering that some patent applications may be involved in China's national security, they need to be submitted to the patent administrative department under the State Council in advance for a confidential review. In addition, the law has also made specific provisions on the procedures of confidential review to ensure the applicant can obtain the review's conclusion in the shortest time.

3) Adopting the standard of absolute novelty when granting patents. According to the previous Patent Law, although some technologies that have not been published have been publicly used in foreign countries or corresponding products have been sold, so long as such products are not publicly used or no corresponding products are sold in China, its novelty will remain. In order to improve the quality of Chinese patents and effectively use the rights of the patent that has been published in foreign countries, the revised Patent Law adopts the standard of absolute novelty, i.e. to cancel the geographic restriction on novelty judgement, and a Chinese patent may only be granted on the premise that this patent must be unknown at home and abroad. The revised Patent Law also stipulates that patent rights shall not be granted for the design of two-dimensional printing primarily for the purpose of identification.

After years of efforts, the protection scope of the Patent Law for the patent holder has become more extensive, with more specific protection measures, and the overall regulations are geared to international standards. But current patent rights still encounter significant problems such as the difficulty in obtaining evidence, long time periods, high costs and low compensation, and the occasional occurrence of wilful infringement, repeated infringement, group infringement and cross-regional chain infringement. In this regard, the Patent Law was prepared to conduct the fourth amendment from 2011, and the draft of the fourth amendment formally began to solicit comments from society in August 2012; the final revision will be published in 2014.[18] This amendment will strengthen the functions of the patent administrative organs, and improve administrative channels for the ways to protect patents in addition to the single way of civil litigation in order to shorten the period of right protection, reduce the cost of right protection and enhance the confidence of right holders in the patent system. However, the fourth amendment has strengthened the functions of administrative organs, which have aroused controversy among all walks of life. No clear conclusion has been reached on whether patent right protection shall focus on juridical or administrative means, and it is also difficult to reach a consensus on how to divide the duties and functions pertaining to the judgement of patent infringement. Therefore, in order to solve such problems, more effort needs to be made to promote the development of the patent law system.

In recent years, patent right protection has attracted more attention from manufacturing and marketing enterprises, especially in the high-tech sector. The protection of intellectual property has become a powerful tool for companies in competing for market share; therefore, in addition to market competition, all kinds of enterprises have started a battle in patent rights. On one hand, patent litigation can bring huge profits, while on the other, it can contribute to the improvement of intellectual property protection.

The most common thing to see in a patent infringement litigation case is the use of a patent belonging to others without authorisation. There are two main difficulties in litigation: first, identifying the act of infringement, that is, to find out whether the technology adopted by the defendant is included in the protection scope of the invention; and second, deciding any loss arising from the infringement, and here there are significant difficulties in obtaining evidence. For example, in 2004, Guangdong Provincial Higher People's Court made a final decision on a case where Sony Corporation filed a lawsuit against Roofer Technology (Shenzhen) Co., Ltd for patent infringement.[19] Sony has the patent right for inventing "battery device and installing unit for battery device" granted by China's State Intellectual Property Office , while Roofer Technology was found to have manufactured, sold and offered for sale the patented products without authorisation. As

---

[18] See the website of China's State Intellectual Property Office: http://www.sipo.gov.cn/ztzl/ywzt/zlfjqssxzdscxg/xylzlfxg/

[19] (2004) Yue Gao Fa Min San ZhongZi (YGFMSZZ) No. 269

a result, Sony filed for an order to immediately stop the infringement and destroy the infringing products and moulds.

The first difficulty is to identify the act of infringement. In this case, Sony suggested that Roofer had infringed products involving different models, but this was not fully supported by the court, since an infringement decision is generally made on the basis of the comprehensive coverage principle, which states that a corresponding comparison shall be made between all necessary technical features stated in the patent claim and all technical features of the allegedly infringing product, and the product of which the technical features are comprehensively covered by the patent claim will be identified as an infringing product. After investigation, the court found that the technical features of some products appealed by Sony did have the same necessary technical features of the patents involved, while some products were not comprehensively covered by the technical features of the patent claim. Therefore, the court identified only partial patent infringement. The difficulty of infringement identification mainly lies in the fact that there are more and more technical features in a patent claim, meaning that it takes a long time to compare them individually. This time delay weakens the protection for the patent holder.

The second difficulty is to decide the loss arising from an infringement. Even if an infringement is identified, it may hard to identify specific compensation. For example, in this case, as Sony did not provide direct evidence for its actual loss arising from Roofer Technology's infringement, it was difficult to identify the amount of compensation for infringement; although the court seized Roofer Technology's financial books at the plaintiff's request, the books were incomplete, and not suitable for auditing. Roofer Technology refused to provide complete accounting records, and insisted that no profits were obtained from the infringement, making it impossible to identify its profits from the infringement. In this case, after taking into account the patent type, the nature of infringement, the impact of infringement, the size and attitude of infringement, the court identified the amount of compensation for the infringement. Although the amount of compensation decided in this case was in line with the expectations of the plaintiff, the patent holder cannot avoid the fact that it is difficult to identify losses caused by the infringement because of the difficulty in obtaining relevant evidence.

In the process of a country's economic development, the simulation of foreign advanced technologies is inevitable. China has been criticised for its mass production of "cheap copies". But with the increase in trade between China and the rest of the world, Chinese law and international treaties have become more closely linked, and China's independent research and development (R&D) ability has improved. These trends have helped to gradually reduce the "cheap copy" problem, and today even Chinese products are being "copied".

In one case, Holley Communications filed a lawsuit against Samsung Kejian for patent infringement[20]. Here, it was a Chinese company that owned the independent intellectual property Here, it was a Chinese company that owned the independent intellectual property rights through R&D investment, and first started the dual-mode and dual-standby market, but was "copied" by international brands. In April 2007, Holley Communications filed a lawsuit against Shenzhen Samsung Kejian Mobile Communications Technology for infringing upon Holley Communications' patent of Approaches of Mobile Communications with Dual-mode of CDMA/GSM and Telecommunications Equipment. In May, Samsung launched a vigorous counter-attack and applied to the Patent Re-examination Board of SIPO, declaring Holley Communications' patent to be invalid, and requiring revocation of the patent granted. After hearing the case, the Patent Re-examination Board made a re-examination decision in December 2007 that the patent remained valid. One year later, Hangzhou Intermediate People's Court made the first-instance verdict that Samsung had infringed upon Holley Communications' patent, and should compensate Holley Communications with Rmb50m. Although Holley Communications achieved the verdict it wanted, the case lasted for more than 20 months from the date of the first-instance verdict; in litigation against patent infringement, it is painful for patent holders to experience a long wait. Moreover, it involved an appeal case that consumed nearly three years before Zhejiang Provincial High Court made a final judgement in 2012[21], and the final results were very unfavourable to Holley Communications: the court of final instance believed the right of Holley Communications to the patent involved should be protected by law, but according to the technical appraisal conclusion, Samsung did not use the methods described in the patent claim for its particular model, and therefore Samsung did not commit a patent infringement as it did not fall within the scope of protecting the right to the patent involved. After five years of litigation, Holley Communications failed to achieve the desired result, showing the toughness of patent litigation. In another case, on 10 June2011, TechFaith Wireless Technology (Beijing) Limited initiated an action against Samsung's DSDS (Dual SIM and Dual Standby) phones for infringing upon its patent rights, and claimed that almost all Samsung's DSDS phones had the same technical features using TechFaith DSDS patent rights. DSDS technologies were first developed and used by Chinese companies, but as Chinese mobile phone companies lacked awareness of patent protection, they were unable to enjoy the profits from such innovation. Based on this experience, Chinese companies have gradually learned to protect their own interests through intellectual property laws.

---

[20] (2007) Hang Min San Chu Zi(HMSCZ) No. 108 - Civil Judgement
[21] (2009) Zhe Zhi Zhong Zi (ZZZZ) No. 64

2. Copyright law

The Copyright Law of the People's Republic of China was enacted in 1990. In order to meet the needs of China's accession to the WTO, the Copyright Law was amended or supplemented in respect of those aspects that were inconsistent with the TRIPS Agreement issued by the WTO.

In order to further improve China's legal system of copyright and intellectual property rights and meet the practical needs of deciding cases about disputes over intellectual rights between China and the US, a second revision was made to the Copyright Law in 2010. This revision was mainly in response to China's first case concerning WTO intellectual property rights in 2007, and its contents mostly related to accusations against China's intellectual property right law and enforcement measures raised by the US, which claimed that that the provisions of China's copyright law were inconsistent with China's obligations under the TRIPS Agreement, including: (1) thresholds for criminal procedures and penalties to be applied in cases of wilful trademark counterfeiting or copyright piracy; (2) disposal of goods confiscated by customs authorities that infringe intellectual property rights; (3) failure to hold criminally responsible or impose criminal penalties for unauthorised copying or unauthorised release of copyright works; and (4) denial of copyright and related rights protection and enforcement to works that have not been authorised for publication or distribution within China. Finally, the panel report supported the claims involving China's copyright law, as Section 1 of Article 4 of the previous Copyright Law provides: "The works being prohibited from publication or distribution according to law shall not be protected by this Law", for which the US held that this clause showed that China refuses to protect copyright and related rights to works that have not been authorised for publication or distribution within China, and this practice has violated China's obligations under Article 5(1) of the Berne Convention included in articles 9.1 and 41.1 of the TRIPS Agreement. In response to this decision, China made a second amendment to the Copyright Law in 2010, and deleted the first section of Article 4 in order to prevent a recurrence of similar misunderstanding in the future, and specified the registration system of works and pledge registration agencies.

Given the practical needs of prevailing copyright protection, China started a third revision to the Copyright Law in 2012. Meanwhile, in order to better promote the application of the Copyright Law in judicial practice, the Regulations for the Implementation of the Copyright Law, serving as an interpretation for the Copyright Law, was amended for a second time in January 2013 to make further additions to and descriptions of the provisions with weak operability or unclear reference in the Copyright Law, so that the Copyright Law can protect copyright in a more feasible manner.

In June 2014, the Legislative Affairs Office of the State Council promulgated the Copyright Law (Draft Amendment for Review)[22], and this amendment has integrated the system of rights, adjusted the authorisation mechanism and market trading rules, and improved relief measures. On the basis of the Regulations for the Implementation of the Copyright Law, the Draft Amendment for Review has raised the amount of penalties, enriched the enforcement measures of administrative organs regarding copyright, and importantly strengthened the rights of seizure, copyright protection and infringement prevention so as to effectively solve the identification of copyright in practice. The Draft Amendment for Review has also amended the objects, contents and ownership of right and protection period in respect of copyright protection. These substantial changes indicate that copyright protection and the regulatory system will be developed in a more rigorous and complete manner.

3. Trademark law

The Trademark Law of the People's Republic of China was enacted in 1982, and the first revision was made in 1993, followed by a second revision in 2011 upon China's accession to WTO and a third revision in 2013. In order to meet the needs of reform and opening up as well as economic development, the main aspects of these revisions are to: simplify the application procedures of intellectual property rights, standardise the application process and shorten the application period; expand the scope of protection of intellectual property, e.g. expand the constituent elements of a trademark, and increase new categories such as three-dimensional logos, colour combinations and sound marks, and allow applicants to apply for a trademark in terms of goods with several categories in a single application; intensify the crackdown on intellectual property infringement, specify a higher limit on tort compensation and punish repeated infringements more severely while reducing the burden of proof of the infringed. These measures will help to further strengthen the protection of intellectual property right-holders, maintain a fair market order, promote the application of intellectual property rights and effectively give full play to the competitiveness of science and technology.

In order to better implement the national intellectual property strategy, on 30 August 2013, the Standing Committee of the National People's Congress amended the Trademark Law, and the revised law became effective in May 2014. Further-

---

[22] See the website of the Legislative Affairs Office of the State Council: http://www.chinalaw.gov.cn/article/xwzx/fzxw/201406/20140600396195.shtml

more, in order to support the implementation of the Trademark Law, the State Council revised the Regulations for the Implementation of the Trademark Law on 29 April 2014, which came into force in the following month.

The revised Trademark Law has two prominent features. First, it strengthens protection for trademarks, and clarifies the time limit for handling trademark registration, simplifies the procedures for trademark registration and improves registration efficiency; in terms of trademark infringement cases, this law specifies punitive compensation, intensifies actions against trademark infringement and clarifies the protection system of well-known trademarks to ensure fair and orderly competition. Second, the new Trademark Law also imposes necessary and reasonable restrictions on trademark rights. For example, the alleged infringer shall not be liable for compensation if the said holder is neither able to prove its actual use of the registered trademark during the three years prior to the lawsuit, nor able to prove other losses suffered as a result of the infringement; well-known trademarks are prohibited from being used for advertising. These provisions have effectively achieved the right balance and constraints.

In summary, there have been two main routes for the legal construction of China's intellectual property system in the last decade. First, in order to fulfil its commitments to the WTO and gradually adjust China's intellectual property law to adapt to its obligations under the WTO Agreement, a number of intellectual property laws and regulations were amended or new laws and regulations were enacted around 2001. Second, with the accumulation of lessons in respect of intellectual property protection in the last decade, the construction of China's current intellectual property law system has reached new heights, and with the innovation of science and technology, and communication technology, some of the clauses appear to be inadequate or even anachronistic, and a number of issues that were not considered have been highlighted; the intellectual property laws are under adjustment in order to keep abreast of the times.

Mastering independent intellectual property regarding the core technologies of the information industry is an important means to improve a country's industrial competitiveness. Soon after China acceded to the WTO, domestic manufacturing enterprises, especially high-tech companies, were in a passive position in intellectual property, and lost many famous cases. However, with the accumulation of experience and training of professionals, China's intellectual property system is being improved; especially in previous amendments, the principle of strengthening intellectual property protection has been adopted. In recent years, the number of patent and trademark applications in China has grown significantly, and lawsuits concerning intellectual property reflect the improved awareness of Chinese enterprises for the creation of intellectual property rights to the protection of intellectual property rights.

Land and real estate law

Land is an irreplaceable means of production, and houses are the most important property in the lives of the people. In order to properly regulate legal relations, legislative bodies and the government have introduced a series of laws and regulations, and with the passage of time, these laws and reg-ulatory documents are constantly being improved. Laws and regulations concerning land and real estate include civil laws, administrative laws and social laws, all of which will be addressed in this chapter in addition to civil legal norms.

Before 2008, in addition to some principle provisions of the Land Management Law concerning the overall planning of land use, China's land planning law system mainly consisted of the City Planning Law[23] adopted by the Standing Committee of the Seventh National People's Congress and the Administrative Regulations on Village and Town Planning and Construction[24] enacted by the State Council. Over time, this legislative model has led to a lack of overall connection between urban and rural planning, and has failed to the new situation of China's rapid economic and social development. In addition, as the provision of "one law with one regulation" was principled for planning preparation and modification; in particular, it imposed very weak management on rural planning, which should be improved immediately.

On the basis of summing up the experience of implementing these laws and regulations, the Standing Committee of the 10th National People's Congress adopted the Urban and Rural Planning Law that went into effect on 1 January 2008, while the City Planning Law was repealed. The new Urban and Rural Planning Law is not a simple combination of the aforementioned laws and regulations, but the overall consideration of urban and rural development, which clearly puts forward the concept of balanced urban and rural development. In terms of specific system settings, the new law has the following innovations:

First, the Urban and Rural Planning Law emphasises that social and public interests shall be placed in a central position. For example, with regard to the construc-

---

[23] Adopted in December 1989

[24] Promulgated in June 1993

tion and development of urban areas, priority shall be given to the construction of infrastructure and public service facilities, so as to encourage public finances to be invested in such projects.

Second, from the preparation of planning to organisation and implementation, this law always adheres to the protection of arable land, natural resources, cultural resources and scenic resources.

Third, the Urban and Rural Planning Law improves the approval system for construction project planning. While retaining the working system of the land use permit, the planning permit on construction projects (planning permit for rural construction), the circumstances and procedures of issuing a written proposal of location are also specified, and a distinction is made between the type of construction engineering and management procedures to improve the conditions of relevant permits and simplify licensing procedures.

Fourth, this law improves public participation and social supervision mechanisms. In accordance with the provisions, urban and rural planning shall be made available to the public before being submitted for approval, and the period of announcement shall be at least 30 days. The organ establishing the planning shall fully consider the opinions of experts and the general public, and attach an explanation on the adoption of relevant opinions and an explanation to the material filed for examination and approval. Village planning shall be consented to through villagers' meetings or villagers' representative meetings before it is filed for examination and approval.

Fifth, this law establishes a clear system of urban and rural planning and strict planning development processes. A chapter specifies the conditions to amend urban and rural planning and change the procedures of approval, making planning more flexible and able to adapt to the rapid development of a city.

In terms of land reserve law, the State Council gave an instruction in 2001 that "local governments shall carry out the reserve system through acquisition for construction land on a trial basis", after which the land purchase and reserve work around China progressed very quickly. However, there were still some problems.

Therefore, on 19 November 2007, the Ministry of Land and Resources, the Ministry of Finance and the People's Bank of China jointly promulgated the Administration Measures for Land Reserve, where the following key contents were specified:

First, the scope of land reserve. Land that can be included in the scope of land reserve includes state-owned land recovered by law, land purchased by law, land acquired via the exercise of pre-emptive rights and other types of land acquired legally. All parts of the country shall reasonably determine the size of the reserved land in line with the needs of the land market.

Second, institutions. Land reserve institutions should be the agencies that are approved by the government at city or county level with an independent legal entity and affiliated to land and resource administrative departments. In addition, land reserve institutions should give necessary pre-development for the reserved land, especially those being included in the reserved land after legal expropriation, so that it can be supplied.

Third, funds. The loan that a land reserve institution applies to banks and other financial institutions shall be a secured loan, and the size of borrowings shall be consistent with the current land reserve plan along with the budget of land reserve funds, which shall be filed to the financial department at the same level for approval, so as to ensure that the loan does not go beyond the plan or size.

Land registration and housing registration have been covered in the aforementioned Property Law. But the law does not make detailed provisions for the registration system; thus, in order to regulate land registration acts, pursuant to the Property Law, the Land Administration Law, the Urban Real Estate Administration Law and the Regulations on the Implementation of the Land Administration Law, and on the basis of raising the legal level of, and making amendments to the Rules for Land Registration[25], the Measures for Land Registration was promulgated by the Ministry of Land and Resources and came into effect on 1 February 2008. The Measures for Land Registration mainly specifies the concept, principles, validity, types, contents and procedures of land registration and various basic systems regarding land registration.

The Measures for Land Registration has standardised the system of land registration. As for housing registration, other laws are promulgated for it. After the development of the Property Law, the promulgation of real estate registration law is required so as to implement the provisions of the Property Law on real estate registration. But considering it will take some time to introduce real estate registration law, and during this period, in order to further standardise housing registration and protect the legitimate rights and interests of the parties concerned, the Ministry of Housing and Urban-Rural Development formulated the Measures

---

[25] Enacted in 1989 and revised on 28 December 1995

[26] Additions, modifications and improvements have been made to the Measures for Housing Registration based on the Administration Measures on the Registration of Urban House Title.

for Housing Registration[26] according to the provisions regarding real estate registration. Thus, the current Real Estate Registration Law can be divided into at least two parts, and such coexistence is contrary to the basic provision of the Property Law on the unified registration of real estate. It is likely that, with further improvement of China's real estate registration system, the current land registration and housing registration systems will be subject to change.

Conclusion

In various types of civil rights, laws and regulations related to property rights and obligatory rights have been developed, while the system of personal rights still lags behind. Until now, China has no formal legislation regarding personal rights. These rights are mostly regulated by judicial interpretations, and the new Tort Law only involves a few issues about personal right protection. Obviously, this is contrary to global trends as most countries have attached great importance to the protection of personal rights. Many cases related to personal rights turn out to have highly significant meanings in their judicial practices.

One of the problems for China's personal rights development is that many personal interests endure for a very long time before they are identified as personal rights by legislators and judges; mostly, they are recognised as "personal benefits" and cannot be raised to the level of personal rights, not to mention the protection of rights. Taking privacy rights for example, before the introduction of the Tort Law, there were several judicial interpretations mentioning the protection of "privacy", but privacy protection at this stage was attached to reputation right, and did not become an independent right. Instead of attributing privacy right to the scope of reputation right, the Interpretation of the Supreme People's Court on Several Issues Regarding the Ascertainment of Compensation Liability for Mental Damages in Civil Torts promulgated by the Supreme People's Court on 10 March 2001 clearly provides that infringement upon privacy may be directly brought to the court for compensation for mental damages. The judicial interpretation provides a sufficient basis for judicial practice to raise the protection of "privacy" interests to the legislation of privacy right. Articles 2 and 62 of the Tort Law specify the protection of privacy rights, and formally establish the right to privacy as a "civil right", rather than "civil interests"; Article 62 includes the privacy tort provision that medical institutions and healthcare workers are obliged to protect the privacy of patients. The decision to protect privacy rights is a big step forward in terms of human rights in China. However, once the right to privacy has been infringed, how it is it remedied? In this regard, the Tort Law makes no special provisions applicable to the conditions about compensation for mental damage as set forth in general provisions, namely Articles 6 and 22 of this Law. A problem involved in the right to privacy is how to distinguish between personal privacy and public interest, because privacy protection must give way to public interest if it involves the latter. Unfortunately, China's legislature does not usually arrange the legislative order logically. For example, the Tort Law was enacted prior to the law of personal rights, which leads to a dilemma that the limited content of the Tort Law cannot always meet the needs of protecting individual rights. Therefore, the problems of privacy protection and restriction of public interest remain to be solved through further improvement and development of China's legal system regarding privacy rights.

When it comes to the rights to privacy, the "human flesh search" has been a popular topic in recent years. This is where a question about something or someone is raised on the internet, and in response to this question, many internet users strive to find out the truth about this matter and expose the details they have found.

In terms of the Property Law, although the law is widely praised, there are still some problems. For example, the "accretion" system is not stipulated, which is a deficiency from the legal perspective. Article 115 of the Property Law provides the system of "principal property and accessory property", but the relationship between the two cannot completely reflect the content of the accretion system. This is because the former is mainly designed to solve the attribution of accessory property after the transfer of principal property, while the latter tries to identify real rights, especially the ownership in static conditions. In this regard, some scholars suggest that judicial issues can be analysed in reference to the scholar's proposal draft[27].

Commercial law

Reform and opening up has injected a powerful force in China's economic development. Entering the 1990s, the central government made it clear that it would establish a socialist market economic system by focusing on economic construction. Since then, state-owned enterprises (SOEs), collective enterprises and other enterprises have been permitted by law to coexist in the capital market. Thus, three economic systems - the individual economy, the private economy and the foreign economy - have since coexisted in the socialist market economy system.

However, as state-owned enterprises are a product of the planned economy era, which cannot be easily removed, SOE reform has been a priority for the Chinese government, and this work has continued into the early 21st century. Partnership is an important modern enterprise system, and amendments have been made to

---

[27] Sun Xianzhong, General Instructions on the Property Law of China (2nd Edition), Law Press, February 2009

the law in order to move with the times, playing an important role in regulating the behaviour of partnerships and safeguarding the legitimate rights and interests of partners and partnership enterprises. The Company Law was promulgated in 1993, followed by amendments in 1999 and in 2004. These amendments only involved partial modification to individual provisions, and were unable to fundamentally overcome the institutional and structural defects of the old law; therefore, a third comprehensive revision was made to the Company Law in 2005. In the capital markets, the National People's Congress made two amendments to the Securities Law (1999), mainly in the following aspects: the first was to improve the system of securities issuance and trading, and the second was to strengthen the protection of the interests of small investors. In 2008, the State Council promulgated the Regulations on the Supervision and Administration of Securities Companies and the Regulations on the Risk Disposal of Securities Companies to refine and implement the relevant provisions of the Securities Law and other laws. Later, the implementation of the Law of the People's Republic of China on Securities Investment Fund set the stage for the development of China's fund industry.

SOE restructuring

The Chinese government wants to keep public ownership as the mainstay of the economy and allow diverse forms of ownership to develop side by side. SOEs play a highly important role in the economy, and at the start of the reform and opening-up process in the late 1970s, SOE reform was put on the agenda. Enhancing the vitality of enterprises, particularly large and medium-sized ones that are owned by the public, is the central link of the city-based economic system reform. On 2 September1980, the State Council approved the Report on the Work of Expanding the Autonomy of Enterprises on a Trial Basis and Future Opinions submitted by the National Economic Commission, giving approval to give state-owned industrial enterprises greater autonomy in terms of human resources, finance, materials, production, supply and marketing,. Although it was not obvious at the time, SOEs were showing signs of breaking free from subordination under government agencies, and their property rights were also showing signs of independence.

In May 2003, the State Council formulated the Provisional Regulations on the Supervision and Administration of State-owned Assets of the Enterprises to provide clear and enforceable rules on the regulation of "administration of personnel, affairs and assets", marking the creation of a new management system for state-owned assets.

Partnership enterprise law

The Partnership Enterprise Law of the People's Republic of China promulgated in

1997 has played an important role in protecting the legitimate rights and interests of the partnership and its partners, encouraging private investment and promoting economic development. However, with economic development, especially after China's accession to the WTO, the defects of the old Partnership Enterprise Law became increasingly apparent, and the demand for change was increasingly urgent. Hence, in April 2006, the Partnership Enterprise Law (Amendment) was adopted by the Standing Committee of the National People's Congress and came into force on 1 June 2007.

The Partnership Enterprise Law enacted in 1997 defines the partnership and expands the scope of partners. It limited partners to natural persons, with legal persons and other similar subjects not allowed to become partners; the revised law provides that natural persons, legal persons and other organisations can establish partnerships. Meanwhile, particular legal persons are not allowed to be general partners, as provided in Article 3 of the new law: "A wholly state-owned company, state-owned enterprise, listed company, or a public welfare institution or public organisation shall not become a general partner." However, these subjects are not prohibited by law to become a partner with limited partnership. The second main aspect of the law was to increase the limited partnership system. In a general partnership, each partner must jointly bear unlimited liabilities of the partnership, while a limited partnership is organised by partners with unlimited liabilities and those with limited liabilities. There must be at least one partner with unlimited liabilities in a limited partnership, on which basis partners with limited liabilities neither directly manage the company's affairs nor represent the partnership, but assume limiting liabilities in terms of the amount of investment. This system is conducive to the development of venture capital industries.

The third main aspect is an increase in the special general partnership system. This system is similar to the general partnership except that the partners shall assume limited liabilities under special circumstances. The scope of partners to assume unlimited liabilities shall be limited to the business scope and fault of the partner, who shall not bear any debts arising from the duties or faults of other partners. This system allows professional service organisations such as law firms, accounting firms and other partners to avoid excessive risks, which are favourable for their own development and growth, and for the development of business in different places.

The fourth main aspect is a clarification of the partnership's income tax. According to the features of the partnership and in combination with practical experience, the revised Partnership Enterprise Law clarifies whether the partnership needs to pay income tax. Pursuant to Article Six of the revised Partnership Enterprise

Law, "the partners of a partnership shall, according to the tax regulations of the state, respectively pay taxes on the partnership's incomes derived from production, business operation and other sources."

The final main aspect concerns bankruptcy. It is believed that the partners shall assume limited liabilities for the partnership's debts, and where a partnership's property is insufficient to repay the debts to creditors, it shall have the right to claim recovery from the partners. Therefore, this argument holds that it has little meaning for the bankruptcy of a partnership. However, it is still advantageous for the partnership to go bankrupt if it cannot repay its debts, as it may repay creditors in proportion through bankruptcy and take into account the interests of all creditors. In addition, the acts of a company illegally transferring properties will be revoked if the transfer occurs within one year before declaring bankruptcy, and it may recover a portion of the property, thereby protecting the interests of creditors. The revised Partnership Enterprise Law stipulates that creditors may make an appropriate choice according to different situations[28]: (1) apply to a people's court for bankruptcy of the partnership according to law; or (2) requires the partners to pay off such debts. When a partnership is declared bankrupt according to law, its general partners shall still bear unlimited joint and several liabilities for the debts of the partnership.

Company law

The Company Law enforced in 1994 and the Securities Law enforced in 1999 are two important laws for the regulation of capital markets. They form the cornerstone of the legal system of China's capital markets. These two laws have played an important role in regulating the organisation and behaviour of companies, protecting the legitimate rights and interests of companies, shareholders and creditors, and regulating the acts of participants in the stock market. However, with the continued reform of the economy and financial system and the development of a socialist market economy, the market has undergone great changes, and many new situations have arisen; these two laws cannot fully meet the objective needs of these new situations and are therefore in urgent need of modification.

In October 2005, the National People's Congress revised the Company Law and brought it into effect on 1 January 2006.

On 28 December2013, the Sixth Session of the Standing Committee of the 12th National People's Congress adopted the amendment of the Company Law mainly

---

[28] Article 92 of the Partnership Enterprise Law

covering 12 changes and adjusting the order of provisions. This new Company Law, which took effect on 1 March2014, was another major breakthrough in China's company laws since the amendment in 2005.

The Company Law 2005 and the Company Law 2013 are the two most eye-catching amendments since China's company law was promulgated, fully demonstrating the maturity and improvement concerning company laws in China over the last decade. Compared with the former Company Law, the Company Law 2005 has been amended and reformed in an unprecedented manner. Most important have been the improvements in the company's capital and corporate governance system.

In terms of the capital system, the Company Law 2005 relaxes the restriction on the access threshold for a company's capital as follows:

First, it provides that the minimum amount of registered capital of a limited liability company shall be Rmb30,000, and the minimum amount of registered capital of a joint stock limited company shall be Rmb5m, significantly lowering the minimum amount of a company's registered capital.

Second, the Company Law 2005 diversifies the forms of a shareholder's capital contribution, as prescribed in Article 27:"A shareholder may make capital contributions in cash, in kind or intellectual property rights, land-use rights, or other non-monetary properties that may be assessed on the basis of currency and may be transferred according to the law, excluding the properties that shall not be treated as capital contributions under any law or administrative regulation."

Third, the Company Law 2005 cancels the provision of the former Company Law that the establishment of a company shall be subject to approval and commonly complies with the doctrine of registration for the establishment of a company.

Fourth, the Company Law 2005 creates the incorporation of a company by stock flotation. According to Article 78: "The incorporation of a company by stock flotation means that the promoters establish a company by subscribing to some of the shares that should be issued by the company and offering the remaining shares to the general public or to a group of specified people for subscription." In addition, Article 79 of the Company Law 2005 provides that, to establish a joint stock limited company, there shall not be less than two but not more than 200 promoters.

Fifth, the Company Law 2005 puts up special provisions on one-person limited liability companies. Since then, only a single natural person is allowed to establish a limited liability company in China, which has been included in the adjustment scope of the Company Law. Meanwhile, in order to prevent the shareholder of a one-person company mixing the company's property with his/her own property and harming the interests of the company's creditors, the revised Company Law has established the following five risk prevention systems:

1. Carry out the strict capital principle on a one-person company: the minimum amount of registered capital of a one-person limited liability company shall be Rmb100,000 in a lump sum;

2. A one-person limited liability company shall give a clear indication that it is solely-funded by one natural person or legal person in its business licence;

3. One natural person is allowed to establish a one-person limited liability company, which shall not establish any more one-person limited liability companies;

4. A one-person limited liability company shall make a financial report at the end of every fiscal year and have the report audited by an accounting firm;

5. In the event of debt disputes, the shareholder of a one-person company must prove the independence between the company's property and his/her own property; where the shareholder of a one-person limited liability company is unable to prove that the property of the one-person limited liability company is independent from his/her own property, he/she will lose his/her rights to bear the limited liabilities only in terms of his/her contribution to the company.

Compared with the laws of other countries concerning a one-person company, the above provisions are more stringent. The provisions have provided institutional facilities for the establishment of companies, which are conducive to encouraging business investment, promoting economic development and increasing employment.

The breakthrough of the Company Law 2005 is also reflected in the amendments made on paid-in capital and building a flexible authorised capital system, namely, the amount of the initial capital contributions made by all shareholders shall not be less than 20% of the registered capital, the margin shall be paid off by the shareholders within two years from the day when the company is established; for an investment company, it may be paid off within five years.[29]

---

[29] According to Article 26 of the Company Law: "The registered capital of a limited liability company shall be the total amount of capital contributions subscribed to by all shareholders registered in the company registration authority. The amount of the initial capital contributions made by all shareholders shall not be less than 20% of the registered capital, nor less than the statutory minimum amount of registered capital, the margin shall be paid off by the shareholders within two years from the day when the company is established; for an investment company, it may be paid off within five years.

The breakthrough of the Company Law 2005 is also reflected in the improvements to the share transfer system. Particularly noteworthy is the relaxation of restrictions on the share transfers of promoters, directors, supervisors and senior managers of a joint stock limited company. For example, the period of prohibiting transferring shares of a company held by the promoters of this company is shortened to one year, and the directors, supervisors and senior managers of the company may transfer the shares held by them during the term of office, and the shares transferred by any of them each year shall not exceed 25% of the total shares of the company he/she holds. The shares of the company held by the aforesaid persons shall not be transferred within one year from the day when the stocks of the company were listed and are traded in a stock exchange. After any of the aforesaid persons is removed from his/her post, he/she shall not transfer the shares of the company he/she holds. Compared with the "one-size-fits-all" provision of the former, the[30] Company Law 2005 is more reasonable and conducive to the value growth of shares[31].

In capital markets, the most radical change of the Company Law 2005 is to increase the system of "disregarding the personality of corporate" or "piercing the corporate veil". In other words, where any of the shareholders of a company evades the payment of its debts by abusing the independent status of a legal person or the shareholder's limited liabilities, if it seriously injures the interests of any creditor, it shall bear several and joint liabilities for the debts of the company.

Changes to the Company Law 2005 are also reflected in improving the corporate governance system, and particularly highlighting the mechanism of protecting the rights of shareholders, especially minority shareholders. In today's corporate governance, due to the fact that shares are dispersed, "shareholder centralism" has been replaced by "board centralism", and directors and senior managers have become the actual controller of the company, making minority shareholders ex-

---

The minimum amount of registered capital of a limited liability company shall be Rmb30,000. If any law or administrative regulation prescribes a relatively higher minimum amount of registered capital of a limited liability company, the provisions of that law or administrative regulation shall be followed."

[30] Article 142 of the new Company Law

[31] Pursuant to Article 147 of the former Company Law: "Shares of a company held by its sponsors may not be assigned for a period of three years commencing from the date of the company's establishment."

The directors, supervisors and general manager of the company shall report to the company the number of the company's shares held thereby, and may not assign such shares while they are in office.

tremely vulnerable. One of the focuses of the modern Company Law is to protect the interests of minority shareholders and other stakeholders by taking reasonable measures. In this regard, the Company Law 2005 makes a series of provisions:

First, it gives minority shareholders the right to request the convening of, to convene and to chair the general meeting of shareholders. Second, Article 22 provides for the right of minority shareholders to revoke a resolution. Third, it allows a joint stock limited company to adopt a cumulative voting system, with the aim of preventing major shareholders from manipulating the voting of directors and supervisors by taking advantage of their voting rights, and correcting existing drawbacks in the voting system of "one man, one vote". Fourth, it implements a shareholder's right to information; for example, the Company Law 2005 grants shareholders of a limited liability company the right to review the company's accounting books; but if the company has legitimate reason to believe that the shareholder's requests to review the books has an improper motive and may impair its legitimate interests, it may reject such a request. It should be noted that the Company Law 2005 does not grant the shareholders of a joint stock limited company the right to review the company's accounting books based on the characteristics of a large number of shareholders. Fifth, the shareholders of a limited liability company may exercise the appraisal right as dissenters to withdraw the company[32]. Sixth, it clarifies the right of shareholders to request the dissolution of the company when the company reaches an impasse. Seventh, it specifies the rights of shareholders to litigation and subrogation rights; according to Article 152 of the Company Law 2005, where a director, supervisor or senior manager violates the provisions of the law, regulations or the articles of association when performing his/her duties, causing losses to the company, "the shareholder(s) of the limited liability company or joint stock limited company separately or aggregately holding 1% or more of the total shares of the company for 180 consecutive days or more may request in writing the board of supervisors or the supervisor of the limited liability company with no board of supervisors to initiate a lawsuit in the people's court..." Eighth, it limits the right of the associated shareholder (i.e. the actual controller) to vote and trade. For example, pursuant to the Company Law 2005, if a company intends to provide a guarantee to a shareholder or actual controller of the company, it shall make a resolution through the shareholder's meeting or shareholders' assembly. The shareholder as mentioned in the preceding paragraph or the shareholder dominated by the actual controller as mentioned in the preceding clause shall not participate in voting on the matter as mentioned in the preceding clause. Such a matter requires affirmative votes from more than half of the other shareholders attending the meeting[33].

---

[32] Article 75 of the new Company Law

[33] Article 16 of the new Company Law

The Company Law 2013 has further relaxed the capital requirements on basis of the Company Law 2005, and simplified registration procedures, including a number of modifications considered effective in promoting the development of small and medium-sized enterprises (SMEs), the transformation of government functions and the simplification of company establishment. The main contributions of the Company Law 2013 to the advancement of China's rule of law are mainly reflected in the following aspects:

The Company Law 2013 has further reformed the capital system. For one thing, it cancels the restrictions that the minimum registered capital of a limited liability company, a one-person limited liability company and a joint stock limited company shall respectively reach Rmb30,000, Rmb100,000 and Rmb5,000,000, and also no longer imposes restrictions on the proportions of the initial capital contribution and monetary investment. Cancellation of the minimum registered capital is one of the highlights of the amendments to the new Company Law, which is also inevitable given the historical development of the capital markets. This revision achieves a shift from capital credit to asset credit. As the limited liability system of a company may put creditors at greater business risk, the minimum registered capital is designed to ensure the interests and risk balance of shareholders and creditors and such capital credits can provide the minimum guarantee for the interests of creditors. However, a company's independent liability is to be liable for its debts with its total assets, and the scope of a company liable for any other person or organisation shall depend on its total assets held, rather than its registered capital. The longer a company continues to exist, the larger the difference between the assets and the capital. Therefore, for its potential creditors, a company's registered capital does not have a great reference value in terms of its solvency; for a non-listed company, as it is not obliged to disclose its financial statements, potential creditors evaluate the company mainly through its usual credit status, actual operations and quality of management, in which assets have become a criterion to evaluate the company's credits, rather than the capital. Second, this revision can objectively reduce the threshold for entrepreneurship, encourage self-employment and stimulate economic development. The cancellation of the minimum registered capital indicates the realisation of no threshold for establishing a company, which will definitely promote the development of SMEs.

In addition, the company's capital system changes from a paid-in capital system to a capital subscription system. The Company Law 2013 cancels the original provision that the amount of initial capital contributions made by all shareholders shall not be less than 20% of the registered capital and the margin shall be paid off by the shareholders within two years from the day when the company is established; for an investment company, it may be paid off within five years; for a one-person limited liability company, it shall be paid off in a lump sum. Instead, the amount, means and time limit of contribution may be agreed by the shareholders of a company. From the lump-sum payment prescribed in the Company Law 1993 to the payment in instalments provided in the Company Law 2005 and even to the current capital subscription system, fundamental changes have taken place in the capital requirements for establishing a company.

When a company is founded, shareholders no longer bear the obligation to actually pay certain funds to ensure the business capacity and credibility of the company; instead, shareholders only need to subscribe the company's total registered capital. However, the nature of a shareholder's capital contribution obligation remains unchanged, as he/she is still obliged to contribute to the registered capital, and the implementation of capital subscription system has only changed the time limit of contribution of shareholders, but the nature of the obligation of contribution and legal capital system remains unchanged. Although the minimum registered capital is cancelled, the registered capital upon registration of a company is still necessary and the shareholder's obligation of capital contribution is a statutory as well as a legal obligation. It is agreed that shareholders may decide the registered capital amount of the company and the amount of their own subscription at their sole discretion. Once a company is registered in the industrial and commercial authorities, shareholders must pay the amount payable in line with the subscribed capital, and it is legally provided that the registered capital has its validity to be published.

After the new Company Law was amended in 2014, in the context of cancelling the restriction on the minimum registered capital and practising the complete capital subscription system, anyone may freely set up a company with a registered capital of millions or even tens of millions of renminbi, while he/she does not need to pay even a single cent or is subject to a time limit for payment. Therefore, the trustworthiness of shareholders is particularly important; China's personal credit mechanism is not yet perfect, and ordinary people must go through many departments and complicated procedures in order for their personal credit to be checked, and it is difficult to find personal credit information. China must build a comprehensive and reliable credit information platform concerning market subjects as soon as possible in order to balance the interests of shareholders and creditors.

The Company Law 2013 has also reformed the registration system of a company. The new law abolished the requirement to include paid-in capital as an item of business licence registration, and deleted the provision that the capital contribution for establishing a company must be verified by an accounting firm as set forth in the original Article 29. The cancellation of capital verification procedures can not only simplify the procedures for establishing a company, but also reduce the cost of its establishment.

one-person company mixing the company's property with his/her own property and harming the interests of the company's creditors, the revised Company Law has established the following five risk prevention systems:

1. Carry out the strict capital principle on a one-person company: the minimum amount of registered capital of a one-person limited liability company shall be Rmb100,000 in a lump sum;

2. A one-person limited liability company shall give a clear indication that it is solely-funded by one natural person or legal person in its business licence;

3. One natural person is allowed to establish a one-person limited liability company, which shall not establish any more one-person limited liability companies;

4. A one-person limited liability company shall make a financial report at the end of every fiscal year and have the report audited by an accounting firm;

5. In the event of debt disputes, the shareholder of a one-person company must prove the independence between the company's property and his/her own property; where the shareholder of a one-person limited liability company is unable to prove that the property of the one-person limited liability company is independent from his/her own property, he/she will lose his/her rights to bear the limited liabilities only in terms of his/her contribution to the company.

Compared with the laws of other countries concerning a one-person company, the above provisions are more stringent. The provisions have provided institutional facilities for the establishment of companies, which are conducive to encouraging business investment, promoting economic development and increasing employment.

The breakthrough of the Company Law 2005 is also reflected in the amendments made on paid-in capital and building a flexible authorised capital system, namely, the amount of the initial capital contributions made by all shareholders shall not be less than 20% of the registered capital, the margin shall be paid off by the shareholders within two years from the day when the company is established; for an investment company, it may be paid off within five years.[29]

---

[29] According to Article 26 of the Company Law: "The registered capital of a limited liability company shall be the total amount of capital contributions subscribed to by all shareholders registered in the company registration authority. The amount of the initial capital contributions made by all shareholders shall not be less than 20% of the registered capital, nor less than the statutory minimum amount of registered capital, the margin shall be paid off by the shareholders within two years from the day when the company is established; for an investment company, it may be paid off within five years.

has any merger or split-up, alters its form of corporation, suspends its business, goes through dissolution or bankruptcy, it shall be subject to the approval of the securities regulatory authority under the State Council." It goes on to state: "Where a securities company establishes, purchases or cancels a branch, alters its business scope or registered capital, increases the registered capital with major changes in shareholding structure, reduces registered capital, alters its shareholders or actual controllers who hold more than 5% of its stock rights, alters any important article of its constitution, has any merger or split-up, alters its form of corporation, suspends its business, goes through dissolution or bankruptcy, it shall be subject to the approval of the securities regulatory authority under the State Council."

In recent years, with the development of China's capital markets, various types of criminal acts associated with financial capital and securities have become even more common. Cases of market manipulation, false statements and insider trading have increased year by year, with regard to which the Securities Law has awarded severe administrative penalties. However, it is far from enough to simply rely on administrative penalties, and such violations in securities markets may also be curbed with the support of civil compensation liabilities and criminal penalties. China's criminal law has begun to make great efforts to crack down of financial crimes; for example, Article 180 of the Criminal Law makes reference to "the crime of trading on non-public information", which is targeted for the act of rat trading[34]. In September 2010, Han Gang, a former fund manager at Great Wall Fund Management, was arrested and transferred to judicial authority, initiating the criminal detention of fund managers in China. In August 2009, the Shenzhen Branch of the CSRC (China Securities Regulatory Commission) made a surprise inspection of 14 fund management companies within its jurisdiction, where Han Gang was found to privately engage in rat trading. During this inspection, the Shenzhen Branch of the CSRC found Tu Qiang, a fund manager at Invesco Great Wall, and Han Gang and Liu Hai, fund managers at Great Wall Fund, were suspected of being involved in trading stocks by using non-public information. The amount in the alleged accounts ranged from several hundred thousand renminbi to several million renminbi. Tu Qiang and Liu Hai were not held criminally responsible because their trading amounts did not reach the amount as prescribed by the Criminal

---

[34] Rat trading refers to fund managers buying shares via their personal trading accounts (agency heads, traders and their relatives or individuals closely related) ahead of large purchases of the same shares by their fund companies. Using this method, they can illegally profit from a rise in share price following the larger transactions.

Law, or their illegal acts occurred before the promulgation of the Amendment of the Criminal Law (VII)[35].

In addition, administrative penalties and criminal cases relating to insider trading are gradually increasing. As it needs to prove that the perpetrator has actually "known" the trading information in insider trading, it must also be proved that the acts of the perpetrator are causally associated with the information known in insider trading involving the transmission of information. As it is very difficult for the CSRC and judicial authorities to collect direct evidence, it is often necessary to rely on indirect, or circumstantial evidence to determine whether there is insider trading. In this regard, China's judicial authorities have referred to a large number of insider trading cases filed by the SEC to courts, and scholars have written many papers on this subject. On 1 June 2012, China's Supreme People's Court issued judicial interpretation on Several Issues Concerning the Specific Application of Law in the Handling of Criminal Cases of Engaging in Insider Trading or Leaking Insider Information to comprehensively specify the sentencing guidelines and other legal issues about sentencing guidelines on the part of insiders, personnel illegally obtaining insider information, the sensitive period of insider information, insider trading and the disclosure of insider information. This interpretation has not only fully absorbed the research results of legal theories at home and abroad, but also drawn on the successful judicial experience in foreign countries.

The judicial interpretation also disclosed the details about the case of insider trading and leaking insider information by Huang Guangyu. The case has had tremendous influence in China, because Huang Guangyu is the President of Gome, China's largest nationwide retail chain of consumer electronics products. Huang Guangyu featured in "China Rich List" on three occasions. He held a status in China similar to that of Sam Walton, founder of Wal-Mart, in the US. On 30 August 2010, Beijing Municipal Higher People's Court made a final decision on the case of Huang Guangyu, who was sentenced to 14 years' imprisonment, a fine of Rmb600m and the confiscation of property totalling Rmb200m.

Meanwhile, civil proceedings about insider trading cases are in progress. On 22 November2012, the third session on civil compensation applied by Zhongguancun investors against Huang Guangyu's insider trading case was called in Beijing Second Intermediate People's Court. This was China's first civil case arising from insider trading; however, the investors still lost the lawsuit. The case drew great attention, and Ma Pingchuan, a lawyer from Guangdong International Business Law Firm, said in an interview with Yangcheng Evening News: "In practice, there

---

[35] Because the Fourth Section of Article 180 is added by the Amendment to the Criminal Law (VII).

are no clear criteria concerning the identification of insider trading, the consequences that may arise and the cause-and-effect relationship, so it is easy to create a situation where the court may make different decisions on the same case. In China, in terms of compensation for the victims of insider trading, there are still many problems to be solved from legal empowerment to the realisation of realistic relief."

Regulatory system and law enforcement system of capital markets

The regulatory and law enforcement systems of capital markets are also being improved. Since the unified regulatory system was established in 1998, in order to meet the needs of market development, the securities and futures regulatory system has gradually been improved. In 2004, the CSRC changed the cross-region regulatory system and set up CSRC branches by administrative regions.

In terms of law enforcement, the CSRC set up inspection agencies[36] in individual branches, and established an agency responsible for investigating market manipulation and insider trading in 2002[37]; the Ministry of Public Security set up the Securities Crime Inspection Office co-located with the CSRC. In 2007, the law enforcement system underwent major reforms, established a unified inspection mechanism, set up the Administrative Punishment Committee, Chief Inspection Office and the Inspection Corps under the CSRC to strengthen the inspection resources of CSRC branches.

Split-share structure reform

In the last decade, one of the major institutional reforms has been the split-share structure reform. In the early days of capital markets, A-shares were divided into tradable shares and non-tradable shares; different levels of mobility gave rise to different values to these two types of share. During the course of reform, the way of consideration (such as bonus shares and warrant distribution) was taken between non-tradable shareholders and tradable shares to balance the interests of each other, and non-tradable shareholders transferred a portion of gains from equity listing to tradable shareholders. On 29 April 2005, the CSRC issued the Notice

---

[36] In 1995, the China Securities Regulatory Commission (CSRC) established an inspection department responsible for investigating illegal acts concerning securities and futures markets. In September 2000, the CSRC set up nine inspection offices in Tianjin, Shenyang, Shanghai, Jinan, Wuhan, Guangzhou, Shenzhen, Chengdu and Xi'an, with responsibility for investigating illegal cases concerning securities and futures within the jurisdiction.

[37] No. 2 Inspection Office; the original inspection office was renamed No. 1 Inspection Office, responsible for investigating fraud of securities issuance, false statements and other unlawful cases.

on the Pilot Reform of the Split-share Structure of Listed Companies to start the split-share structure reform on a trial basis. This reform has fundamentally eliminated the interest and price splits of state-owned shares, legal person shares and tradable shares; different types of tradable shareholders have the tradable rights to share listing and the rights to earnings of share prices, and different shares are priced based on a unified market mechanism. In early 2008, the split-share structure reform was basically completed.

Establishment of a multi-level capital market system

In the last decade, China's capital market system has gradually undergone multi-level development. Shenzhen Stock Exchange took the lead in setting up an SME board in May 2005, and established the Growth Enterprise Market (GEM) in 2012, commonly known as the "second-board market". A third-board market has also been developed. In 2006, unlisted companies in Zhongguancun Science Park entered the transfer agent system to offer and transfer their shares, known as the "new third board". Since then, China's multi-level capital market system has been gradually established.

Laws and regulations on listed companies

In the last decade, China's listed companies have experienced continuous growth and development; they have become an intermediary force to promote enterprise reform and drive industrial growth. But being affected by institutions, mechanisms and environmental factors, a large number of listed companies have been subject to imperfect governance structure, non-standard operations and low quality, seriously affecting the confidence of investors and restricting the healthy and stable development of capital markets.

In November 2005, the State Council approved and forwarded the Opinions on Improving the Quality of Listed Companies issued by the CSRC, thus initiating the governance on listed companies. Specific measures include:

First, it improved the regulatory system of listed companies. The jurisdiction monitoring accountability system for listed companies implemented in 2004 was a major reform of the regulatory system of listed companies, putting forward the requirement of "territorial regulation, clarification of rights and responsibilities, responsibilities to people, mutual cooperation". It further clarified the work responsibilities and positioning of the agencies dispatched by the CSRC and improved the timeliness and effectiveness of regulatory work.

Second, it strengthened information disclosure. The CSRC promulgated the Administrative Measures for the Disclosure of Information of Listed Companies[38] to further improve the information disclosure rules and regulatory processes and help to improve the transparency of operations of listed companies.

Third, it standardised corporate governance. In order to improve corporate governance, the CSRC has introduced a number of related regulations such as Guidelines for Articles of Association of Listed Companies[39] and Code of Corporate Governance for Listed Companies[40], and introduced the independent director system.

Fourth, it has cleared up defaults in listed companies. The CSRC has introduced provisions to strictly restrict the controlling shareholder and other related parties from occupying the funds of listed companies and the policy of "paying debts with equity" on a trial basis.

Fifth, it has established an equity incentive mechanism. In January 2006, the CSRC issued the Administration Measures for Equity Incentive Plans of Listed Companies (For Trial Implementation) for the purpose of promoting listed companies to further establish and improve their incentive and restraint mechanisms, which has had a profound impact on the standard operation and sustainable development of listed companies.

Sixth, it has promoted market-oriented mergers and acquisitions. By revising the Administrative Rules on Acquisition of Listed Company and information disclosure standards, the issuance of shares for subscribing assets to specific objects was started on a pilot basis to promote listed companies to grow stronger and larger. It also encouraged the controlling shareholders of listed companies to centralise high-quality assets and advantageous projects to listed companies, so that the merger and acquisition of market-oriented listed companies and the overall listing of enterprises can be significantly increased. In September 2007, the CSRC set up a review sub-committee for mergers, acquisitions and restructuring of listed companies to be responsible for reviewing the application of a listed company for merger, acquisition and restructuring, so as to further standardise the review system and enhance the transparency of review work.

When answering reporters' questions on the Administration Measures for the Material Asset Restructuring of listed Companies (Exposure Draft) and the Deci-

---

[38] It was promulgated and brought into effect on 13 December 2007
[39] Amended in 2006
[40] Enforced on 10 January 2002

sion on Amending "the Administrative Rules on Acquisition of Listed Company" (Exposure Draft), a spokesman of the CSRC stated that this revision was aimed at carrying through the market-oriented regulatory concept of "relaxing governance and strengthening supervision", and further "streamlining administration" on the basis of full argument, while supporting arrangements will be made to strengthen information disclosure, enhance supervision and urge intermediaries to exercise due duties. For example, in terms cancelling or simplifying administrative approvals, the revision: first, substantially cancel administrative approvals for material purchase, sale and replacement of assets of listed companies; second, cancel the prior-event approval for tender offers; third, cancel the approval for exemption in respect of two tender offers. The revision also improves the pricing of listed company share issues and cancels the negotiation-based pricing mechanism of bankruptcy reorganisation of listed companies.

Sponsor system and issuance pricing mechanism

Since March 2001, the approval system has been formally put into effect in China's IPO securities market. Compared with the examination and approval system, the authorised system is more scientific and reasonable. It has relaxed supervision and given companies more freedom, but it remains quite different from an international registration system. From 2001 to the beginning of 2004, the new share issuance in China's securities market was mainly recommended by lead underwriters, but the amount recommended was subject to channel restriction[41]. Until February 2004, after the implementation of the Interim Measures for the Stock Issuance and Listing under the Sponsorship System, the recommendation system of lead underwriters was formally shifted to the sponsor system, which is designed with reference to the UK's "AIM (alternative investment market)" system, and stipulates that sponsor agencies and sponsor representatives shall be engaged by a joint stock limited company that applies for an initial public offering and listing, and a listed company that issues new shares or convertible bonds. This system is an important exploration to establish a market restraint mechanism for issuance and listing.

In order to implement the requirements of the Securities Law, sum up the experience after the implementation of the sponsor system in a timely manner, enrich

---

[41] Channel restriction is a system where regulatory authorities determine the number of issuance channels of various comprehensive securities companies, and a securities company shall recommend the issuing company in accordance with the procedure of issuing one company before reporting another. The system is designed to limit the number of issuers recommended by securities companies through administrative means, and to control the number of companies to be listed and the speed of expansion.

and perfect the sponsor system in response to market needs and give full play to the role of the sponsor system, the CSRC revised the Interim Measures for the Stock Issuance and Listing under the Sponsorship System and renamed it the Administrative Measures for the Sponsorship Business of the Issuance and Listing of Securities, which went into effect on 1 December 2008. To facilitate the construction of China's GEM and perfect relevant supporting systems, the CSRC carried out a further revision of the Measures on13 May 2009 to enrich and improve the sponsor system and deepen the reform of the issuance system.

In terms of the issuance and pricing mechanism, with the increasing pricing power of institutional investors, the CSRC promulgated the Several Issues Concerning the Trial Implementation of Price Inquiry System for Initial Public Offering of Shares Circular at the end of 2004 to abolish the price approval system for stock issuance and carry out the price inquiry system[42]. Later, the Administration Measures for Securities Issuance and Underwriting[43] were introduced to further perfect the inquiry system.

Other laws and regulations

In order to adapt to the amendments to the Company Law and the Securities Law, the National People's Congress and departments under the State Council made a summary and adjustment of relevant laws, regulations and rules. In addition to these normative documents, other important laws and regulations include:

In April 2001, the Standing Committee of National People's Congress adopted the Trust Law of the People's Republic of China, which came into effect on 1 October 2001, since when China's trust industry has embarked on the process of legalisation and standardisation.

In June 2004, in order to regulate the securities investment activities and protect the legitimate rights and interests of investors and other relevant parties, the Standing Committee of National People's Congress adopted the Securities Investment Fund Law of the People's Republic of China. On 28 December 2012, the Standing Committee of the 11th National People's Congress revised this law and the new Securities Investment Fund Law took effect on 1 June 2013.

---

[42] Inquiry objects include fund management companies, securities companies, trust and investment companies, finance companies, insurance institutional investors and qualified foreign institutional investors (QFII) that meet the conditions as prescribed by the CSRC as well as other institutional investors approved by the CSRC.

[43] In September 2006

In August 2006, the Standing Committee of National People's Congress formulated and passed the Enterprise Bankruptcy Law of the People's Republic of China (the Enterprise Bankruptcy Law) to regulate the bankruptcy of enterprises and comprehensively protect the interests of all parties. In order to better support the implementation of the Enterprise Bankruptcy Law, Provisions (I) and (II) of the Supreme People's Court on Several Issues concerning the Application of the Enterprise Bankruptcy Law of the People's Republic of China were issued in 2011 and in 2013 respectively to give guidance on applicable laws concerning bankruptcy cases in the form of judicial interpretation.

The CSRC promoted the drafting and formulation of the administrative regulations in connection with the Company Law and the Securities Law, and after sorting out and integrating relevant rules, normative documents and self-regulations, it successively promulgated a series of regulations and normative documents such as the Code of Corporate Governance for Listed Companies (effected on 10 January 2002), Measures of China Securities Regulatory Commission for the Implementation of Freezing and Sealing-up (effected on 1 January 2006), Rules for the General Meetings of Shareholders of Listed Companies (effected on 16 March 2006), Guidelines for Articles of Association of Listed Companies (effected on 16 March2006), Administration Measures for Securities Settlement Risk Fund (effected on 1 July 2006), Regulatory Measures for Professional Qualifications of Directors, Supervisors and Senior Management of Securities Companies (effected on 1 December 2006) and Detailed Implementation Rules for the Non-public Issuance of Stocks by Listed Companies (effected on 1 September 2011), basically forming the regulatory system supporting the Company Law and the Securities Law.

Conclusion

In the last decade, the development of China's commercial laws has been universally recognised. By drawing on the experience of more advanced countries, we have spent just a few years going through a process that took decades elsewhere, quickly bringing China into line with international standards and fulfilling the promises made in its accession to the WTO. However, negative repercussions were unavoidable, and some problems have emerged. The country's rapid adoption of a market economy has inevitably led to the problem of unbalanced development.

Looking at the last decade, we should first focus on the amendments to the Company Law. This law, amended in 2005, is a major event in the history of China's Commercial Law. Some scholars believe that "the new Company Law has been a real revision since 1993, which is considered to be a major event in the history of the Company Law". The benefits of this new law are obvious, but there are also many deficiencies. The first deficiency is the fact that legal policies are still unreasonable; for example, the scope of business and the powers of companies are still subject to considerable restrictions, while harsh conditions are imposed on one-person liability limited companies. In addition, the capital verification system remains inflexible, the requirement for residence of promoter of a joint stock limited company is retained, and strict restrictions are imposed on derivative litigation. Second, legislative technology is still relatively rough, and institutional construction remains undistributed; for example, legal control is deficient in the negative effect on reinvestment, standards of judicial review are still required for the system of piercing the corporate veil and fiduciary duties, sound procedural safeguards need to be introduced for relevant corporate litigation, and related transactions are deficient in system processing.

In term of capital markets, with the resolution of historical issues and the gradual improvement of the legal system, capital market size has expanded rapidly with increasingly active transactions.[44] But China's nascent capital markets, after all, are passing through a transition period, and laws and regulations as well as institutions are not yet perfect. For example, the existing delisting mechanism is deficient in terms of flexibility, placing an emphasis on losses for three consecutive years. This standard has played a positive role in strengthening corporate profitability and prompting delisting risk, making the standard excessively inflexible. Moreover, the existing delisting mechanism adopts a single standard without different delisting criteria for different markets, causing the market mechanism of "survival of the fittest" to be realised incompletely.

Furthermore, the overall size of institutional investors in China's capital market is small, although great developments have been made in recent years. Institutional investors, mainly consisting of securities investment funds, have also been formed, and their role in the market continues to strengthen; nevertheless, the investment scale of insurance capital and pensions in the stock market remains small. Compared with foreign institutional investors, Chinese institutional investors are characterised by a short-term outlook, and current institutional investors show great homogeneity in terms of investment philosophy and investment targets, which are not conducive to the long-term healthy development of the market.

---

[44] According to the Report on China's Capital Market Development published by the CSRC, as of the end of 2007, there were 1,550 companies listed on the Shanghai and Shenzhen stock exchanges, with a total market capitalization of Rmb32,700bn, equivalent to 133% of GDP. In the same year, IPOs on the stock market aggregated Rmb459.58bn, ranking first in the world. The daily turnover reached Rmb190.3bn, becoming one of the most active markets in the world.

Third, the legal system of China's private equity investment has been relatively slow, and a number of problems that need to be addressed urgently have become a stumbling block to the development of private equity, of which the most crucial is to strengthen the building of laws and regulations. Although the revised Partnership Enterprise Law has helped cleared the way for private equity investment, there has been no law to make comprehensive or concrete provisions on management and flows of private capital, as the Interim Measures for the Administration of Start-up Investment Enterprises is only a framework-based law without supporting operational provisions. Therefore, there are no effective guidelines and norms for the development of private funds, but in this sense, a space has been left for future innovation. The government's position on this area is unclear, and there are no competent administrative departments responsible for fostering SMEs, thus ignoring the risks arising from the development of private equity investment and its potential impact on financial systems. In terms of market exist mechanism, China does not have diversified and well-developed exist channels as exist in Western countries, and there is no effective exist channel for venture capital funds. For a long time, the support needs of private companies and innovative technology companies, in particular, have not been given adequate attention, and the stock market has imposed higher requirements for listed companies, with inadequate development of the second-board market, slow and tortuous OTC (over-the-counter trading) development, and unstable property transactions, all of which make it difficult for venture capital to exit. In short, much remains to be done to help the development of private equity in China. The author believes that the most important thing is to develop a law concerning investment companies as soon as possible; in addition, the government should proceed from taxation and other financial policies to enhance government support and financial aid in private equity investment.

The Interim Measures for the Administration of Private Securities Investment Fund Business enacted in June 2013 reflect the function to give full play to industrial self-regulation, and the legislative idea to carry through appropriate administrative supervision, which mainly provides and refines the matters as expressly specified by law such as conditions for registration of private equity fund managers, criteria for qualified investors, fund publicity and promotion, fund filing and practitioner management.

In order to implement the Law of the People's Republic of China on Securities Investment Fund and the Several Opinions of the State Council on Further Promoting Healthy Development of the Capital Market (Guo Fa (GF) [2014] No. 17), regulate the activities of private investment funds, protect the legitimate rights and interests of investors and related parties, and promote the healthy development of private investment fund industry, the CSRC drafted the Interim Measures for the Supervision and Management of Private Equity Funds (Exposure Draft)[45] on 11 July 2014, putting forward normative requirements for private equity sales behaviour, scope of investment, private equity service agencies and their employees engaging in private equity fund services. There are signs that further standardised measures for private equity fund management are coming soon.

---

[45] See CSRC Website: http://www.csrc.gov.cn/pub/zjhpublic/G00306201/201407/t20140711_257649.htm

Chapter 3

China's criminal law in the last decade

— The balance between human rights protection and social security

Introduction

When the People's Republic of China (PRC) was founded, the new government faced national reconstruction in all aspects. The time was not ripe to draft a criminal code. In order to meet the demands of the social reform movement, the government enacted several separate criminal laws. These laws had a limited coverage and criminal cases were handled mainly on the basis of national policies. The enactment and promulgation of the Criminal Law in 1979 is considered as China's first criminal code in the 30 years following the establishment of the PRC. The Criminal Code of 1979 comprises 13 chapters with 192 articles, but all the provisions are relatively simple. With the deepening development of reform and opening up, China has been transformed. While promoting social reform, the market economy has also given rise to new types of crime. In order to deal with the disjunction between criminal laws and social development, the top legislative body successively enacted 24 separate criminal laws. It also added accessory criminal law norms to 107 non-criminal laws and made a series of minor revisions and amendments to the Criminal Code of 1979. In March 1997, the Eighth National People's Congress reviewed and passed the Criminal Law of the People's Republic of China, otherwise known as the Criminal Code of 1997, which consists of general, specific and supplementary provisions, and comprises 15 chapters with 452 articles. While inheriting the system of the Criminal Code of 1979, the Criminal Code of 1997 also reorganised and included 24 separate criminal laws and the criminal law norms of 107 non-criminal laws enacted between 1981 and 1997. The Criminal Code of 1997 is relatively comprehensive in terms of system and content. Unlike the criminal law norms developed before, the 1997 version stipulates three basic modern criminal law principles: Legally Prescribed Punishments, Equality upon the Criminal Law, and Balance of Crime, Responsibility and Penalty. This separation has strengthened the function of criminal law in guaranteeing human rights.

Although the Criminal Code of 1997 is a comparatively complete criminal code, some new developments have emerged in China's society since 1997. This is especially true in the 10 years following China's accession to the WTO in 2001, with the rapid strengthening of the economy and the acceleration of social transformation. In this environment, the legal sense and the people-oriented concept have become deeply rooted in people's minds and their understanding of crime and penalty has changed. In 2006, the central government clearly put forward the requirement to implement a policy that combined punishment with leniency, fully reflecting the improvement and development of China's criminal policy in terms of legal concept. In order to keep up with the pace of social development, the Standing Committee of the National People's Congress has made five amendments to criminal law in the past 10 years. In addition, it has passed four legislative interpretations for criminal law. These criminal law amendments and legislative interpretations have facilitated an improvement of China's criminal norms, guaranteed the stability of laws, and effectively mitigated the hysteresis quality of law. It can be concluded that China has achieved remarkable improvement in the lawmaking of criminal law in the past decade, in terms of the method, technique and content of lawmaking.

First, in terms of lawmaking method, criminal law amendment has become the only lawmaking method. In the last decade, all changes to criminal laws have been realised through amendments by the Standing Committee of the National People's Congress. In response to social development, the Standing Committee has introduced five criminal law amendments in total, and has not issued any separate or accessory criminal law. Compared with the latter two methods, the amendment method has combined the timeliness and scientificity of lawmaking, and maintained the unity of criminal law. In a sense, the establishment of the amendment method is a sign of the maturity of China's criminal law lawmaking model.[46]

Second, in the technical aspect, the structure and expression of criminal law lawmaking have gradually matured, and are reflected in two main aspects. On one hand, the lawmaking structure has become more well-established. The structure of the Criminal Law of 1997 has been adhered to by all the criminal law amendments introduced in the last decade, of which the first four amendments made changes by adding, removing or amending partial contents of the specific provisions of criminal law. The 8th Criminal Law Amendment has made a breakthrough. For the very first time, it also amended and added the content of the general provisions of criminal law. The changes to the general provisions, such as the adjustment of the prison term served after commutation, the limitation of commutation for death sentence with reprieve, the expansion of the

---

[46] Zhao Bingzhi, the Four Features and Two Directions of Criminal Law's Amendments, the Procuratorate Daily, 2 March 2009

scope of recidivism, and the adjustment of the maximum jail term for cumulative punishment, fully adapt to the changes in criminal law. As a result, the harsh punishments associated with certain crimes are somewhat tempered by these changes, which give prisoners the opportunity to be released from jail early. On the other hand, the legislative language of criminal law has become more accurate, rigorous and concise, and it has put more emphasis on the clarity and operability of the provisions. Take Article 3 of the 7th Amendment to the Criminal Law[47] as an example. This article summarises the specific tax evasion means of the original tax evasion crime as "cheat" and "subreption". It also expresses general guidance on conviction and sentencing. These specific amounts have been changed to "relatively large amounts" and "huge amounts". This article changes the expression for the specific amount involved in tax evasion crime[48] of the 1997 Criminal Law, which makes the provisions more suitable for the demands of social development, and makes the expression more rigorous and accurate.

Third, with regard to the content of lawmaking, it has fully reflected the active response of criminal law to social development and juridical practice. Specifically, there have been three features in the amendments of criminal law during this period. For one thing, based on the demands of economic and social development of different periods and combined with the requirements of juridical practice, these amendments have adjusted the content of criminal law and added a number of

---

[47] In Article 3 of the 7th Amendment to the Criminal Law, Article 201 of the Criminal Law was amended to read: "Where any taxpayer files false tax returns by cheating or concealment or fails to file tax returns, and the amount of evaded taxes is relatively large and accounts for more than 10% of payable taxes, he shall be sentenced to fixed-term imprisonment not more than three years or criminal detention, and be fined; or if the amount is huge and accounts for more than 30% of payable taxes, shall be sentenced to fixed-term imprisonment not less than three years but not more than seven years, and be fined...Where any withholding agent fails to pay or fails to pay in full the withheld or collected taxes by cheating or concealment, and the amount is relatively large, he shall be punished under the preceding section."

[48] Article 201 of the 1997 Criminal Law reads: "Tax payers found guilty of forging, altering, concealing or indiscriminately destroying accounts books, entry proofs, or making unsubstantiated expenditures, or failing to enter or enter lower income items, or failing to submit tax returns after being notified by the tax authorities, or submitting a false return, or failing to pay taxes or pay less, or evading taxes exceeding 10% but less than 30% of payable taxes, or evading taxes again after two administrative sanctions for tax evasion, shall be punished with imprisonment or criminal detention of less than three years, with a fine of more than 100% but less than 500% of the evaded tax amount; for cases with evaded tax amount exceeding 30% of payable taxes, or exceeding Rmb100,000, with imprisonment of more than three years but less than seven years, with a fine of over 100% but less than 500% of the evaded tax amount. "Withholding agents using the preceding means to refuse payment and full payment of withheld or collected taxes, which are more than 10% of payable taxes or over Rmb10,000, shall be punished in accordance with the preceding section."

new crime types. For example, the 4th Criminal Law Amendment added two new crimes: employing child labourers to engage in dangerous and heavy work, and smuggling of waste. In the 5th Criminal Law Amendment, two new crimes of credit card management nuisance and damaging weaponry, military installations and military communications under negligence have been added. For the 6th Criminal Law Amendment, eight new crimes were added, including false bankruptcy, major safety accident crime in large-scale mass activities, and concealment and false reports about accidents. The 7th Criminal Law Amendment added eight new crimes, such as using undisclosed information to trade, organising and leading pyramid selling activities, and bribery by influence. Ten new crimes were added in the 8th Criminal Law Amendment, including dangerous driving, producing and selling substandard foods, and forcing people to work. In addition, based on the criminal policy of combining punishment with leniency and the practical needs of juridical practice, the penalty structure and system have been actively improved, and the constitutive requirements and legal penalty of related crimes have been constantly adjusted, reflecting a strong practicality. Third, in order to adapt to the changing reality, the outdated criminal provisions have been repealed to improve the scientificity of criminal law. In the 8th Criminal Law Amendment, three legal provisions of criminal law have been cancelled, including Section 2 of Article 68 which states that criminals should be given a lighter or mitigated punishment or be exempted from punishment if they surrender and perform major meritorious services after committing the crime, Section 2 of Article 205 and Section 2 of Article 206. In conclusion, the lawmaking process of China's criminal law in the past decade has also led to the law becoming more mature, and signified the overall progress of China's socialist legal construction. It has promoted, and will continuously promote, the development and improvement of China's socialist criminal law construction.

Progress and development of China's criminal law in the last decade

In the 10 years following the end of 2002, based on the Criminal Law of 1949, China's criminal law has been continuously improved in the form of amendment in line with the demands of social reality and juridical practice. On 28 December 2002, the Standing Committee of the Ninth National People's Congress passed the 4th Amendment to the Criminal Law of the PRC at its 31st meeting. On 28 February 2005, the Standing Committee of the 10th National People's Congress passed the 5th Amendment to the Criminal Law of the PRC at its 14th meeting. On 29 June 2006, the Standing Committee of the 10th National People's Congress passed the 6th Amendment to the Criminal Law of the PRC at its 22nd meeting. The 7th and 8th Amendments were separately passed by the Standing Committee of the National People's Congress in February 2009 and the Standing Committee of the 11th National People's Congress on 25 February 2011.

The 4th Amendment to the Criminal Law of the PRC

With the emergence of the new conditions and problems in juridical practice, and the revisions of several laws such as the Customs Law and Pharmaceutical Administration Law, some parts of the 1997 Criminal Code required timely amendment after its enactment[49]. The Standing Committee of the National People's Congress passed the 4th Amendment to the Criminal Law of the PRC in its 31st meeting on 28 December 2002. The positive effects of the 4th Amendment on the improvement of China's criminal legislation are mainly reflected in the following aspects.

Two important livelihood protection measures have been involved in the 4th Amendment, including amendments about the crime of producing and selling substandard medical equipment (Article 1)[50] aimed at guaranteeing the safe use of medical equipment, and the newly added crime of employing child labourers to engage in dangerous and heavy work (Article 4)[51] aimed at protecting the interests of minors.

The crime of producing and selling substandard medical equipment originally was added as a supplement to the Criminal Code of 1979 in the Decisions about the Crime of Fake and Shoddy Products of 1993, and then amended and improved in the 1997 Criminal Code. However, the repackaging and sale of medical equipment such as disposable syringes and infusion tubes that were collected in huge quantities by some entities and individuals was widely practised despite repeated prohibition since 1997. Although the crime of producing and selling substandard medical equipment was defined in the Criminal Law of 1997, this crime had the constitutive requirement of serious harm on human health, leading to a very limited judicial application. On the basis of consequential offence, the 4th Amendment for the first time added the potential damage offence into this crime. It states

---

[49] Huang Taiyun, Understanding and Application of the 4th Amendment to China's Criminal Law. People's Procuratorial Monthly, 2003, Issue 3

[50] Article 145 is revised to read: "Whoever produces medical apparatus and instruments or medical hygiene materials that are not up to national or trade standards for safeguarding human health or sells such things while clearly knowing the fact, which is harmful enough to seriously endanger human health, shall be sentenced to fixed-term imprisonment of not more than three years or criminal detention and shall, in addition, be fined not less than half, but not more than two times, the amount of earnings from sales; if serious harm is caused to human health, he shall be sentenced to fixed-term imprisonment of not less than three years but not more than 10 years and shall, in addition, be fined not less than half, but not more than two times, the amount of earnings from sales; if the consequences are especially serious, he shall be sentenced to fixed-term imprisonment of not less than 10 years or life imprisonment, and shall, in addition, be fined not less than half, but not more than two times, the amount of earnings from sales or be sentenced to confiscation of property. "

[51] One article is added after Article 244 as Article 244(a), which reads: "Where a unit, in violation

that criminals will be convicted and punished if the crime is serious enough to cause serious damage to human body health, which greatly lowers the threshold of being criminalised and is quite important in protecting the medical and health security of the masses.

The crime of producing and selling substandard medical equipment originally was added as a supplement to the Criminal Code of 1979 in the Decisions about the Crime of Fake and Shoddy Products of 1993[52], and then amended and improved in the 1997 Criminal Code. However, the repackaging and sale of medical equipment such as disposable syringes and infusion tubes that were collected in huge quantities by some entities and individuals was widely practised despite repeated prohibition since 1997. Although the crime of producing and selling substandard medical equipment was defined in the Criminal Law of 1997, this crime had the constitutive requirement of serious harm on human health, leading to a very limited judicial application. On the basis of consequential offence, the 4th Amendment for the first time added the potential damage offence into this crime[53]. It states that criminals will be convicted and punished if the crime is serious enough to cause serious damage to human body health, which greatly lowers the threshold of being criminalised and is quite important in protecting the medical and health security of the masses.

The protection of minors' interests has gradually been included in China's various laws and regulations since the end of the 20th century. The illegal use of child labour has been clearly forbidden in laws such as the Minors Protection Law (1991), the Labour Law (1994) and the Compulsory Education Law (1986), and in administrative regulations and rules such as the Regulation of Forbidding the Usage of Child Labour issued by the State Council in 2002 and the Regulation of Special Protection on Minor Workers issued by the Department of Labour in 1994. However, these laws, regulations and rules failed to have the sufficient

---

of the laws and regulations on labour administration, employs a minor under the age of 16 to do physical labour of ultra-intensity, or to work high above the ground or in a pit, or to work under explosive, inflammable, radioactive, poisonous and other dangerous conditions, if the circumstances are serious, the person who is directly responsible shall be sentenced to fixed-term imprisonment of not more than three years or criminal detention and shall, in addition, be fined; if the circumstances are especially serious, he shall be sentenced to fixed-term imprisonment of not less than three years but not more than seven years and shall, in addition, be fined.

[52] Gao Mingxuan, the Breed, Birth, Development and Improvement of China's Criminal Law, 1st Edition. Peking University Press, 2012, P350.

[53] Yang Xinjing. Criminal Law's Amendments and Juridical Explanation, 1st Edition. China's Procuratorate Press, 2005, P159.

compelling and deterrent forces. In practice, some unlawful firms are motivated by interest to illegally employ minors under 16 to engage in dangerous and heavy work, which caused many tragedies. The incident of a "slave child" in a clothing workshop brought about poignant reflection in society. This incident occurred on 10 July 2001. Liu Li, a child labourer, died of heatstroke after continuously working under high temperature for 16 hours in an individually owned clothing workshop in Wuhan, Hubei province. The death of Liu Li attracted the attention of society on "child labour workshops". Wuhan's law enforcement officers then carried out a surprise inspection and found more than 20 garment factories concealed in an incomplete passenger transport centre building. Each of those factories employed about 10 child workers, aged around 12 or 13 years old[54]. Public opinion seethed with indignation after the scandal was revealed. The issue of protecting minors' interests was put on the table again. Addressing this painful social phenomenon, the 4th Amendment added the crime of employing child labour to perform dangerous and heavy work into the criminal law, which regulates the employment of child labour to engage in dangerous and heavy work as a crime for the first time, and regulates criminal penalties. With the compelling force of criminal law and the deterrent power of the penalties, the provisions on the crime of employing child labourers to engage in dangerous and heavy work in the 4th Amendment to the Criminal Law defends the protection of minors' interest. It demonstrates the value orientation of China's criminal law and reflects the great legislative advance of China's criminal law in the protection of minors' interests.

Unlike the criminal law amendments introduced previously, the 4th Amendment puts more emphasis on environmental protection. Among the nine legal provisions in this amendment, three of them relate to environmental protection and include four charges: the crime of illegally logging and destroying plants specially protected by the state in Article 6; the crime of illegal acquisition, transportation, processing and sale of national key protection plants and national key protection plant products in Article Six; the crime of illegal acquisition and transportation of unlawful and excessive felling of trees; and the crime of smuggling waste in Article 7.

With rising awareness of the importance of protecting wild plants, China has successively joined international conventions such as the Convention on Inter-

---

[54] Liu Ziling, the Shocking View of the Workshop Employing Child Labour. Hua Shang Daily, 14 August 2011 Access on 13 May 2013 from http://hsb.hsw.cn/gb/newsdzb/2001-08/14/2001-08-14-10bkll7.htm

national Trade in Endangered Species of Wild Fauna and Flora (1981)[55] and the Convention on Biological Diversity (1994)[56]. However, China's efforts to protect flora and fauna remain insufficient and the legal protection system is not complete. Obvious inadequacies can be found in the criminal protection of precious trees, especially other plant resources under the state's key protection. As the basic law of China, the criminal law has not played a sufficiently important role in this aspect[57]. Article 344 of the 1997 Criminal Law regulates the crime of illegally logging and destroying precious trees. However, as society has developed, new problems have emerged during the implementation of this crime. In accordance with regulations about the protection of the wild plants, several other precious wild plants under the state's key protection also have importance to the economy, culture and scientific research. However, in practice, the issue of destruction of rare wild plants is quite serious, and the suggestion had been made that the criminal law should include relevant regulations to address this issue[58]. Against this background, the 4th Amendment meets the demands of society and expands the term "precious trees" to "precious trees or other plants under the state's key protection" in the amendment. It also adds the crime of illegal acquisition, transportation, processing and sale of national key plants under protection and national key plant products under protection, which improves the connection between different legal provisions and increases the strength of legal protection.

The 1979 Criminal Law has regulated the crime of unlawful felling of trees and the crime of excessive felling of trees. The crime of illegal acquisition of the unlawful and excessive felling of trees was added during amendments made to the 1997 version of the Criminal Code with the aim of curbing unlawful felling and excessive felling of trees by punishing downstream crime[59], which

---

[55] Meng Xianlin, Fulfilment of United Nations Convention on the International Trade in Endangered Species of Wild Fauna and Flora by China. Wild Animals. 1997, Issue 4

[56] Wang Xianfu & Guo Ke, Achievement and Prospect on China's Fulfilment of Convention on Biological Diversity, Guangxi Plants. 2006, Issue 3

[57] Liu Jie, Legislative Improvement to Criminal Law and the Newly Added Crimes in the 4th Amendment to the Criminal Law. Journal of Xiangtan Institute of Technology. 2003, Issue 2, Volume 5.

[58] Gao Mingxuan, the Breed, Birth, Development and Improvement of China's Criminal Law, 1st Edition. Peking University Press. 2012. P570

[59] Section 3 of Article 345 in the 1997 Criminal Law: Those who, in order to make a profit, illegally purchase timber from illegal or wanton logging in a serious manner are to be sentenced to less than three years of fixed-term imprisonment or criminal detention or control and, in addition, be sentenced to a fine. They may also be only punished by a fine. In especially serious cases, those offenders are to be sentenced to not less than three years and not more

has indeed had a positive impact. However, in practical terms, there is no reason for the existence of the two restrictions of "the aim of getting profit" and "in forest areas", which must be met when constituting this crime in the original legal provisions. Based on actual legal cases, all cases of this crime type are motivated by profit. And with increasing efforts in tree planting, the boundary between forest areas and non-forest areas is no longer obvious. The vast forests in non-forest areas also need protection. Therefore, the 4th Amendment has amended the constitution of the crime by deleting these two restrictions. Additionally, it added "transportation" as a criminal behaviour. This crime was finally amended as the crime of illegal acquisition and transportation of unlawful and excessive felling of trees[60], which further improved China's criminal regulations over forest protection.

In the Criminal Law of 1997, there is a general regulation that smuggling overseas solid waste into China will be punished under the crime of smuggling. However, no specific punishment regulations in the provision of smuggling crime in the criminal law can be referred for smuggling solid waste.[61] Specific to this legislative loophole, the 4th Amendment to Criminal Law added the crime of smuggling waste in the provision of smuggling crime. At the same time, in order to prevent lawbreakers from taking advantage of this legal loophole, the amendment also includes smuggling liquid and gaseous wastes in this crime. The enactment of the 4th Amendment provides the legal basis to punish the crime of smuggling waste. In 2004, the People's Procuratorate of Nantong Municipality filed a public prosecution on China's biggest waste smuggling case since the foundation of the new China. With the aim of making large profits, Gong Jianchang, the defendant, imported the waste molybdenum catalyst into China to extract the metal. Significant toxic gas and hazardous substances were released during the extraction, which gave rise to serious air and water pollution. The Intermediate People's Court of Nantong Municipality convicted and punished the defendant with the crime of smug-

---

than seven years of fixed-term imprisonment and, in addition, be sentenced to a fine.

[60] In Article 7 of the 4th Amendment to the Criminal Law, Article 345 of the Criminal Law is revised to read: "Whoever illegally purchases and transports timber from illegal or wanton logging, if the amount involved is relatively large, shall be sentenced to fixed-term imprisonment of not more than three years, criminal detention or public surveillance and shall in addition, or shall only, be fined; if the amount involved is huge, he shall be sentenced to fixed-term imprisonment of not less than three years but not more than seven years and shall, in addition, be fined.

[61] Ibid as footnote 2, p3

gling waste[62]. It is fair to say that the provisions on the crime of smuggling waste in the 4th Amendment have not only closed the loophole in criminal law, but also helped to maintain the order of customs management. Besides, it can prevent waste from polluting China's environment after being smuggled, which is positive for environmental protection in China.

The 4th Amendment added the crime of delinquency in judgement and adjudication execution and the crime of abusing power in judgement and adjudication execution in Article 8[63], which has strengthened the accountability of crimes in the field of law enforcement in China.

The Criminal Law of 1997 has set the crime of bending the law for the benefit of relatives or friends and the crime of refereeing by perverting the law in civil and administrative cases. But in juridical practice, corruption also exists in the execution phase, except during investigation, prosecution and trial. Some law enforcement officers exhibit favouritism and commit irregularities. They deliberately put off the execution of cases that can be executed, or illegally enforce litigation preservation measures and compulsory execution measures, which cause great loss for the parties involved and serious social harm. The 4th Amendment to the Criminal Law added a new provision after Article 399 of the original criminal law. It introduced two types of crimes, namely the crime of delinquency in judgement and adjudication execution and the crime of abusing power in judgement and adjudication execution in the effort to fight against misconduct in law enforcement, which has a positive meaning in maintaining justice.

Besides, corresponding to the amendment of the Customs Law of 2000 and targeting smuggling activity in border waters such as rivers and lakes, the 4th Amendment also expanded the special scale of smuggling crime, making contributions to the improvement of defining smuggling crime in China.

---

[62] Xu Degao and Jin Hua, Four Companies Fined and Two People Sentenced for Smuggling More than 3,400 Tons Waste Catalyst. The Procuratorate Daily, 2004, Issue 3839

[63] Section 3 of Article 7 in the 4th Amendment to the Criminal Law: "Any judicial officer who, being seriously irresponsible or abusing his power in execution of judgements or orders, does not take preservation measures in litigation in accordance with the law, or does not perform his statutory duty of execution, or unlawfully takes preservation measures in litigation or takes compulsory enforcement measures, thus causing heavy losses to the interests of the parties or other persons, shall be sentenced to fixed-term imprisonment of not more than five years or criminal detention; and if especially heavy losses are caused to the interests of the parties or other persons, he shall be sentenced to fixed-term imprisonment of not less than five years but not more than 10 years.

The 5th Amendment to the Criminal Law of the PRC

On 28 February 2002, the Standing Committee of the 10th National People's Congress passed the 5th Amendment to the Criminal Law of the PRC at its 14th meeting. Based on the needs of China's economic development since the reform and opening up, and new problems in juridical practice, the 5th Amendment puts great emphasis on legislative improvement of credit card-related crimes by adding the crime of hindering credit card management in Article 1 and amending the crime of credit card fraud in Article Two. The provisions of the 5th Amendment mainly reflect the progress of China's market-oriented reform in the aspect of government by law.

During the early years of reform and opening up, China had a relatively single-function financial market. Financial activities were restricted and credit card-related criminal cases were uncommon. There was no relevant legislation at that time. However, with the development of China's financial market and the demand of juridical practice, legislation over bank card crime in China has progressed from nothing and gradually improved and developed. The enactment of the new Criminal Law of 1997 marked the establishment of China's legislative system of bank card crime. In 1999, the People's Bank of China, its central bank, issued the Measures for the Management of Bank Card Business[64]. It clearly stated the distinction between bank credit cards and debit cards, which triggered a debate among criminal law scholars over whether debit cards belonged to credit card fraud crime. In order to unify understandings and define the scope of credit cards in criminal law, the Standing Committee of the National People's Congress issued and implemented the Explanation for Credit Card-Related Provisions in the Criminal Law of PRC on 29 December 2004[65]. It provides an expanded explanation for the concept of credit cards in the criminal field to include both credit cards and debit cards in the term "credit card" in criminal law. Although the introduction of this explanation resulted in different concepts of credit card in the fields of crime and finance, it has had great significance in cracking down on credit card-related crimes.

---

[64] Article 5 of Chapter 2 in Regulations on the Bank Card Business states that, bank cards including the credit cards and the debit cards.

[65] The Explanation for Credit Card-Related Provisions in the Criminal Law of the PRC clearly states that the credit cards involved in the Criminal Law refer to electronic payment cards that are issued by commercial banks or other financial institutions, and have all or part of the functions such as consumption payment, credit loans, settlement by transferring accounts, and depositing and withdrawing cash.

With the development of China's financial markets and economic globalisation since reform and opening up, the bank card, as a modern settlement tool, has been widely used. According to the People's Bank of China, the total amount of bank cards issued in China reached 800m at the end of 2004, ranking second in the world[66]. The total value of bank card transactions in China reached Rmb18,000bn in 2003[67]. With the increasing reach and development of the credit card business, the type and nature of credit card-related crimes has diversified, resulting in increasing harm to society. In 2002, Guangdong province cracked a major case of forged international credit cards with the case code of JK1[68], with 20,000 forged credit cards being seized during the action. The credit cards of 20 internationally known banks including First Pacific Bank of Hong Kong, the Atlantic Bank of Macao, the Hong Kong and Shanghai Banking Corporation, the MBNA Bank of Britain, American International Group or AIG, Overseas Union Bank of Singapore and Shinpan Corporation of Japan had been forged, and the amount involved in this case was about Rmb320m. Given the worsening trend of credit card-related crime in China, in terms of incidence, diversification and seriousness, the 5th Amendment improves regulation in this area. Based on the crime of forged and altered financial tickets in Article 177 of the criminal law, it added provisions on the crime of hindering the credit card management. This amendment also included one more aspect of credit card fraud crime by convicting the behaviour of fraudulently procuring credit cards through false identification as a credit card fraud crime, which can help China to tackle the challenges arising from marketisation reform. The amendment and improvement for the provisions of credit card-related crimes in the 5th Amendment highlight actions taken by China's legislative body to close the net of justice for credit card-related crime, effectively cracking down on new types of credit card-related crimes and improving legislative protection of financial order.

The implementation of the 5th Amendment reflects the further improvement of China's criminal law and regulation system over credit card-related crimes. In April 2008, in the Approvals about How to Determine the Nature of the Be-

---

[66] See Wang Bixue, Credit Cards: New Direction of Financial Crimes. People's Daily, 30 March 2005

[67] See Wu Jing, Legislation to Punish Credit Card-Related Crimes. People's Daily, 28 October 2004

[68] Liang Ruiguo and Xia Xiaolu, A Super-Large Case Of Forging International Credit Card Coded JK1 Uncovered in Guangdong, Published on the website of the Public Security Ministry, http://www. mps.gov.cn/n16/n1237/n1402/97421.html, accessed on 9 May 2013

haviour of Picking up other People's Credit Cards and Using Them at an ATM, the Supreme People's Procuratorate regulated that the behaviour of stealing other people's credit cards and using them at an ATM belonged to the situation of "false usage of other people's credit cards" in Article 1996 of the criminal law. This behaviour will be investigated for criminal responsibility as credit card fraud if it constitutes a crime. On 16 December 2009, the Supreme People's Court and the Supreme People's Procuratorate jointly introduced the Explanations for Some Questions in the Specific Application of Laws When Handling the Criminal Cases of Hindering the Credit Card Management. This judicial explanation refines the legal issues in credit card-related crimes, clears up some difficult questions about the application of laws in handling criminal cases involving credit cards, and improves the operability of credit card-related criminal law in juridical practice.

The 6th Amendment to the Criminal Law of the PRC

On 29 June 2006, the Standing Committee of the 10th National People's Congress passed the 6th Amendment to the Criminal Law of the PRC at its 22nd meeting. This amendment comprises 21 provisions, adding nine new crimes such as failing to report, or making up reports on, safety accidents, false bankruptcy, infringing listed companies in bad faith, and distorting the law to arbitrate, and amending 12 legal provisions such as the crime of major liability accident, the crime of negligently causing serious labour safety accidents, the crime of illegally disclosing or not disclosing important information, the crime of bribery for non-government workers and the crime of offering bribes to non-government workers. Compared with previous criminal law amendments, the 6th Amendment has a larger adjustment range and a wider span in content, which generates a widespread discussion in theoretical and practical fields. This amendment has the following positive meanings for the legislation and juridical practice of China.

The crime of workplace accidents, especially coalmine safety accidents, in China has been rising in recent years. There were four serious mining accidents in China in 2005 alone, with more than 100 miners killed and wounded in each case. These accidents include gas explosion at Sujiawan coal mine in Fuxin city[69] on 14 February, a water inrush accident at Xingning coal mine in Guang-

---

[69] See Reports about 2.14 gas explosion at Sujiawan coal mine in Liaoning, available on http://www.sczfsafety.cn/ArticleShow.aspx?id=2c97707f-358f-4899-b38c-ee4e1228cb04. Accessed on 1 June2013

dong province on 7 August[70], a coal-dust explosion at Dongfeng coal mine in Qitaihe on 27 November and the 7 December gas explosion at Liuguantun coal mine in Tangshan. According to statistics, a total of 127,000 people in China were killed in production accidents in 2005[71]. The 6th Amendment adjusted and amended the criminal law with an emphasis on improving the legal system of workplace accident crimes and enhancing public safety. The 6th Amendment amended the crime of major liability accident in Article 1 and the crime of negligently causing serious labour accidents in Article 2. It also added three new crimes including compelling workers to violate regulations and work at risk in Article 1, major accidents in large-scale activities in Article 3 and failing to report, or making up reports on safety accidents in Article 4. The role played by the 6th Amendment in improving the criminal legal system of accident is the inevitable demand of China's current juridical practice.

China's Criminal Law of 1997 includes provisions on the crime of major liability accident[72]. The subjects of this crime are the same as in the 1979 Criminal Law, being limited to workers in factories, mines, forest farms, construction enterprises, and other enterprises and public institutions. However, with the transformation of China's economic structure, emerging entities such as self-employed ventures and cooperative joint ventures have emerged and it's difficult to impose criminal liability on them under the original criminal law. Due to the narrow range of criminal subjects, provisions on the crime of major liability accidents in the original criminal law could not meet the demand in punishing and preventing major accidents. This is especially true when some producers and operators aggressively pursue economic profits and compel workers to work against job regulations,

---

[70] See water inrush accident at a private coal mine in Xingning, Guangdong province. Available on Sina.com,

http://news.sina.com.cn/z/mzmkts/, Accessed on 1 June 2013

[71] You Liang, Statistical Bulletin of 2005. Available on Xinhua News,

http://news.xinhuanet.com/photo/2006-03/01/content_4241854.htm, Accessed on 1 June2013.

[72] Article 134 of the 1997 Criminal Law reads: "The staff and workers of factories, mines, forestry centres, construction enterprises or other enterprises and institutions who do not submit to management and violate the rules and regulations or force workers to work in a risky way in violation of the rules, thereby giving rise to major accidents involving injury or death and causing other serious consequences, are to be sentenced to not more than three years of fixed-term imprisonment or criminal detention; when the circumstances are particularly odious, to not less than three years and not more than seven years of fixed-term imprisonment.

which has resulted in frequent liability accidents and caused great losses to people's life and health, as well as to corporate property. Against this background, the 6th Amendment amended the original provision of the criminal law and expanded the subject of this crime from workers of enterprises or public institutions to all people involved in production or operation. It included self-employed entrepreneurs, labour contractors and people serving in production or operation without a licence, all of whom can be responsible for accidents, but could not be punished under the original criminal law. It also increased the maximum legal penalty for direct responsible persons. Besides, in order to curb the occurrence of compelling workers to work against job regulations, the 6th Amendment added the crime of impelling workers to violate regulations and work at risk[73]. Through these amendments, the 6th Amendment has comprehensively enhanced the investigation and punishment over the crime of major liability accidents.

The crime of major labour safety accident[74] originated in the Criminal Law of 1997. Before that, there were no related provisions in China's criminal law. In practice, most labour safety accidents were regulated by Article 92 of the Labour Law of the PRC[75], which was put into force in 1995. With the rapid development of China's economy and the emergence of private enterprises and individual enterprises, labour safety accidents occurred at a high frequency. Coal mine accidents continued to spread, which made state organs appreciate the necessity to legislate. The Criminal Law of 1997 was the first to in-

---

[73] Section 2 of Article 1 in the 6th Amendment to the criminal law reads: "Whoever forces another person to work under hazardous conditions in violation of rules, thereby causing an accident involving heavy casualties or causing other serious consequences, shall be sentenced to fixed-term imprisonment of not more than five years or criminal detention; and if the circumstances are especially flagrant, he shall be sentenced to fixed-term imprisonment of not less than five years."

[74] Article 135 of the 1997 Criminal Law reads: "Any factories, mines, forestry centres, construction enterprises or other enterprises and institutions that have labour safety facilities that fail to conform with state regulations and do not take measures to prevent hidden dangers after a request was made by relevant departments or the unit's staff and workers, thereby giving rise to major accidents involving injury or death or other serious consequences, personnel who are directly responsible are to be sentenced to not more than three years of fixed-term imprisonment or criminal detention; when the circumstances are particularly odious, the sentence is to be not less than three years and not more than seven years of fixed-term imprisonment."

[75] Article 92 of the 1995 Labour Law reads: "The employer whose labour safety facilities and labour sanitation conditions fall short of state regulations or who fails to provide labourers with necessary labour protection articles and labour protection facilities shall be ordered by labour

troduce this type of crime, but it had a drawback in that the crime of major liability accident was narrowly defined. For the same reason, the 6th Amendment amended this crime. It removed the enumerative regulations about the crime subjects in the original legal provisions and simplified the facts about this crime, which improved its applicability in juridical practice. Besides, when it comes to punishment over labour safety accidents, except for expanding the range of application for the crime of major liability accident, the 6th Amendment also added the crime of failing to report or falsely reporting safety accidents, which can help to crack down on the serious threat to life and property caused by people acting in their own selfish interests. The emphasis on labour safety in the 6th Amendment is the highlight of this criminal law amendment, reflecting the criminal law's function in protecting people's livelihood.

The 6th Amendment also added the crime of major accidents in large-scale activities. In recent years, cases involving great personal casualties or property loss happened frequently at such events due to a violation of safety management regulations. One example is a stampede accident that happened during the Spring Lantern Show in Miyun county, Beijing. On 25 February 2004, Mihong Park in Miyun county held the 2nd Spring Lantern Show. One visitor fell from a park bridge and caused a stampede among other visitors. A total of 37 people died and 15 were injured in this accident[76]. There are differences between safety accidents in large-scale cultural activities and liability accidents in production and operation. The criminal law did not provide specific punishment over these safety accidents, and they were usually settled in the form of civil compensation. In fact, the organisers of some large-scale activities were seriously irresponsible. Cases with serious consequences that occurred due to management negligence were quite common. It is quite necessary for the criminal law to define clear responsibilities of relevant organisers and improve protection over public safety. In this regard, the 6th Amendment added the crime of major safety accidents at

---

administrative departments or other relevant departments to make corrections, or be fined. Those involved in serious cases shall be reported to people's governments at or above county level so that they can order it to stop production. Criminal responsibilities shall be fixed upon the persons in charge according to stipulations in Article 187 of the Criminal Law should the failure on the part of the employer to take measures against possible accidents result in serious accidents and cause losses of labourers' life or properties.

[76] See Stampede Accident Happening during the Spring Lantern Show in Beijing's Miyun county, from Xinhua News. Available on http://www.bj.xinhuanet.com/myzn/myzn.htm, accessed on 1 June 2013.

large-scale activities[77] to provide the clear legal basis for the judicial act in relevant criminal cases, which is an important progress for China's criminal law in protecting people's livelihood.

The most visible contribution of the 6th Amendment on legislation lies in its provisions on crimes in the economy. China's economy has been growing rapidly since the reform and opening up, and there have been tremendous changes, especially in terms of enterprises and finance. Difficulties have arisen from the relative stability of the criminal law compared with rapid changes in the economy. In this situation, the 6th Amendment must take its responsibilities in the reform and evolution of criminal law in the economy. Amendments to financial crime and enterprise crime account for more than half of the contents of the 6th Amendment.

To be specific, the provisions on enterprise crimes in the 6th Amendment are mainly reflected in two newly added crimes, covering false bankruptcy in Article 6 and infringing listed companies against good faith in Article 9, and the amendments for three crimes: illegally disclosing or not disclosing important information in Article 5; bribery for non-government workers in Article 7; and offering bribes to non-government workers in Article 8.

One-third of the contents of the 6th Amendment is made up of provisions on crimes in the financial sector. This reflects the rapid evolution and development of China's criminal law in finance, where three new crimes have been added: cheating loans, bills acceptance and finance tickets in Article 10; breach of entrusted property in Article 12; and illegally using funds in Article 12. It is also reflected in the amendments to five crimes: manipulating the securities and futures markets in Article 11; illegally providing loans in Article 13; not recording deposits in book in Article 14; illegally issuing financial tickets in Article 15; and money laundering in Article 16.

There had been six amendments to the criminal law prior to this amendment. But the 6th Amendment has the widest coverage and the most content with the purpose of meeting the demands of a fast-changing economic and financial system. All the economic crimes mentioned above reflect the serious circumstances, serious consequences and huge amounts involved as the premise for the constitution

---

[77] One article is added after Article 135 of the Criminal Law to be Article 135a, which reads: "Where a large-scale mass activity is held in violation of safety provisions, thereby causing an accident involving heavy casualties or causing other serious consequences, the person directly in charge and the other persons directly responsible shall be sentenced to fixed-term imprisonment of not more than three years or criminal detention; and if the circumstances are especially flagrant, the said persons shall be sentenced to fixed-term imprisonment of not less than three years but not more than seven years.

of the crime. This is because, considering the short history of China's financial and security markets and the relatively large amount of non-standard conditions, lawmakers introduce the relatively stricter constitutive requirements (compared with foreign countries) to financial crime. For example, in the US and Japan, the crimes of securities insider trading crime or the rigging of stock prices only needs the implementation of these acts. Elements such as the serious circumstances or causing serious consequences are not necessary for the constitution of crime in these countries[78].

The most important feature of the 6th Amendment in legislative content is the timely response to the demand of economic and social development. In response to the new conditions emerging during the development of the market economy, regulations concerning the crime of breaking market economic order have been enriched. For example, targeting financial risks arising from the Asian financial crisis, the decisions to punish the fraudulent purchase of foreign exchange, the evasion of exchange control and illegally buying and selling foreign currency have been passed to add new crimes and adjust legal penalties, which has effectively guaranteed the safety of China's finance and economy[79]. The 6th Amendment also paid full attention to the important role played by criminal law in punishing and preventing corruption. These measures are all contributions made by the 6th Amendment to China's criminal law in the economic sector. They reflect the value orientation of China's criminal law in severely cracking down on illegal business behaviour, punishing economic corruption, and preventing and controlling financial risk, which has had a positive and progressive significance.

The 7th Amendment to the Criminal Law of the PRC

In February 2009, the Standing Committee of National People's Congress passed the 7th Amendment to the Criminal Law of the PRC. This amendment amended and adjusted the relevant provisions on the crime of corruption and bribery, the crime of disrupting the order of the socialist market economy, the crime of infringing citizens' rights and the crime of impairing the administration of social order. The general tendency of amendments to criminal law has been the increase overall penalties, expand criminal scope and the specification of criminal accusations and facts since the implementation of the 1997 Criminal Law. The 7th Amendment followed this tendency and made some adjustments. For example, the criminal

---

[78] Gu Xiaorong, New Changes in Punishing Financial Crimes Brought by the Sixth Criminal Law Amendment. Politics and Laws, 2006, Issue 4

[79] Lei Jianbing, New Progress in China's Criminal Law since 1997: On the Occasion of the Enactment of the 6th Criminal Law Amendment. The National People's Congress of China, 10 July 2006.

facts about the crime of tax evasion were described in a summarized legislation model. The legal penalty of kidnapping was also lowered, which was quite rational. But the strictness of the criminal law net and the aggravation of penalty is still the general tendency[80]. The expression of criminal law legislation should be reasonably detailed and the net of criminal law should be rationally expanded. The legislative power of criminal law should further reflect the tendency of democratisation to realise the positive interaction between theory and practice. Generally speaking, the 7th Amendment has the following highlights.

The 7th Amendment reflects the increase of China's efforts in anti-corruption, which are mainly embodied in the expansion of the definition of the crime of bribery and the increase in penalty term for the crime of holding a huge amount of property from unidentified sources.

The crime of bribery by influence was added after Article 388 of the criminal law through Article 13 of 7th Amendment[81], which expands the crime of bribery to people around government leaders. In practice, it has been common for some state functionaries' relatives or others with close relations to take advantage of these functionaries' positions to seek interests for others and accept bribes. According to the criminal law before this amendment, bribery was a job-related crime conducted by state functionaries. Non-government workers could not form part of this crime by themselves alone. But if this behaviour cannot be punished as a crime, the relatives of state functionaries or other people with close relations to them would accept bribes without any scruple, which can severely damage China's efforts to construct a clean government. In past juridical practice, the court could only list people around leaders as the accomplices of bribery law. With the implementation of the new criminal law amendment, people around government leaders can independently become the subject of a bribery crime, which addresses the shortcomings of the original criminal law. It has also fixed

---

[80] Yang Gaofeng, Breakthrough and Deficiency in the Legislation of the 7th Criminal Law Amendment, Law Science Magazine, 2009, Issue 6

[81] Article 13 of the 7th Criminal Law Amendment reads: "Where any close relative of a state functionary or any other person who has a close relationship with the said state functionary seeks any improper benefit for a requester for such a benefit through the official act of the said state functionary or through the official act of any other state functionary by using the advantages generated from the authority or position of the said state functionary, and asks or accepts property from the requester for such a benefit, and the amount is relatively large or there is any other relatively serious circumstance, he shall be sentenced to fixed-term imprisonment not more than three years or criminal detention, and be fined; if the amount is huge or there is any other serious circumstance, shall be sentenced to fixed-term imprisonment not less than three years but not more than seven years, and be fined; or if the amount is extremely huge or there is any other extremely serious circumstance, shall be sentenced to fixed-term imprisonment not less than seven years, and be fined or be

the problem debated for years in criminal theory about whether the acceptance of property form others by using the advantage of their former position or status with decommissioned state functionaries should constitute bribery, which has had positive repercussions for the punishment of bribery crime.

In its 14th article, the 7th Amendment also amended Section 1 of Article 395 in the criminal law about the crime of holding a huge amount of properties derived from unidentified sources[82] by increasing the penalty term for this crime. Before this amendment, Article 395 of the original criminal law only provided a range for the legal penalty of this crime, that is, a fixed-term imprisonment of not more than five years or criminal detention. Such a light penalty could easily be exploited by the corrupt officials. Some corrupt officials refused to confess the sources of their huge amounts of property after their crime was uncovered because the higher the value of the unidentified property, the less their bribery amount will be. This made the crime of holding a huge amount of property derived from unidentified sources something of a shield for some corrupt officials who were facing legal punishment. In China's juridical practice, many subjects of bribery crime cannot provide legal sources for their property. The maximum five-year legal penalty obviously cannot always reflect the seriousness of the crime. The 7th Amendment created two ranges of legal penalty and increased the maximum penalty to 10 years in prison, which reflects the principle of compatibility of crime, responsibility and penalty. So it was proper to raise the maximum legal penalty, which now better reflects China's anti-corruption efforts and serve as a deterrent to corrupt officials.

Based on recent economic developments, the 7th Amendment has included rat trading cases in the security and futures sector as a crime, and has increased the punishment of the crime of disrupting the order of the socialist market-oriented economy.

---

sentenced to confiscation of property. Where any state functionary who has left his position, any close relative of him or any other person who has a close relationship with him commits the act as prescribed in the preceding section by using the advantages generated from the former authority or position of the said state functionary, he shall be convicted and punished under the preceding section.

[82] Article 14 of the 7th Criminal Law Amendment reads: "Where the property or expenditure of any state functionary obviously exceeds his legitimate income, and the difference is huge, he shall be ordered to explain the sources. If he fails to do so, the difference shall be determined as illegal income, and he shall be sentenced to fixed-term imprisonment not more than five years or criminal detention; or if the difference is extremely large, shall be sentenced to fixed-term imprisonment not less than five years but not more than 10 years. The difference of the property shall be recovered.

In recent years, most financial institutions such as fund companies, commercial banks, insurance companies, securities companies and futures companies have been involved in investing and financing, or client asset management. They manage large amounts of customer funds that they invest in financial products. Before using client funds to buy financial products such as securities or derivatives, futures or option contracts, some asset management institutions can make excessive profits by buying these financial products at a low price in advance in their own name, or through making use of another person's name or telling their relatives and friends, and then selling them after the price has risen due to their clients' funds. Since most of these practitioners hide in the dark and steal profits from rising financial products, such behaviour is known as rat trading. This behaviour seriously breaches the order of financial management, damages the fairness, justice and openness of the market and seriously damages the interests of the client and the reputation of the financial industry.

Against this background, the 7th Amendment amended Section 1 of Article 180 about the crime of insider trading and disclosing inside information in Article 2 of this amendment[83] by adding the relevant provisions on rat trading. Besides, in order to severely punish the crime of rat trading, the 7th Amendment adds one new section as Section 4 in Article 180. It states that: "Practitioners of the financial institutions like securities exchange, futures exchange, security companies, futures brokerage companies, fund management companies, commercial banks and insurance companies, and the employees of relevant regulatory authorities or industry associations will be punished in line with the regulations of Section 1 if they violate the rules and use other undisclosed information other than the inside one acquired through their position to be involved in the trading activities of securities and futures relating to the information, or directly tell or imply others to do the related trading."

The 7th Amendment takes the protection of personal information as an important issue for the first time and adds new provisions to clearly investigate criminal liability for the crime of leaking personal information in sectors such as finance and telecommunications. The emphasis on the protection of personal information is an important progress and development in China's criminal law.

---

[83] Section 1 of Article 2 in the 7th Criminal Law Amendment reads: "Whoever has inside information on securities or futures transactions or illegally obtains inside information on securities or futures transactions, and prior to the release of the information that involves the issuance of securities or securities or futures transactions or other information that has a material effect on the transaction price of securities or futures, buys or sells the said secu-

The rapid development of technology in China and the fast emergence of information networks have transformed people's lives. While enjoying the convenience brought by new technologies, people also face fresh challenges from the information age. Nowadays, the personal information can be easily acquired and abused, which results in various social problems. Before the enactment of the 7th Amendment, the cases of "human flesh search" caused great disquiet in China. In 2006, the case of a woman abusing a cat gave rise to the first public example of a human flesh search. On 28 February that year, a network user with the name "broken glass" released a video recording of a cat being abused by a woman, which caused great anger among the public. Some netizens voluntarily began to trace the details of this woman. Within six days, they found and publicised her name, age and work unit, which resulted in her dismissal from her employer. Her peaceful life was also destroyed.

This kind of case has happened again and again. For example, the incident of a "death blog" occurred on 9 January 2008 when a post was published in the social network site, Tianya Community. It reposted a full blog about how Jiang Yan had committed suicide due to her husband's affair. The news caused heated discussion and condemnation in the online community, which resulted in the revelation of detailed information about Jiang Yan's husband and his mistress. Some radical netizens even found the address of these two people's parents and wrote hurtful comments, which greatly damaged the lives of these people.

Another nationwide human flesh search event occurred more recently. On the night of 24 May 2013, a network user named Kongyouwuyi posted an article on the Sina microblog. He said that he found some Chinese words indicating that Ding Jinhao had carved his name in Egypt's Luxor Temple. This user said that he felt "quite embarrassed at this saddest moment in Egypt". Uproar was caused after this microblog was released. Within a day, more than 11,000 comments had been made and the microblog had been reposted 83,000 times. Hundreds of thousands of people posted comments on the internet with regard to the poor behaviour of Chinese visitors in general. Some netizens also found Ding Jinhao's personal information such as his identity as a junior middle school student through human flesh search. On 25 May, Ding's parents publicly apologised for their child's behaviour,

---

rities, engages in the futures transaction related to the inside information, leaks the said information, or explicitly or implicitly advises others to engage in the aforesaid transaction activities shall, if the circumstances are serious, be sentenced to fixed-term imprisonment not more than five years or criminal detention, and/or be fined one to five times the illegal gains; or if the circumstances are extremely serious, shall be sentenced to fixed-term imprisonment not less than five years but not more than 10 years, and be fined one to five times the illegal gains.

and pleaded for the opportunity to make reparations. In China, the human flesh search has caused considerable controversy, but since it is a by-product of the modern internet age, there is no effective prevention method in China's current legal system.

Personal information protection has become an urgent legal issue in China. The Edison Chen scandal in 2008 underscored the importance of protecting the personal information of members of the public. In 2008, some unidentified people released nude photos of the actor and musician Edison Chen with various women. These photos attracted wide attention and caused heated online discussion. The victims included A-listers of the entertainment world such as Gillian Chung, Cecilia Cheung and Bobo Chan. After the images were released, people involved had to stop acting or take temporary retreat. Their personal lives and work were seriously damaged. The Edison Chen scandal exposed the defects of China's criminal law in protecting citizens' privacy. Unlike in other countries, China has not enacted a law of personal information protection. So, there is no legal regulation in China over the illegal violation of personal information, such as when, for example, personal information on medical history, house purchases, job applications or bank card applications is sold.

As a growing number of serious information leaks occurred, personal information protection became an important focus of the 7th Amendment. This amendment finally added a new article after Article 253 of the criminal law to introduce the crime of selling or illegally providing citizens' personal information[84] and the crime of illegally acquiring citizens' personal information[85].

Although there is provision about the crime of selling or illegally providing citizens' personal information and the crime of illegally acquiring citizens' personal information in the 7th Amendment, it is mainly focused on the employees of state organisations or of financial, telecoms, transport, educational and medical organisations. So this provision cannot solve some cases in China's juridical practice. For example, the question remains as to whether the widely-concerned human flesh search should be regulated as a crime. There is no consensus between

---

[84] Section 1 of Article 7 in the 7th Criminal Law Amendment reads: "Where any staff member of a state organ or an entity in such a field as finance, telecommunications, transportation, education or medical treatment, in violation of the state provisions, sells or illegally provides personal information on citizens, which is obtained during the organ or entity performance of duties or provision of services, to others shall, if the circumstances are serious, be sentenced to fixed-term imprisonment not more than three years or criminal detention, and/or be fined."

[85] Section 2 of Article 7 in the 7th Criminal Law Amendment reads: "Whoever illegally obtains the aforesaid information by stealing or any other means shall, if the circumstances are serious, be punished under the preceding section."

academia and legal practitioners. It is a plain truth that human flesh search has severely damaged citizens' basic rights and interests. However, in order to protect the safety of citizens' personal information, is it necessary to investigate the criminal liability of the initiator of the human flesh search? Some people think that it should not be included in the regulation of criminal law for two reasons. For one thing, in line with the modest and restrained principle of criminal law, this behaviour should not be regulated by criminal law when there are other methods. The infringement of others' privacy can be solved by civil methods, for example. If the collection of personal information has infringed a citizen's reputation, the subject of this behaviour can be prosecuted for criminal liability by the crime of defamation. For another, since the draft of personal information protection law has not been finished and the protection scope of personal information has not been defined, it is currently premature to include human flesh search into criminal law.[86] This opinion is highly endorsed in this paper. It is true that human flesh search can have significant negative influence on the people concerned. But in order to avoid the disadvantages of "emotional criminal law", it should be cautious when considering whether human flesh search should be included as a crime. If human flesh search was included in criminal law, it may be helpful in protecting the safety of personal information. But in a society with diversified values, it would result in a restraint on citizens' social activities and influence social development.

The 8th Amendment to the Criminal Law of the PRC

On 25 February 2011, the Standing Committee of the 11th National People's Congress passed the 8th Amendment to the Criminal Law of the PRC at its 19th meeting, which became effective on 1 May 2011. This amendment addresses the demands from various aspects of China including the current economic and social development, policy adjustment and progress with nomocracy. It has the greatest number of amendments and is the most important amendment in the last 10 years of China's legal construction.

The major contributions of the 8th Amendment to China's nomocracy progress are mainly reflected in the following aspects.

The 8th Amendment abolishes the death penalty for 13 crimes, which is the single greatest contribution made by this amendment.

---

[86] See Shen Yuzhong, Legitimacy of Personal Information Protection and Criminal Law Intervention: Discussion about Article 7 of the 7th Criminal Law Amendment. Journal of Yanshan University, 2009, Issue 2, Volume 10

According to the 8th Amendment, starting from 1 May 2013, the death penalty will be eliminated from 13 economic and non-violence crimes. This amendment has reduced the number of crimes for which death penalty could be imposed from 68 to 55. These 13 crimes are smuggling cultural relics, smuggling precious metals, smuggling precious animals or precious animal products, smuggling general goods and articles, financial ticket fraud, financial document fraud, letter of credit fraud, issuing fraudulent special VAT invoices to defraud export tax refunds and deduct tax invoices, forging and selling forged special invoices for VAT, theft, initiating criminal methods, illegally excavating and robbing ancient cultural sites or ancient tombs, and illegally excavating and robbing the fossils of ancient human being or ancient vertebrates.

The deletion and adjustment of death penalty crimes in the 8th Amendment reversed the trend of previous criminal legislation that only added new death penalty crimes but never reduced them. Some scholars point out that it remains China's long-term criminal policy to keep and strictly apply the death penalty. But it is the first time that China has reduced the number of death penalty crimes since the enactment of China's criminal law in 1979, and this is a sign of the respect for life and guarantee of human rights. However, some scholars also point out that, although the 8th Amendment appears to abolish the death penalty for a number of crimes, the death penalty has been rarely applied in these crimes. Although the 8th Amendment did not drastically amend the death penalty, the reduction of death penalty crimes for the first time in legislation still has groundbreaking significance.

It is worth mentioning that, although China has retained the death penalty, the design of the legal system has limited its application, including a limitation on the subject, condition and procedure of the death penalty application. The most prominent feature should be that the Supreme People's Court has reclaimed the right of death penalty review. The ownership of the death penalty review right can directly affect the processing procedure of death penalty cases, which is quite important in practice. China's death penalty review right has been modified over a long period of time. The right first appeared in the Organic Law on People's Court of the PRC enacted in 1954. It was controlled by the higher people's courts, and the Supreme People's Court only played an assistant role. In the decision passed by the 1st National People's Congress in 1957, it stated that, "all the death penalty cases will be judged or approved by the Supreme People's Court from now on". This realised the first withdrawal of the death penalty review right for the Supreme People's Court. With the worsening of social security and an increase in the number of cases that should be legally punished by the death penalty, the death penalty review right was decentralised to the higher people's courts to approve death penalty cases in an effective and timely manner and fight against vicious crimes. On 31 October 2006, the Standing Committee of the 10th National People's Congress passed the Decision about Amending the Organic Law of People's Court, which makes it clear that death penalty cases should be submitted to the Supreme People's Court to approve except for the one sentenced by the Supreme People's Court according to law. This decision came into force on 1 January 2007. Since then, the death penalty review right has finally returned to the Supreme People's Court. It was reported that 15% of death penalty cases were not approved in the first year after the death penalty review right was reclaimed and uniformly executed by the Supreme People's Court. It was the first time that the Supreme People's Court reprieved more death sentence cases than there were new death penalty cases[87]. This data proves that the reclamation of the death penalty review right has played a remarkable role in protecting life and human rights.

The uniform execution of death penalty review right by the Supreme People's Court makes the procedure of death penalty review more strict, which adds a legal shield for defendants and can help to reduce the occurrence of unjust and fraudulent cases. The Wu Ying case is the best example[88]. Wu Ying used to be the legal representative of Zhejiang Bense Holding Group. Private lending is quite common in Zhejiang province and Bense Group made its fortune from this business. Promising to provide a high investment return, Wu Ying borrowed huge amounts of funds from the public and she was finally arrested on suspicion of fraud. In December 2009, Jinhua Intermediate People's Court sentenced Wu Ying to death for the crime of fund-raising fraud. In January 2012, the Higher People's Court of Zhejiang made the judgment of second instance for Wu Ying's case of fund raising fraud and affirmed the death penalty on her. The release of the second instance judgement caused public outcry. It was widely believed by the public that, although Wu Ying did commit the crime, her criminal behaviour was not serious enough to warrant the death penalty. The Supreme People's Court did not approve the death sentence on Wu Ying in April 2012 and returned the case to the Higher People's Court of Zhejiang to retry it. Zhejiang Higher People's Court made the final judgement and sentenced Wu Ying death penalty with a two-year reprieve for the crime of fund raising fraud. The turnaround of Wu Ying's case in the review stage of the death penalty largely

---

[87] Pei Zhiyong, Looking Back the Death Sentence Review, Available on the Chinese court net, http://www.chinacourt.org/article/detail/2009/11/id/380622.shtml, Accessed on 7 May2013.

[88] See: Wu Ying: Debate under the Knife, Available on Hexun net.
http://opinion.hexun.com/2012/helpwuying/. Accessed on 23 April 2013

reflects the active response to current legislation and proper respect to social practice from criminal judicature. This means that, if the legislation cannot be changed frequently, especially when there is serious conflict between legislation and practice, the criminal judge should take the changed situation into consideration and make a convincing judgment in response to social practice and people's demands. This reflects the unification between legal effects and social effects.

Both the reduction of death penalty crimes in the 8th Amendment and the return of the death penalty review right highlight the respect for human rights and life from China's criminal law, and reflect the progress and development of China's rule of law.

In recent years, with the rapid development of China's market economy, the phenomenon of damaging people's livelihood has become more serious. The public have increasingly stronger demands for a criminal law that protects people's livelihood. Given the problems that exist in Chinese society such as road safety, food safety, withholding workers' pay and environmental pollution, the 8th Amendment adds a number of protection measures over people's livelihoods. The focus on social hot spots and livelihood issues is a bright spot of the 8th Amendment, and it also reflects an important change in China's criminal law. These changes are mainly reflected in the following aspects.

In order to punish dangerous driving, which has caused great public anger, the 8th Amendment made it a crime[89] in Article 22. In recent years, numerous accidents have occurred as a result of drink-driving. According to some statistics, from January to August 2008, a total number of 3,206 traffic accidents happened due to drunk driving, which caused the death of 1,302 people. Among these accidents, 2,162 accidents and 893 deaths were caused by drivers who had been driving after drinking, and 1,044 accidents and 409 deaths by drunk drivers[90]. The crime of drink-driving is happening at a high frequency and the damage is becoming more serious. Some serious drink-driving cases in recent times, such as the ones involving Sun Weiming in Nan-

---

[89] One article is added after Article 133 as Article 133A: "Whoever races a motor vehicle on a road with execrable circumstances or drives a motor vehicle on a road while intoxicated shall be sentenced to criminal detention and a fine."

[90] Supreme People's Court, Notice of the Supreme People's Court on Issuing the Guiding Opinions on Issues Concerning the Application of Law to the Crime of DWI and the Relevant Typical Cases, No. 47 [2009] of the Supreme People's Court, 11 September 2009

jing[91], Zhang Mingbao and the guilty Land Rover case in Jixi[92] have attracted national attention. The 8th Amendment incorporated dangerous driving into criminal regulations to meet public demands to punish drunk driving, which reflects the democratisation of legislation in a certain sense. The incidence of drink-driving cases has dropped dramatically in some places. Take Beijing as an example: 1,024 drink-driving cases were found by Beijing traffic police from 1 May to 30 May 2011, which represented a fall of 81% compared with the previous year. Among these accidents, 89 of them were caused by drink-driving, which means a year-on-year decline of 79%. The inclusion of drink-driving in criminal law has been to the benefit of society[93].

After the enactment of the 8th Amendment, on 22 April 2011, the Standing Committee of the 11th National People's Congress amended the Road Traffic Safety Law of the PRC[94] at its 20th meeting. The Road Traffic Safety Law of the PRC added punishment measures such as the revocation of a driving licence and the investigation of criminal liability for drink driving to link with the regulations about the crime of drink-driving. After this amendment, China's Criminal Law has tied in more closely with the Road Traffic Safety Law in punishing and preventing drink-driving, and therefore has improved the effectiveness in preventing drink-driving.

It should be noted that the 8th Amendment is inadequate in regulating the crime of drink-driving. The related provisions only list two types of dangerous driving behaviour — racing driving and drink-driving — and do not consider conditions such as driving under the influence of drugs and driving without a licence. Some scholars suggest that it should add the wording of "this kind of dangerous driving behaviour" as the catch-all regulation to the provisions, which can leave room to add new types of dangerous driving in

---

[91] See Cai Yugao and Wang Junyong, Looking Back 2009: Warnings from Drunk Driving Accidents. Available on the website of the Public Security Ministry, http://www.mps.gov.cn/n16/n983040/n2032785/n2032879/2255838.html, Accessed on 21 May 2012. Reprinted from Xinhua Agency.

[92] See Wang Mingliang, Theoretical Interpretation of the Hot Criminal Cases. Chinese People's Public Security University Press, 2010. pp25-26

[93] See Liu Yang. Higher Law Enforcement Requirements and Stricter Procedure Requirements in Investigating Drunk Driving. People's Public Security Daily, 4 June 2011.

[94] See the Standing Committee of the National People's Congress's decision about Amending the Road Traffic Safety Law of the PRC. Available on http://www.gov.cn/flfg/2011-04/25/content_1851694.htm

the future[95]. Considering the high incidence of drink-driving and racing driving, it is understandable that the 8th Amendment listed these two types of dangerous driving. As circumstances change, it will be feasible to add new forms of dangerous driving behaviour in future criminal law amendments.

The Supreme People's Court, the Supreme People's Procuratorate and the Ministry of Public Security issued the Instructions for Problems of Applying Laws in Dealing with the Criminal Cases about Drunk Driving on 18 December 2013. This document further regulates and details the related law-enforcement standards. It makes it clear that drivers driving on the road with a blood alcohol level higher than 80mg/100mg will be considered as drink-driving and they will be convicted and punished for the crime of dangerous driving. It also states that, "the authentication opinion on the blood alcohol level test will be the basis to identify whether the suspects are drunk. If they have met the drunk standard stated in Article 1 of this instruction as a result of a breath test determining the blood alcohol level, the test results can be used as the basis to identify them as being drunk should they run away before the blood test". In order to prevent suspects from evading liability, it also states that: "If the suspects drinks again before the breath or blood test with the aim of escaping legal punishment when they face the legal inspection of public security organs, they should be identified as being drunk when their blood alcohol level test results meet the standards stated in Article 1."

In order to improve the protection of food safety, the 8th Amendment introduced hard-hitting measures to enhance the punishment over the crime of producing and selling substandard foods in Article 24 and the crime of producing and selling toxic and hazardous foods in Article 25. In recent years, many food safety scandals have occurred in China. From the Sudan red incident to illegal cooking oil, from the melamine incident of Sanlu milk powder to the clenbuterol incident of Shuanghui ham, from the dyed steamed buns in a Shanghai supermarket to the gel-injected shrimp in Tianjin's aquatic products market, these food safety incidents have caused alarm among the public. It is quite urgent to enhance the punishment over food safety problems. Against such a background, through improving the criminal penalty starting point and removing the limitation on fine penalties, the 8th Amendment changed the prevailing situation in which the fines imposed upon the food producer and seller are relatively low. Besides, there are also provisions specially regulating the supervisors of food safety in the 8th Amendment. In previous criminal law, when the supervision and management departments on food safety have violated criminal law for misconduct, they were

---

[95] Gao Mingxuan, The Breed, Birth, Development and Improvement of China's Criminal Law, 1st Edition. Peking University Press, 2012, P349

usually convicted and punished for the crimes of authority misuse or of duty dereliction. On this occasion, the 8th Amendment added the crime of duty dereliction in food supervision in Article 49[96], which further highlights the supervision and administration function of the administrative law enforcement departments and sounds the alarm for the functionaries of state organs responsible for food supervision.

Food safety concerns people's vital interests. Facing the ever worsening situation of China's food safety, after the enactment and implementation of the Food Safety Law of PRC and the Implementation Regulation of PRC's Food Safety Law in 2009 by the Chinese government, the 8th Amendment once again focuses on food safety in its provisions. This reflects the tough legal attitude towards food-related illegal behaviour. It has had positive and practical significance for the prevention and punishment of China's food safety problems.

In order to protect the interests of workers, the 8th Amendment has newly added the crime of refusing to pay remuneration to workers in Article 41[97]. Refusing to pay remuneration or deliberately not paying workers' wages has become a serious problem in China. The importance of worker remuneration, especially for the ever-growing number of migrant workers, is quite obvious. China does not yet have a complete social security system and labour rewards are almost the only guarantee for workers to make a living. Deliberately not paying workers' wages is a serious challenge to the workers' right to live. It could easily lead to serious criminal cases if it is not handled well. In recent years, mass disturbances have been reported about workers appealing to the higher authorities for help or even attacking state organs due to employers deliberately not paying wages. Vicious incidents have resulted from migrant workers failing to get their wages. Cases such as the

---

[96] Article 49 of the 8th Criminal Law Amendment reads: "Where a state functionary with food safety supervision and management functions abuses his powers or neglects his duties, if any serious food safety accident or other serious consequence is caused, he shall be sentenced to imprisonment of not more than five years or criminal detention; or if any especially serious consequence is caused, be sentenced to imprisonment of not less than five years but not more than 10 years. Where the crime as provided for in the preceding section is committed by the state functionary by making falsehood for personal gains, a heavier penalty shall be imposed on him.

[97] Article 41 of the 8th Criminal Law Amendment reads: "Whoever evades payment of a relatively large amount of labour remuneration by transferring property or escaping and hiding or refuses to pay a relatively large amount of labour remuneration though capable, and still refuses to pay even after being ordered to do so by the relevant government department, shall be sentenced to imprisonment of not more than three years or criminal detention and/or a fine; and if there are serious consequences, shall be sentenced

Wang Binyu case[98] and the 16 September case about migrant workers asking for wages from Tiandi Huicheng Development Company in Zhumadian city[99] are the most prominent examples. Before the 8th Amendment was enacted, there was no effective relief approach in China's legal system for the practice of deliberately not paying workers' wages. The 8th Amendment incorporates this behaviour into criminal law for the first time, providing a shield for workers to ask for wages by using the deterrent force of criminal penalty, which has the obvious progressive significance.

However, provisions in the 8th Amendment about the crime of refusing to pay worker remuneration are too general, which has caused many practical problems. On 14 January 2013, the Judicial Committee of the Supreme People's Court passed the Explanation from the Supreme People's Court for Questions in Applying the Laws When Trying Criminal Cases of Refusing to Pay Labour Remuneration. This criminal law juridical explanation further supplements the legal provisions about the crime of refusing to pay worker remuneration, which increases the operability of the law.

To deal with the ever worsening environmental pollution situation, the 8th Amendment amends the provisions about the environmental pollution-related crimes by lowering the threshold to be convicted and by increasing environmental protection efforts. In recent years, China has seen many environmental pollution accidents. Famous cases include major water pollution of the Songhua River caused by an explosion at PetroChina's Jilin Petrochemical Company in 2005[100], the blood lead poisoning incident in Shaanxi's Fengxiang county in 2009[101] and the

---

to imprisonment of not less than three years but not more than seven years and a fine. Where an entity commits the crime as provided for in the preceding section, a fine shall be imposed on it, and its directly responsible person and other directly liable persons shall be punished according to the provision of the preceding section. Whoever commits an act as mentioned in the preceding two sections without serious consequences but pays labour remuneration before a public prosecution is instituted and assumes the corresponding compensatory liability according to law may be given a mitigated penalty or exempted from penalty.

[98] Chen Rongfei and Xiao Min, Theoretical Research on the Criminalization of Deliberately not Paying Workers' Wages at the Background of the 8th Criminal Law Amendment

[99] Zhang Bao, One dead and several injured in the bloody case caused by migrant workers' requesting for wages in one construction site of Zhumadian. Henan Workers' Daily

[100] See He Yong, Cannot let enterprises run away after polluting the environment when dealing with the pollutions. Review of Economic Research, 2011, Issue 48

[101] See Lu Tingting, Reviewing the Conflicts between Rural Economic Development and Environ-

pollution incident of Zijin Mining in 2010[102]. The number of environmental pollution accidents indicates the gravity of China's environmental protection situation. However, in the original criminal law, the adjustment range of major environmental pollution accident crime was too narrow, which resulted in insufficient punishment for several environmental pollution-related crimes. Against such a background, the 8th Amendment amended the crime of major environmental pollution accident to the crime of environmental pollution, and the term "hazardous waste" to "hazardous substance" in Article 46[103], which expands the range of the behaviour regulated by the criminal law. Besides, it also amended the expression of causing major environmental pollution accidents to seriously polluting the environment, and removed the constitutive element of the serious consequence of causing serious losses to public or private property or personal injury, which greatly lowers the conviction standards for the behaviour of environmental pollution.

The amendments to environmental pollution-related crimes in the 8th Amendment reflect the increasing attention that China has put on environment criminal law. However, current environmental conditions in the country are still not good. Since 2012, air pollution incidents have been frequent and the situation has become so bad that China's major cities' PM 2.5 indicators have exceeded the standard. This reflects the limited role played by China's law in preventing and controlling environmental pollution. How to realise the effectiveness of the environment criminal law in preventing environmental pollution will be an important task for China's criminal law in its development.

The 8th Amendment has not only improved the protection of people's livelihood by amending or adding the articles in specific provisions, but also reflects greater consideration of the public in the general provisions. For example, in Article 11 of the 8th Amendment, the declaration of no significant adverse effects on the

---

mental Protection from the Blood Lead Incident of Fengxiang. Modern Business, 2009, Issue 30.

[102] See Gao Qiaoping, Reflection from the Pollution Accident of Zijin Mining: Risks and Prevention of Ecological Environment Safety. Peking University legal information network. Available on http://article.chinalawinfo.com/article_print.asp?articleid=68322, Accessed on 12 May 2013, Reprinted from the Law Research Society of Environment and resources in China Law Science Association

[103] Article 46 of the 8th Criminal Law Amendment reads: "Whoever, in violation of the state provisions, discharges, dumps or disposes of any radioactive waste, any waste containing pathogens of any infectious disease, any poisonous substance or any other hazardous substance, which has caused serious environmental pollution, shall be sentenced to imprisonment of not more than three years or criminal detention and/or a fine; or if there are especially serious consequences, be sentenced to imprisonment of not less than three years but not more than seven years and a fine.

community has been considered as one of the premises for probation. In Article 16, it states that, "it needs to consider the influence on the community where the criminals live when deciding whether to give them parole".

The 8th Amendment has increased humanistic provisions for the aged and minor citizens involved in crimes. The following provisions are about elderly citizens involved in crimes. (a) In Article 1 of the 8th Amendment, it states that a person reaching the age of 75 may be given a lighter or mitigated penalty if he/she commits an intentional crime; or shall be given a lighter or mitigated penalty if he/she commits a negligent crime. (b) Article 3 states that the death penalty shall not be given to a person aged at least 75 at the time of trial, unless he/she has caused the death of another person by especially cruel means. (c) Article 11 states that where a convict sentenced to criminal detention or imprisonment of not more than three years meets the following conditions, probation may be announced, and probation shall be announced if he/she attains the age of 75. In total, three provisions about elderly criminals have been added in the 8th Amendment, which lowers the punishment level and fully reflects a humanistic attitude to elderly people. However, it cannot be denied that the conditions in the 8th Amendment for lenient punishment on elderly criminals are still quite strict. For one thing, the age limitation for the lenient punishment is quite high; 75 exceeds the current average lifespan of China's male citizens. So, these provisions may sound good, but the practical application is quite limited.

The 8th Amendment also increases the provisions about providing lenient punishment to minor criminals, which are mainly reflected in the following aspects. (a) It adds the provision that the recidivism system does not apply to minors. Article 6 of the 8th Amendment states that one person shall not be considered as a recidivist if he commits the crime under the age of 18. (b) This amendment also adds the provision that minors can be exempted from the reporting obligation. Article 19 of the 8th Amendment states that, whoever is given a penalty lighter than imprisonment of five years for a crime committed under the age of 18, shall be exempted from the reporting obligation. (c) Article 11 states that, where a convict sentenced to criminal detention or imprisonment of not more than three years meets the following conditions, a probation may be announced, and a probation shall be announced if he is under 18.

The 8th Amendment is the one that amends the widest range and has the most important implications for China's criminal law since the criminal law was enacted in 1997. It has played a great role in further improving the scientific development of the legislation and judicature of China's criminal law. Aside from this amendment, the Standing Committee of the National People's Congress also issued two judicial explanations on 24 April 2014. In the judicial explanation for Article 266 of China's criminal law, it states that: "An act of obtaining social insurance benefits such as endowment, medical, job-related injury, unemployment, or maternity insurance benefits or any other social security benefits by fraud, falsification of certifications, or any other fraudulent means shall be an act of fraudulently obtaining public or private property as prescribed in Article 266 of the Criminal Law". In the explanations for Articles 341 and 312, it states that: "The act that with the aim of eating or the other aims, people know or should know what they illegally purchase are rare or endangered wild animals under the state's priority protection and products made thereof shall be an act of illegally purchasing rare or endangered wild animals under the state's priority protection and products made thereof as prescribed in Section 1 of Article 341 of the Criminal Law".

We still notice that the Supreme People's Court has individually or jointly with the Supreme People's Procuratorate issued judicial explanations to provide a detailed provision for the punishment over the following criminal behaviour that have severely impaired social safety.

(a) The criminal activities of making up and deliberately spreading false terrifying information

Interpretation of the Supreme People's Court of Several Issues on the Application of Law in the Trial of Criminal Cases about the Fabrication and Intentional Dissemination of False or Terrifying Information (Code [2013] No. 24, adopted at the 1,591st session of the Judicial Committee of the Supreme People's Court on 16 September 2013)

(b) The criminal activities of defamation through information networks

Interpretation of the Supreme People's Court and the Supreme People's Procuratorate on Several Issues concerning the Specific Application of Law in the Handling of Defamation through Information Networks and Other Criminal Cases (Code [2013] No. 21, adopted at the 1,589th session of the Judicial Committee of the Supreme People's Court on 5 September 2013 and the 9th meeting of the 12th Procuratorial Committee of the Supreme People's Procuratorate on 2 September 2013).

It should be noted that these two judicial explanation documents reflect the severe situation facing the security forces in a highly networked society. It has become a new and important task for the development of China's criminal law legislation and juridical practice to realise the balance between criminal law's two original values of social security, and guaranteeing the free speech and human rights of citizens.

Conclusion

With the development of its economy and the evolution of its society, China's criminal law has continuously been adapted. In China, amendment is the main form for the adjustment and improvement of criminal law. Criminal law amendments have been the touchstone for the progress of China's criminal law. As an important part of the criminal law system in China, the amendments have the advantages of flexibility and timeliness. By adding or amending legal provisions, criminal law amendments can reflect the latest changes in juridical practice and social life. They fix the issues in society that need to be solved urgently while safeguarding social stability and the economic fruits of reform and opening up. Criminal law amendments have made a remarkable contribution to the progress and development of China's criminal law.

The amendments to criminal law in China have been made jointly to department laws, administrative laws and rules and regulations, which has reinforced the relative stability and inter-coordination of the legal system. This can reflect the improvement of China's legislation.

Problems can also be found in the process of promoting the evolution of criminal law with the form of amendment. Some scholars think that it is reasonable for China's legislative body to use amendments to amend criminal law. But five amendments have been introduced in past 10 years by China's legislative body, which means one new criminal law amendment has been enacted every two years. This is too frequent, and it can affect the stability of criminal law. In response, some scholars have suggested that China should use the dual legislation system. By learning from the experience of foreign countries, the introduction of the dual legislation system can help to solve the conflict between stability and the hysteretic nature of the law. Some scholars also say that there is a long time interval between the enactment of criminal law amendments and a criminal explanation from the Supreme People's Court and the Supreme People's Procuratorate, which results in chaos. This problem has indeed always bothered China's juridical practice. During the period after the enactment of a criminal law amendment and before the issue of a relevant criminal explanation, the courts have to use a temporary crime name to try related cases. This results in the same type of cases being tried on the same legal basis by different courts with different crime names, which greatly influence the seriousness and authority of China's criminal law. This paper thinks that this problem can be solved easily. When the amendment is enacted, it should determine the crime names to be added or amended to replace the juridical explanation of the Supreme People's Court and the Supreme People's Procuratorate, and these crime names should be released with the criminal law amendments.

Another widely criticised drawback of China's criminal law amendments is that, in accordance with the existing laws such as the Constitution and Legislative Law, the amendment should be enacted by the National People's Congress, not its Standing Committee. This paper also supports this view. As an important part of the criminal law, the amendments should have the same legislative body as the criminal law. China's criminal law is enacted by the National People's Congress, and so should criminal law amendments. The Standing Committee of the National People's Congress should only have the right to interpret the criminal law and its amendments.

Although there are drawbacks in China's criminal law amendments, they have still made remarkable contributions in promoting the rule of law. The progress and development of China's criminal law in the past 10 years are mainly reflected in the progress and development of criminal law amendments. These five amendments are like the footprints that bear witness to the progress and development of China's criminal law, as well as to the historic moment of China's economic development and social progress.

Chapter 4

Procedural democracy and visible justice

—A review of China's criminal procedural law and civil procedural law in the past 10 years

Overview

As an important part of adjective law, procedural law is judicially defined as "the procedural form through which legal rights are enforced. Different to laws granting and stipulating rights, procedural laws refer to procedural legislations through which courts of law handle legal proceedings. It is machinery instead of product."[104] The rule of law, on the other hand, is defined as "to equally abide by the good law", i.e. an independent judicial office applies the law to all men equally. How to guarantee that the law is equally applied? This is where procedural law can play its role, which is the key to dispute solution and the assurance of human rights. Therefore, the continued improvement of procedural law is indispensable in China's efforts to establish and uphold the rule of law. In the decade-odd years after entry into the new century, two major procedural laws, namely the Criminal Procedure Law and Civil Procedure Law, have undergone noteworthy modifications.

The criminal procedural law

In the history of China's criminal justice, the unjust case of Du Peiwu has been a notable scandal. In the late 1990s, the police of Kunming city, capital of southwest China's Yunnan province, discovered the dead bodies of a man and a woman in a minivan parked on a pedestrian crossing in that city. It was later found out through investigation that the man was the Deputy Director of the Public Security Bureau of a certain county, while the woman was a police officer with the Communication Division of the Public Security Bureau of Kunming. In its investigation, the police confirmed that the two victims were shot dead by a handgun, which turned out to be the Type 7-7 pistol that was carried by the male victim and had gone missing. The Kunming police lost no time in forming a special task force for the case. After a series of investigations, the task force focused its suspicion on Du Peiwu, husband of the female victim and also a police officer in a Drug Addiction

---

[104] Please refer to the entry of "Procedure" in the Oxford Dictionary of Law

Treatment Centre under Kunming Public Security Bureau. However, Du Peiwu, who had been trained in how to use a handgun, categorically denied involvement in the murder case when he was interrogated by the task force. According to the task force's analysis of the case, the two victims, Wang Junbo and Wang Xiaoxiang, were said to be having an affair and the latter was believed to have had an abortion some time before the case, which had angered Du Peiwu. The task force believed that Du Peiwu was the murderer, and at about 2pm on 22 April 1998, Du Peiwu was arrested and sent to the Public Security Bureau of Kunming, where he was interrogated intensively for 10 consecutive days and nights. During this time, he was subject to sleep deprivation and an interrogative method aimed at exhausting the suspect. Unable to withstand such torture, Du Peiwu gave up his claim of innocence and "confessed his crime of murder". Later, on 2 July 1998, the task force consulted with the staff members from public prosecutor's office assigned to the case on coercive measures to be adopted against Du Peiwu. At 8pm that day, the task force announced to Du Peiwu that he had been placed under criminal detention. On 17 December 1998, the Intermediate Court of Kunming, the court of first instance, started to hear the case. It went on to find Du guilty of intentional homicide and sentenced him to death and deprivation of all political rights for life.

However, a U-turn was about to happen more than six months later, when seven suspects of a criminal gang headed by Yang Tianyong, were charged with murder and car robbery in June 2000. Members of the criminal gang admitted to a number of audacious crimes, including shooting and killing two police officers. Prompted by the confession, the police then found the Type 7-7 pistol that was used to murder the two police officers, as well as a mini recorder that was believed to belong to one of the two victims. The product serial number on the invoice for the mini recorder bought by the victim was identical to that on the mini recorder retrieved. It was then pretty clear that Yang Tianyong and his criminal gang had actually murdered the two police officers, and that Du Peiwu had been wrongly convicted. Du, who turned out to be completely innocent, would have been subject to the gravest injustice and the actual murderer would have been spared sentence. This murder case, then, represents an embarrassment for China's criminal justice system.

A similar case to that of Du Peiwu took place in the US, not in China: the sensational OJ Simpson murder case of the early 1990s, which is still fresh in people's collective memory. In that case, the principle of presumption of innocence was carried out throughout the entire proceeding. The prosecution fulfilled its duty to prove the accused guilty while the defence team fully carried out its duty of defending its client; the judge and jury managed to maintain their neutrality and independence in the true sense.

In comparison, what Du Peiwu endured merits our sympathy. In Du's case, although the investigators were aware of the fact that the crime scene investigation report and photos taken at the scene only recorded that there was a muddy footprint on the clutch pedal, they nonetheless permitted mud on the brake and accelerator pedals, which did not exist at all, to be used by police dogs as a clue to identify the suspect. They later concluded that "the police dogs showed the same reaction" to the fictional mud as that to the smell of the wrongly accused, Du Peiwu. In addition, investigators, as part of the state's law enforcement apparatus, all knew that the Criminal Procedural Law expressly prohibits the use of torture or other illegal means against suspects to extort confession or obtain evidence. However, they nonetheless subjected Du to a 21-day interrogation, during which his arms were handcuffed and twisted behind his back, and he was suspended on the security door and window of the interrogation room for prolonged periods of time. Such cruelty finally broke Du. He promised to his tormentors that he would "say whatever you want me to", and fabricated an account of how he shot and killed the two victims. Furthermore, although the law stipulates that a suspect, from date when he is subject to any coercive measure, shall have access to legal counsel, Du Peiwu was denied such a statutory right and was not permitted to hire a defence lawyer until he had been placed under arrest for three months and 18 days. Even worse, judges hearing his case, who were supposed to remain neutral and uphold justice, not only turned a blind eye to the numerous flaws in the evidence presented by the prosecution and the well-grounded and indisputable case made by the defence lawyer, but also ignored the bloodstained clothes that the suspect took off during the court session to show he had been subjected to torture. Instead, the judges repeatedly required the suspect to produce evidence proving that he didn't kill the two victims, and they went so far as to act against a fundamental principle of criminal procedural law by requiring in the court ruling that the defence lawyer should prove that the accused was guilty, which is actually part of the duties of the prosecution.

The two cases are similar in many aspects: the accused in both cases was the husband of the female victim; two victims were involved and in both cases, they were lovers; in both cases, the police categorised the murder as *crime passionnel*; the trial of both cases was based on the adversarial system; members of the defence team in both cases were leading attorneys of law in their respective countries; the trial process of both cases lasted more than one year; and most important, the "evidence" presented by the prosecution was not completely beyond "reasonable doubt". There are, however, some important factors that differentiated the two cases from each other: the accused in one case was a famous American football star, while that in the other case was a police officer; the victims in one case were ordinary citizens, while those in the other were police officers; the accused in one case was treated in a civilised and legal way during the trial process, while that in the other case was forced to make confessions under torture; the opinions of the defence lawyers in one case were given due consideration by the court while in the other case, the court ignored the defence lawyers' opinions completely. Thus, the fates of the two accused were sealed: while the accused in one case was declared innocent, that in the other case was convicted guilty, sentenced to death, and only escaped death by a hair's breadth.

A thought-provoking question then follows: why the two cases, which are so similar with each other, ended in completely different ways? The answer probably lies in China's Criminal Procedural Law, which was first enacted in 1979 and later revised in 1996. This act, though basically on a par with similar legislation in the US in many aspects, differs from criminal procedure in the US in some key aspects, the most important of which are: first, in the criminal procedural system in the US, the accused are protected from self-incrimination; second, the US follows the rule of excluding illegally obtained evidence; and third, criminal litigation in the US is based on a jury system. It is precisely because of the absence of the above three factors in China's criminal procedural law that the use of torture to obtain confession from the accused persists in spite of numerous efforts to eliminate such practice and illegally obtained evidence is not excluded in court hearing.

The case of Du Peiwu is not an isolated one and possibly the mere tip of an iceberg. The ultimate objective of criminal procedural law is not only to bring offenders to justice, but also more to protect innocent people from being wrongly accused and punished. In this regard, Alan Dershowitz, one of the most prominent attorneys of law, lifetime professor of Harvard University and a member of the defence team in the OJ Simpson murder case, remarked that the US judicial system is one under which "it is better for 10 guilty defendants to go free than for one innocent defendant to be wrongly convicted". In China, however, in spite of the constant claim that "we will always take facts as the basis of justice and avoid wrongly convicting a single innocent person or letting a guilty person go free", in judicial practice, it is always "better wrongly incriminating an innocent person than letting a guilty person go free" when it is hard to establish whether the person in question is actually guilty or innocent.[105]

Criminal procedural law is crucial for protecting human rights. The 1979 Criminal Procedural Law was the first criminal law of the People's Republic of China after its foundation in 1949. After this important legislation was modified in 1996,

---

[105] Page 8, Seeking for Justice: Comparing the OJ Simpson Murder Case of the US with the Du Peiwu Case of China, Wang Daren and Zeng Yuexing, Peking University Press, June 2012

18 years have elapsed, during which time profound changes have taken place in China and the wider world: in 2004, a milestone event occurred in human rights protection in China, the inclusion of the provision that "the state shall respect and protect human rights" into the Constitution of China; in 2007, the Supreme People's Court of China, the highest court law of China, took back the right to review and ratify death penalties from provincial supreme courts, and the newly enacted Property Law took effect; on 1 June 2008, the revised Law on Lawyers took effect. Especially noteworthy was the promulgation of Provisions on Issues Concerning the Review and Assessment of Evidence in Hearing Cases Involving the Death Penalty, and the Provisions on Issues Concerning the Exclusion of Illegally Obtained Evidence in Criminal Litigation on 1 July 2010, which had a profound impact on both the criminal procedural law and criminal litigation in China. All those developments are heralding a new round of revision of the Criminal Procedural Law.

On the other hand, the defects and problems in criminal procedural law, against which the public are highly resentful, have so far failed to be tackled effectively and are actually getting worse. First, the explicit or implicit use of torture to extort confession from suspects has so far failed to be eliminated. The use of torture not only seriously violates the human rights of those interrogated, rendering a violation of procedural justice and rule of law, but has also resulted in a number of high-profile cases where innocent people were wrongly accused and convicted, raising strong public indignation.[106] Second, the difficulties faced by the accused in making a legitimate defence remain unsolved. As a result of the obstacles faced by defence lawyers in gaining access to their clients under custody, relevant documents and evidence as

---

[106] In recent years, a number of sensational miscarriages of justices caused by the use of torture in interrogation have been exposed, a typical example of which is the case of She Xianglin.

On 2 January1994, Zhang Zaiyu, who was the wife of She Xianglin and had been suffering from a mental disorder, went missing. Zhang's family suspected she had been murdered by her husband She Xiainglin. On 28 April of the same year, She Xianglin was put under arrest on suspicion of murder. Later, he was sentenced to the death penalty and deprived of all political rights for life by the Intermediate People's Court of the former Jingzhou region in central China's Hubei province, the court of first instance. Upon She Xianglin's appeal against the verdict, the Higher People's Court of the province reviewed the case and identified at least five points of suspicion in the case and therefore revoked the verdict by the court of first instance and remanded the case for retrial. Since, however, there was a change in the demarcation of relevant administrative divisions, She's case was assigned to the Public Security Bureau of Jingshan county (also in Hubei province) and later heard by the People's Court of Jingshan county and the Intermediate People's Court of Jingmen city consecutively. On 22 September1998, She Xianglin was sentenced to 15 years in prison. The case was turned upside down, however, after Zhang Zaiyu, She Xianglin's wife, returned from Shandong province in northern China and suddenly reappeared in Jingshan county. The People's Court of Jingshan county

well as the relatively higher risks faced in their professional practice, criminal defence as a field of professional legal practice has actually been shrinking. According to surveys, only about 20% of accused criminals are defended by lawyers at trial. Third, the malpractice of illegally extended detention persists and has become one of the deepest-rooted problems in China's criminal justice system. Take the case of Xie Hongwu[107], for example. In that case, which was exposed in southwest China's Yunnan province in 2003, the accused was detained for 28 years in excess of the legally prescribed period of custody. Although the central judicial authorities have repeatedly issued circulars requiring rectification and correction of the problem of illegally extended detention, and launched numerous inspections into law enforcement and judicial authorities, the problem remains unsolved, with new cases of illegally extended detention cropping up while existing ones are being reviewed for remedy. In addition, there are some other prominent problems in criminal judicial practice, including the excessively high percentage of defendants being placed under arrest, refusal by witnesses to testify in court, the adoption of closed hearings by the court of second instance, disguised avoidance of the

---

reopened the case on 13 April of the same year and pronounced She Xianglin innocent. He later received more than Rmb700,000 (about US$100,000 at the prevailing exchange rate) in state compensation on 2 September 2005.

In the years after he was wrongly arrested and imprisoned, family members of She Xianglin made numerous appeals and petitions against his indictment. However, all such appeals and petitions were rejected and She's mother and brother were even detained and threatened for making such appeals and petitions.

According to She Xianglin's accounts, he was subject to severe beating for 10 consecutive days and nights after he refused to admit to the so called crime. This revelation again brought the use of torture in interrogation under the spotlight and turned the case into a national sensation. During one of the interviews he gave after he was released, She Xianglin said: "They used all means possible against me…" "by then I had been subject to physical torture for 10 days and 10 nights. I was feeling completely dumb mentally and was half-asleep from physical and psychological exhaustion. I was bruised all over and barely able to remain standing. All I wished for was some rest and I was ready to obey any instruction they may give as long as they would allow me to have a rest."

Another case involving a wrongly convicted person, Zhao Zuohai, is as widely known as the She Xianglin case in Henan province, a province neighbouring Hubei province.

[107] This is a typical case of three No's: "no files, no conviction and no time limit". Xie Hongwu was taken into custody by the police back in 1974 and was not released from custody until 2002. After being separated from the outside world for 28 years, Xie Hongwu received enormous physical and mental damage. Why does a detention warrant, which is essentially a thin piece of paper, justify the detention of a person for decades? This is a question haunting Zhong Guiwen, a person engaged in providing legal aid. However, as the police chief who signed the detention warrant and interrogators of Xie Hongwu have all passed away, the exact details of how and why Xie Hongwu was arrested will remain unknown forever.

principle of *Reformatio in peius*, and flaws in juvenile litigation procedure. Such problems can only be solved through another round of revision of the criminal procedure law.

Furthermore, new types of crime have arisen over the years and are on the rise, such as terrorism, corruption and juvenile delinquency. In view of all the above problems, China must keep abreast with the times and intensify its fight against crime and improve the procedure by which criminal offenders are prosecuted and punished.

On 14 March 2012, the Fifth Session of the 11th National People's Congress, the national parliament of China, adopted a decision to revise the Criminal Procedural Law and the revised version came into force on 1 January 2013. The latest round of revision involved the addition, deletion and revision of as many as 149 articles of the law (66 new articles were added, 82 existing articles were modified while one article was deleted). In comparison with revisions made to the law back in 1996, which were made primarily to promote China's reform and open-up drive and bring China's criminal procedural law in line with international standards, the latest revisions were more for the purpose of adapting to the rapid transformation of Chinese society. This round of revision was made against the backdrop of the fourth world revolution in criminal procedural law; in the context of China's legal history, on the other hand, this latest round of revision actually embodies the third round of upgrading of China's criminal procedural system. Through a comparison of the Criminal Procedural Law as promulgated in 1979 and the 1996 and 2012 revised versions, it can be clearly seen that the criminal procedural system has undergone three transformations, and is firmly on the road toward the rule of law. The promulgation of the Criminal Procedural Law in 1979 ushered in a comprehensive set of criminal procedural rules, marked an end to the era in which criminal litigation in China was based on judicial rules and policies, instead of a procedural legislation, and kick-started the formation of a criminal procedural system with Chinese characteristics. The 1996 revised version of the law introduced the adversarial system and stipulated that judges should play a more neutral role, thus forming a tripartite litigation structure consisting of the prosecution, the bench and the defence, and making the Chinese characteristics of the system all the more distinctive. For its part, the 2012 revision of the law introduced the provision that human rights must be protected, expanded the rights of the defence, achieving a better balance between the rights of the prosecution and those of the defence and thus making the procedural structure more scientific. Those new developments signified that a Chinese model of criminal procedure had come into existence.

Respecting and safeguarding human rights

In the latest round of revision to the Criminal Procedural Law of China, the highlight is the inclusion of the provision to "respect and protect human rights". Back in 2004, the provision that "the State shall respect and protect human rights" was added to the Constitution of China and has since been enshrined as one of the cardinal principles of the Constitution. The newly revised Criminal Procedural Law, on the basis of concurrently punishing crime and safeguarding human rights, enhances the emphasis on the protection of human rights: to Article 2 of the law, the statement of tasks was added "to respect and protect human rights", which serves as the bedrock of the basic principles, rules and procedures of the entire law. In the context of criminal procedural law, the most important aspect of human rights protection is to ensure the rights that the suspects and the accused are entitled to, the most important of which is the right to defence. In view of this, Section 1 of Article 14 was revised to read as. "The people's courts, the people's procuratorates and the public security organs must ensure that the suspects, the accused and other participants in criminal legal proceedings have access to the right to defence and other litigation-related rights that they are entitled to under law." Although the location of "to respect and protect human rights" in the preamble of the Criminal Procedural Law and its logical relationship with the provisions of "to punish crimes, and protect the people" in Article 1 and "to protect innocent persons from criminal prosecution ...protect the personal, property, democratic and other rights of the citizens" in Article 2 of the law remains to be settled properly, the inclusion of respecting and protecting human rights into the law is clearly positive and therefore should be given credit.

The defence system

The defence system is a core part of the procedural system protecting the rights of suspects and the accused in criminal proceedings. Therefore, whether a country has a properly developed defence system is indicative of the development of the rule of law in that country. Before its Criminal Procedural Law was revised, China's defence system was imperfect in two leading aspects: first, defence lawyers "faced enormous obstacles in gaining access to relevant documentary files, their clients and evidence", which impeded defence lawyers in their professional practice. Second, as a result of Article 306 of the Criminal Procedural Law before it was revised, lawyers rarely tried to obtain evidence during the investigation stage of a case and instead merely tried to challenge the evidence that the prosecution presented during the phase of court trial. Such a "wisely conservative" approach actually neutralised the right granted by the Law on Lawyers to lawyers to obtain evidence.[108]

Through the revision, the following improvements were introduced into the defence system: first, the status of the defence lawyer as "defender" during the investigation stage of the case was confirmed. Before the revision, the Criminal Procedural Law provided that the suspect may have access to legal counsel, but it fell short of confirming the lawyer retained by the suspect for the investigation stage as defender of the suspect. In contrast, the revised Criminal Procedural Law provides in express terms that the attorney of law retained by the suspect can act as defender in the criminal legal proceeding during the investigation stage of the case. Second, the procedures in connection with the defence lawyer's access to his or her client are improved. In order to effectively overcome the difficulties that lawyers face in gaining access to their clients, the revised Criminal Procedural Law incorporated certain elements of the Law on Lawyers and made practical adaptation to such elements. The revised law stipulates that if the defence lawyer applies to meet the suspect or accused on the strength of his or her lawyer's professional practice permit, a certificate issued by the law firm that the lawyer works for, or an official letter issued by competent legal assistance authority in connection with such meeting, the detention facility shall timely arrange for such meeting within 48 hours. However, in cases where the suspect is accused of a crime relating to state security, terrorism or especially serious bribery, the defence lawyer's access to the suspect during the investigation stage shall be subject to approval by the investigation authority concerned[109]. The inclusion of such a provision into the Criminal Procedural Law is, in this author's opinion, necessary in that the Law on Lawyers was adopted by the Standing Committee of the National People's Congress while the Criminal Procedural Law was adopted by the National People's Congress and therefore given a heavier weight by the judicial authorities in practice. Third, lawyers' right to gain access to legal files

---

[108] According to Article 306 of the Criminal Law: "If, in criminal proceedings, a defender or agent ad litem destroys or forges evidence, helps any of the parties destroy or forge evidence, or coerces the witness or entices him into changing his testimony in defiance of the facts or give false testimony, he shall be sentenced to fixed-term imprisonment of not more than three years or criminal detention; if the circumstances are serious, he or she shall be sentenced to fixed-term imprisonment of not less than three years but not more than seven years.

Where a witness's testimony or other evidence provided, shown or quoted by a defender or agent ad litem is inconsistent with the facts but is not forged intentionally, it shall not be regarded as forgery of evidence." This Article, perceived as a "Sword of Damocles" suspended over the heads of lawyers, greatly hinders them in their professional practice.

[109] Article 37 of the new Criminal Procedural Law

and records is expanded. According to the revised Criminal Procedural Law, the defender of the suspect in a case has the right to read, copy or duplicate all files and records of the case[110]. Fourth, provisions concerning the jurisdiction over the prosecution of the defence lawyers for criminal liabilities are modified. If a defender is suspected of a criminal offence in connection with his or her professional practice in a case, the defender should be referred to as an investigation authority other than that in charge of the case. Fifth, the defence lawyer has a right to confidentiality in connection with information involved in the cases for which they are retained. The defence lawyers are granted the right to keep confidential all information of their clients that they may come into their professional practice. However, when a defence lawyer becomes aware during his or her professional practice that his or her client or indeed any other person is preparing to or is already engaged in any crime jeopardising state security, public safety or the personal safety or any other person, then the defence lawyer must inform competent judicial authorities in a timely manner. Sixth, the scope to which legal assistance is applicable (stages of a case and categories of cases) is expanded. The revised Criminal Procedural Law extended the coverage of legal assistance from trial to the stages of investigation and prosecution assessment[111]. Furthermore, two new categories of case were added to those for which defenders shall be appointed under the law, namely, cases in which the suspects or the accused may be sentenced to life imprisonment, and cases in which the suspects or the accused are mental patients who are not completely incapable of recognising or controlling their conduct.

The reforms made to the defence system are highly significant. They allow defence lawyers to fully engage in the investigation stage of a case, and exercise their litigation-related rights during that stage. This is not only conducive to encouraging the prosecution to improve their investigation approach but also to protecting the legal rights of suspects. However, in circumstances where the detention house authorities fail to provide defence lawyers with timely access to their clients, the revised version failed to stipulate any remedial measures. Though the scope of perpetrators of the crime of perjury was extended from "defenders" to "defenders and other persons", such a definition was still unfavourable for defence lawyers; aside from that, the revised version kept the provi-

---

[110] Article 38 of the same law

[111] Article 34: With regard to a case in which the public prosecutor appears before the court to conduct a public prosecution, if the suspect or the defendant has not yet entrusted any defender due to financial difficulty or any other reason, the suspect or defendant may apply to the competent authority for legal aid. If such suspect or defendant is qualified for legal aid, the competent legal aid authority may appoint a lawyer undertaking the duty of legal aid to provide his/her defence.

sion that "[the suspect or accused] shall truthfully answer the questions raised by the prosecution", which is inconsistent with Article 14 of the revised version of the law, which reads that "no person may be forced to prove that he or she is guilty" and therefore a solution must be found for such inconsistency.

The evidence system

In terms of the evidence system, the revised version established the rule that illegally obtained evidence must be excluded. The revised Criminal Procedural Law provided improvements to the evidence system, which is a crucial part of criminal procedural laws. First, the provision that "no person may be forced to prove that he or she is guilty" is added, which will help to reduce the investigators' psychological reliance on oral confessions and thereby contain the malpractice of using illegal means to obtain evidence. Second, the principle that illegal evidence must be excluded is established. Illegal evidence under the revised Criminal Procedural Law falls into two categories, verbal evidence and physical evidence. Illegally obtained evidence, whether verbal or physical, must be excluded. In other words, confessions extorted from suspects through torture and other illegal means, as well as testimonies and statements obtained from witnesses or victims through violence or coercion must be excluded. Illegal physical evidence — items of evidence that are obtained in violence of legal procedure and therefore may seriously impair judicial fairness — shall also be excluded under certain circumstances.[112]

Many countries have made similar provisions in their laws regarding the exclusion of illegal evidence. For example, the US and the UK both follow the "confession exclusionary rule". In the case of China, the Criminal Procedural Law, after the 1996 revision, did not include any exclusionary rule regarding illegal evidence; Article 46 of the revised version was merely a broad declaration of policy and could not be deemed as an exclusionary rule for illegally obtained evidence. Later, the Provisions on Issues Concerning the Review and Assessment of Evidence in Hearing Cases Involving the Death Penalty, which was jointly formulated and promulgated by the Supreme People's Court, the Supreme People's Procuratorate, the Ministry of State Security and the Ministry of Justice (collectively, "the five authorities") and came into force on 1 July 2010, was hailed as a milestone in the process of establishing the exclusionary rule for illegal evidence, because it was jointly issued by the top judicial and law enforcement authorities of the country, even thought that regulatory document was a judicial interpretation in nature. That judicial interpretation defines for the first time in the history of China the scope of illegal evidence, and grants the accused

---

[112] Article 54 of the revised law

with the right to apply for the exclusion of illegal evidence. Furthermore, it also provides that the prosecution must undertake the burden to prove the legality of the evidence they use (if the prosecution fails to prove that such evidence is legal, then such evidence is presumed to be illegal; this means a reversion of the burden of proof). However, some scholars believed that Article 54 was too rigorous. The conditional clause "may seriously impair judicial fairness" makes it hard to exclude illegal physical and verbal evidence in practice and therefore not favourable for the exclusion of illegal evidence. Therefore, the threshold for what qualifies as illegal evidence that "may seriously impact judicial fairness" must be appropriately lowered.[113]

Coercive measures

The revised law also includes new provisions concerning coercive measures. First, qualification conditions for the penalty of residential surveillance are differentiated from those for release on bail pending trial. A provision is added which requires that the punishment of residence assignation and surveillance apply to certain types of cases. Second, the conditions warranting an arrest are altered and the application scope of arrest is restricted. Furthermore, regarding the problem of detention in excess of the statutory period in judicial practice, as frequently exposed, the revised Criminal Procedural Law improved provisions concerning the alteration of coercive measures upon the expiration of the statutory detention period, and thereby enhanced regular review of the justification of detention of suspects. Through investigations and inspections, it was found that an important factor behind the problems of "detention in excess of statutory period and the invariable application of detention against suspects until the conviction thereof" was that whether to adopt coercive measures and what measures should be adopted were decided by the police, prosecution and court, while the suspects were left with no remedial resources against such measures and could do nothing but comply. In view of this, specific provisions were made through this round of revision regarding the following questions: first, the people's courts, people's procuratorates and the police must either release suspects who have been placed under detention upon the expiration of such detention or replace detention with a new and legal coercive measure. Second, the suspects,[114] the accused as well as the agent ad litem, close relatives or defenders were granted the right to apply to change the coercive measure or measures adopted against the suspects or accused, and it was stipulated in clear terms that within three days as of the receipt

---

[113] Interpretation and Comments on the Newest Version of the Criminal Procedural Law, Ji Xiangde et al, Beijing, China University of Political Science and Law Press, March 2012

[114] Article 96 of the revised Criminal Procedural Law

of such application,[115] the competent authority must decide whether to approve the application; third, a regular inspection and review system is established for the necessity and justification of detention of suspects. It must be pointed out, however, that the post-detention review system is different from the pre-arrest necessity review, with the latter focused primarily on whether the denial of arrest may result in falsification or destruction of evidence. The necessity review system for detention is crucial in eliminating the malpractice that a suspect, once placed under detention, will have no resort but to wait until the detention period expires.

Last, under the revised Criminal Procedural Law, it is strictly prohibited to adopt coercive measures against any suspect without notifying his/her family,[116] which prevents the family of the suspect from getting unduly concerned after losing contact with the suspect on the one hand, and ensures that the suspect's family is able to retain a defender for the suspect in a timely manner. This is a positive development, given the reality of judicial practice in China. Nonetheless, the revised Criminal Procedural Law expanded the power of the prosecution in coercive measures, including extending the statutory valid period for coercive summons and callings, reflecting the emphasis on punishing crimes. In addition, as far as the protection of the legal rights of the accused after they are subject to coercive measures and how the competent authorities should fulfil their obligation of notifying the family of suspects after such suspects are placed under detention are concerned, there is still room for improvement.

The interrogation procedure

Under the revised Criminal Procedural Law, the procedure for interrogating suspects during the investigation stage has been reformed and optimised. The high occurrence rate of torture during the interrogation of suspects has been a deep-rooted problem in China's criminal procedural practice. In order to enhance the checks and restraints on state power and effectively control the violation of legal rights,[117] the revised Criminal Procedural Law specifies the statutory procedure for interrogation during the investigation stage, and thereby intensifies the prosecution's supervision of investigative activities, and grants all stake-holders the right to complain against and sue illegal investigative practices. These improvements are helpful to alleviate the strong administrative nature of the existing investigation procedure and lay a solid foundation for the formation of a pre-trial judicial review model.

---

[115] Article 93 of the revised Procedural Law

[116] Interpretation and Comments on the Newest Version of the Criminal Procedural Law, Ji Xiangde et al, Beijing, China University of Political Science and Law Press, March 2012

[117] After a suspect is taken into custody, he or she must be transferred to a detention house within 24 hours; interrogation of a suspect must be conducted within a detention facility. According to Article 121 of the law, when investigators interrogate a suspect, they may keep audio or video records of the interrogation process. In cases in which the defendant may be sentenced to the death penalty or life imprisonment or other serious cases, audio or video records must be kept throughout the interrogation process and the entirety and integrity of such records must be maintained.

Special investigative means

Provisions concerning the use of special investigative means were added to the revised Criminal Procedural Law, in response to the fact that technological investigative means and other special means were frequently used in judicial practice, though they were not sanctioned directly under the Criminal Procedural Law before it was revised. By including such provisions, the revised law bestows formal confirmation of technological investigative means and other special investigative means, specifies expressly the categories of cases in which the police and the prosecution are authorised to adopt such special means, and stipulates in strict terms the confidentiality, destruction and use of information and materials obtained by such special means. While granting the investigation authorities with the right to use technological and secret investigative means, the revised law also specifies the approval procedures for the use of such means. All such provisions, which were included in order to control and punish crimes in an era of rising social problems, have a direct bearing on the privacy of citizens. In view of this, legislators must give them due and careful consideration to further regulate technological and secret investigative means, and ultimately strike a balance between "controlling crimes" and "safeguarding human rights", and ensure that the criminal and judicial review procedure and duration of such investigative means are in line with the inherent rules and patterns of criminal legal proceedings.

Trial procedure

Through the current round of revision, considerable modifications were made to the trial procedure in criminal legal proceedings. One of the most prominent modifications is the inclusion of provisions concerning the appearance of witnesses and expert examiners before the court during the procedure of first instance. Before the current round of revision, though the Criminal Procedural Law stipulated that all persons with information involving a case were obliged to testify in court in connection with that case,[118] no specific provisions were made as to how to fulfil that obligation. The revised Criminal Procedural Law not only requires that witnesses testify in court, but also enhances protection for witnesses, expert

---

[118] According to Article 62 of the law, in cases where the suspects are charged with crimes of jeopardising state security, terrorism, organised crime or narcotics-related crimes, the competent people's courts, people's procuratorates and public security organs shall adopt all necessary protective measures for witnesses, expert witnesses and victims as well as their close relatives who may face danger if they testify during the legal proceedings. Such measures include avoiding the disclosure of personal information such as their real name, domicile and employer; measures to disguise the actual appearance and voice of such persons during the time when they testify, prohibiting designated persons from contacting such witnesses, victims or their close relatives, and special protective measures for the persons and residences of such persons. Such witnesses, expert witnesses and victims may apply for protection if they believe they themselves or their close relatives are in danger.

witnesses and victims. As for summary procedures, the scope of cases to which such procedures are applicable is expanded. In order to effectively differentiate cases eligible for the full and formal procedure and those eligible for the summary procedure and improve the efficiency of litigation, the revised law expanded the application scope of the summary procedure, and merged the "summary procedure" and "summary trial under regular procedure" under the unrevised Criminal Procedural Law and existing judicial interpretations and consolidated the two into one summary procedure.

In addition, the revised law also optimised the procedure of second instance. The first aspect relates to the scope of case categories qualified for open hearing. Under the unrevised criminal procedure, open hearing shall be adopted for the procedure of second instance in principle and only under exceptional circumstances is closed hearing allowed. However, the reversal had been the norm in judicial practice. In order to change the status quo, the revised law prescribed the categories of cases for which open hearing must be adopted (aside from cases in which the prosecution lodged a prosecutorial protest under the unrevised law), and also provided improved procedures for closed hearing cases. Second, detailed provisions were added regarding the remand for retrial to ensure that the principle of Reformatio in peius is effectively followed in judicial practice. Before the revision, the court of second instance may remand a case on the grounds of ambiguity in fact or due to insufficient evidence. However, such a rule was subject to abuse and had undermined judicial fairness. The revised Criminal Procedural Law addressed this flaw and stipulated that "where a case is remanded by the people's court of second instance to the court of first instance for retrial upon the sole appeal by the accused, the people's court of first instance may not hand out a heavier penalty against the accused in the retrial, unless new facts in connection with the suspected crime of the accused are uncovered and the competent people's procuratorate lodges supplementary prosecution on the ground of such facts." Such a provision is a direct embodiment of the Reformatio in peius principle.

Death penalty review and ratification procedure

Another highlight of the revised law is the amendment to the death penalty review and ratification procedure. The attitude of China's judicial authorities towards the death penalty can be summarised as "keep it, yet use it with strict prudence". Reflecting this approach, a review and ratification system has been established in China. A distinctive feature of China's judicial system, this system is meant to be the last-ditch defence against any abuse of the death penalty and it has played a crucial role in ensuring the correct and appropriate application of the death penalty. The review and ratification procedure is not a third-instance trial of a case involving the death penalty, nor is it purely a form of administrative review. Rather, it is a special form of procedure somewhere between a judicial trial and an administrative review. As its name suggests, death penalty review and ratification involves both review and ratification. However, such a procedure for a long time failed to be sufficiently just procedurally in that it had been implemented through written review by the Supreme People's Court of China in a way that was highly administrative in nature. However, the justice of the conviction reached through the trial process is ensured by a just and due procedure, just as Lord Denning, a prominent UK judge, pointed out, wise legislators never treat judges as abstract or impartial persons, because for judges, their being as private individuals is completely mixed up with their social being. In order to eliminate the administrative features of the death penalty review and ratification procedure, a top priority is to increase its litigation elements. As far as back 2007, the Supreme People's Court, the Supreme People's Procuratorate, the Ministry of Public Security and the Ministry of Justice jointly promulgated a regulatory document entitled Opinions on Enhancing the Law-based Handling of Cases to Improve the Litigation Quality of Death Penalty Cases, which stipulates that death penalty review and ratification must comply with a series of procedures, thus injecting some litigation elements into the death penalty review and ratification procedure. Though the document marked a remarkable progress, it was nonetheless quite insufficient. Later, the revised Criminal Procedural Law advanced the litigation-oriented reform of death penalty review and ratification by another step, which is mainly manifested in the following aspects:

First, the Supreme People's Court is required to interrogate the accused when it carries out the review and ratification procedure. Second, the defence lawyers' opinions should be given due consideration if any such opinions are raised during the review and ratification process. Third, throughout the entire review and ratification process of a case, the Supreme People's Procuratorate may present its opinions to the Supreme People's Court, and the latter shall notify the former with the review result.[120]

The community correction system

The community correction system has been created as part of China's enforcement procedure. Community correction, as a mild, humane and economical form of punishment, has attracted the attention of many foreign countries. In view of this, Amendment VIII to the Criminal Law of China has stipulated expressly that "community correction shall be adopted and implemented in accordance with law". This marks another innovation in China's criminal enforcement system and is conducive to the effective implementation of the principle of China's criminal

---

[120] Article 240 of the revised law

justice system, namely, combining leniency with severity. The community correction system has developed rapidly ever since it came into existence in China. The inclusion of provisions concerning this relatively new form of penalty into the Criminal Procedural Law in the latest round of revisions is meant to provide procedural support for the implementation of criminal legislation. However, the provision in the revised Criminal Procedural Law that "community correction shall be enforced by the competent community correction authority in accordance with law" is not feasible in that there is no separate community correction authority, nor is there operable legislation concerning the implementation of this form of punishment. As a result, different agencies or authorities have been assigned with the responsibilities in connection with community correction in different regions of the country. In terms of legislation for this mild form of punishment, there had been nothing but a number of insufficient judicial interpretations and internal rules before the current round of revision was promulgated. Therefore, many expectations have been placed on the amended Criminal Procedural Law, especially the formal launch of state-sanctioned community correction authorities and the drafting of the Law of the People's Republic of China on Community Correction.

Especially noteworthy in the newly amended Criminal Procedural Law are the four types of special procedures: juvenile criminal procedure, criminal reconciliation procedure, forfeiture hearing procedure and the procedure for the compulsory medical treatment of mental patients, with a view to forming a system of special criminal procedures with distinctive Chinese characteristics. Take juvenile criminal cases for example: the amended Criminal Procedural Law expressly provides that defence must be provided for underage suspects and defendants. In addition, for juvenile criminal cases, a social enquiry investigation must be carried out for pre-trial examination that looks into various social factors that influence the suspect's criminal involvement (it is a comprehensive review of a juvenile suspect's background and living environment so that a detailed analysis of subjective and objective reasons for criminal behaviour can be discerned). The revised law also stipulates that a strict arrest procedure shall be applied to juvenile offenders, who must be prosecuted separately from adult co-offenders in their cases so as to protect them from possible negative influences. The revised law also establishes the rule that the interrogation and trial of juvenile offenders must be attended by eligible adults (who are legal representatives, close relatives, school teachers, representatives of local protection organisations for minors, etc). The revised law also creates a conditional non-prosecution system, which is a form of pre-trial diversion. Furthermore, to protect underage offenders, the law provides that crime records of juvenile delinquents must be properly sealed and kept confidential. Although the section on special prosecution procedure is not free of flaws, it has nonetheless filled a gap in China's criminal procedural system, ushered in refined categorisation of procedures in light of actual conditions and marks a step towards advanced, standard and scientific criminal procedure.

Are there any regrettable things about the revised Criminal Procedural Law? The answer is yes. In this author's opinion, the revised law still has the following defects:

First, the revised criminal procedure falls short of writing off the obligation for suspects to "truthfully answer the questions"[121] and therefore fails to actually establish the rule of "voluntary confession". The revised version inherits the provision that "suspects must truthfully answer questions raised by investigators". This provision has become an overly powerful weapon in the hands of investigators and interrogators; since it is up to investigators and interrogators to decide whether suspects have "truthfully" answered their questions, the term "to answer truthfully" may be distorted to become "to answer as required by the investigators". Should investigators find the answers given by suspects to be unsatisfactory, they may be subject to coercive interrogation or even torture. The use of torture to obtain confession in judicial practice is closely related to the stipulation requiring suspects to "answer truthfully". The logical basis of the requirement is the presumption of guilt. In other words, the suspects are actually perpetrators of crime and therefore evidence can be obtained through interrogation, hence the requirement "to answer truthfully".

It can be seen that such a provision is inconsistent with the orientation of contemporary criminal procedure that "no person may be forced to incriminate themselves". However, though that principle has been enshrined in the revised Criminal Procedural Law, the provision requiring suspects to fully answer questions raised by the investigators survives the revision. Such inconsistency is one of the flaws of the revised version, which is detrimental to the efforts represented by the revised law to establish "voluntary confession" and "free confession" principles and contravenes the stated objective of the law to "respect and protect human rights".

Second, it fails to confirm the right of witnesses to refuse to testify under special circumstances. In some Western countries, the privilege to refuse to testify has been confirmed by case law or statutes, including the lawyer-client privilege, physician-patient privilege, husband-wife privilege, clergy-confessor privilege, identity secrecy privilege of intelligence personnel, the privilege of journalists to keep confidential their source of information and the privilege to keep military and government secrets, among others. The revised Criminal Procedural Law still emphasises that witnesses are obliged to testify but fails to provide that they have the right to refuse to testify. Viewed from a humane and cultural perspective, it is more important to keep family bonds than to verify matters of truth, and

---

[121] Article 93 of the unrevised version and Article 118 of the revised version

therefore the privilege of witnesses not to testify against close relatives should be confirmed. In other words, the parents, spouse or offspring of a defendant should be granted the right to refuse to testify against the defendant. Such a move embodies the inheritance of the idea of "tolerance and concealment of crimes for genetic relations" advocated by Confucians in traditional China. It is also line with contemporary ethics.

Third, the death penalty review procedure failed to include the provision that "the opinions of defence lawyers should be given due consideration", which leaves a loophole in the protection of the rights of suspects. The revised law states that, when defence lawyers raise opinions, the court should pay appropriate attention. According to reliable sources, the clause that "the opinions of the defender should be given due consideration" was neglected intentionally since the Supreme People's Court was concerned that if it was included, the Supreme Court would have to inform defendants of their right to retain a defender in all death penalty reviews and would have to appoint a defender for them if they failed to do so. This would greatly increase the workload in connection with death penalty reviews. This author believes that, though respecting and protecting human rights has been adopted as one of the objectives of criminal procedural law, it fails to be properly achieved due to various reasons. The inclusion of "protecting human rights" into both the Constitution and the Criminal Procedural Law marked a giant step forward, but it will take many steps for this notion to be properly implemented in judicial practice.

All in all, the 2012 amendments to the Criminal Procedural Law were made on the basis of those made in 1996 and signified remarkable progress in human rights protection; on the other hand, much remains to be done. As the saying goes: "The life of laws lies in their enforcements." Laws, however perfect they appear, will be worthless if they fail to be properly implemented. In contrast, even highly flawed laws can realise many of the expectations that the public may place on them if they are strictly enforced. Therefore, whatever problems there may be in the latest amended version of the criminal procedural law, as long as the amended version as a whole is conducive to the rule of law and social harmony, and as long as it has become effective after being promulgated, we must make all efforts to promote its implementation and adopt to establish the law as the foundation of criminal justice in China. That should be the most urgent task for us today and in the coming 10 years.

As the saying goes: "Do not spit into a well, for you may have to drink from it." The latest amendment of the criminal procedural law has been completed amid noisy and lively concern from different quarters: the police, the prosecution, the courts, judicial administrative bodies, lawyers and law scholars, and ordinary citizens. As the dust settles, it is clear that this latest round of revision of the law not only marks the high tide mark of a prolonged drive to improve the criminal justice system, but also will be the starting point of a new drive in the same direction. Victory or failure in argument over the law does not matter, for we, as opponents or teammates, share the same objective to improve criminal procedural law.

The civil procedural law

China's current civil procedural law was enacted in 1991 and some of its articles were amended in 2007. In general, the fundamental principles of this law are correct, and most of its provisions are feasible and practical. However, with the development of society, the number of civil cases has been increasing considerably, and new types of cases are emerging. As a result, the law has become insufficient in judicial practice and therefore is in need of further improvement.

On 30 August 2012, amendments made to the Civil Procedural Law were adopted and later came into force on 1 January 2013. This is another milestone in the development of rule of law in China after the revision of the Criminal Procedural Law. There are a number of highlights in the latest amendment of the law, the first of which is protecting litigation rights and enhancing good faith in litigation.

The revised civil procedural law places emphasis on protecting the litigation rights of the parties concerned by adding and creating a series of rules. First, to help the parties produce evidence, the amended law provides that a party has the right to initiate an assessment procedure, invite expert assistance to participate in the litigation and provide expert opinions, and creates a pre-trial evidence preservation system. Second, litigants are granted a wide range of procedure options. For example, Article 122 stipulates that a litigant has the right to reject pre-trial mediation; Article 157 provides that the parties to a case may agree among themselves to follow the summary procedure; Article 199 stipulates that a party to a case may choose the competent court for the retrial of a case; and according to Article 217, after the order of payment becomes ineffective, the party concerned may refuse to go into litigation procedure. All those articles embody respect for the litigants' right to choose procedure and the protection of the litigation rights.

Furthermore, in order to tackle the abuse by some litigants of their litigation rights for the purpose of false or vicious litigation, the latest amended civil procedural law stipulates that the good faith principle should be observed in litigation and be incorporated into specific rules and systems. For example, vicious litigation is prohibited. Where parties to a case collaborate with each other to infringe upon the legal rights of any other party through litigation, the competent people's court must reject the claims of such parties and should, in light of actual circumstances, mete out such coercive measures as fines or detention on charge of hindering civil litigation. If such malpractice qualifies as a criminal offence, for example by securing any effective verdict from the people's court by means of fabrication of facts, or falsification of evidence, or such a verdict is enforced, the offenders must be referred to competent judicial authorities for prosecution. Another example is the prohibition of vicious evasion of debt. When the enforcement procedure is about to start, the debtor or the party against which the judgment is enforced may collaborate with another party to transfer its property through false litigation or mediation, evade its obligations under legal documents. In this case, they should be subject to appropriate punishment.

In addition, a public interest litigation system is created through the latest amendments in response to the frequent occurrence of environmental pollution and food safety accidents. Under the system, the agencies and organisations designated by the amended law may refer to competent people's court conduct that pollutes the environment or infringes on the legal rights of a large number of consumers. The public interest litigation system solves two main problems: the scope of cases and the parties to such litigation; it also leaves room for further legislative improvement, marking a notable step in China's judicial practice and an indication of the progress made to bring the country's civil procedural system in line with more advanced ones elsewhere in the world. In terms of the range of cases qualified for public interest litigation, Article 55 of the amended civil procedural law stipulates that two categories of case, namely, those involving "environmental pollution" and those involving "infringement upon the legal rights of a large number of consumers", are eligible for public litigation. This author believes, however, that such enumeration is not exhaustive; other cases involving "damages to public interest" may also qualify for such litigation, such as cases involving the infringement on state-owned assets and unfair competition, which may also qualify for remedies under this Article.

The parties to public interest litigation must be clearly identified; otherwise, the abuse of litigation rights may occur. In addition, it is necessary to stipulate certain restrictions on the qualification conditions of parties to public interest litigation so as to prevent the abuse of litigation.[122] Under the revised civil procedural law, parities eligible for initiating a public interest legal proceeding are "agencies and organisations concerned designated by law", and the specific eligible agency or organisation is to be identified in line with applicable departmental legislations. However, it must be said that it is highly regrettable that private citizens are excluded from potential plaintiffs of public interest litigation.

---

[122] Article 50 of the revised Civil Procedural Law

As a matter of fact, were private citizens qualified as plaintiffs in public interest legal proceedings, the institutional value of public interest litigation would be all the more prominent. Aside from the eligible potential plaintiffs, public interest legal proceedings are different from ordinary civil proceedings in both procedure and adjudicative rules. Therefore, it is necessary that there should be special provisions for public interest proceedings on issues such as whether the burden of proof is reversed, which party should bear the litigation costs, whether settlement is allowed, and the effect of rulings. However, the latest amended law does not include such provisions, which, in this author's opinion, is understandable: after all, the establishment of a system is a gradual and steady process. In the long run, it is expected that existing problems, and those that may arise in future, will be solved.

Second, the evidence system is improved. Through the latest round of amendment, important modifications were made to the evidence rules in the law, including increasing the allowable types of evidence, confirmation of the expert assistant system, time limit for evidence presentation, more detailed specification of the obligation of witnesses to testify in court, and evidence preservation and evidence assessment.

One, adjustment was made to the allowable types of evidence by including "electrical data" as a type of legal evidence, and renaming the type of evidence formerly called "assessment conclusion" as "assessment opinions"; in addition, the prioritisation of different types of evidence was adjusted, with "accounts by the parties" listed as the first type of legal evidence.

Two, the time limit for evidence production is confirmed as a rule. In addition, conditions for extending such time limits and the treatment of evidence produced after the expiration of such time limits are specified, and the legal consequences of overdue production of evidence were clarified,[123] which is conducive to raising litigation efficiency and preventing evidence raids, and protecting the rights of all parties to the case on an equitable basis. The amended Civil Procedural Law also introduces pre-trial and pre-arbitration evidence preser-

---

[123] According to Article 65 of the amended Civil Procedural Law: "The competent people's court shall, on the basis of the claims of the parties to a case as well as the actual circumstances of the case, specify the evidence that the parties should produce as well as the time limit before which such evidence must be produced. If any party has allowable difficulty in producing the evidence within the time limit, it may apply to the people's court for an extension, and the people's court may permit the time limit to be extended appropriately in light of the application of such party. If any party fails to produce the evidence within the time limit, the people's court shall order such party to provide an account for such failure. Where the party refuses to specify its reason(s) for such failure or the reason(s) provided is not valid, the people's court may, on the basis of actual circumstances, decide either to reject such evidence or adopt such evidence on the condition that such party shall be admonished or fined, as the case may be."

vation.[124] Prior to the current round of amendment, evidence preservation in the civil procedural law of China was limited to in-trial evidence preservation. Though a regulatory document, Provisions of the Supreme People's Court on Evidence Preservation in Civil Legal Proceedings[125] touches upon the issue of pre-trial evidence preservation. However, the document is rather limited in this aspect in that pre-trial evidence preservation was exclusively applicable to specific types of civil cases, including intellectual property cases and maritime disputes. Therefore,[126] in a strict sense, the application of pre-trial preservation of evidence to other types of civil proceedings lacked statutory support. That is why the introduction and confirmation of pre-trial evidence preservation is especially noteworthy. Three, the latest amended version of the law specifies the procedure by which the competent court receives the evidential materials that parties submit. Four, rules in connection with the testimony by witnesses are improved. The amended law provides in clear terms that, in principle, witnesses testify in court; under legally allowed special circumstances, they may testify in writing or by audio and video transmission technology or audio and audio files. Any and all reasonable costs that witnesses may incur by fulfilling their obligation to testify in court shall be borne ultimately by the losing side and advanced either by the applicant for the testimony or the court. Five, the revised law grants parties to initiate the assessment procedure and specifies the way in which an expert witness is selected, the obligation of expert witnesses to testify before the court and the legal consequences they may face if they refuse to do so. Six, an expert assistant system is created, under which a party to a case may apply to the competent people's court to order people with the necessary expertise to appear in court and give opinions on the assessment opinions of the expert witnesses or technical questions.

Third, litigation costs have been reduced and judicial efficiency improved. The newly amended Civil Procedural Law introduces many institutional innovations for the purpose of reducing litigation costs, such as: optimising summary procedures (parties to a civil case to which the regular procedure is applicable may agree among themselves to apply to the court to adopt the summary procedure for the case); it creates a litigation system for small claim cases, for which the ruling by the court of first instance shall be final; the case filing system is

---

[124] Article 81: "Under urgent circumstances where the evidence may be destroyed or is unlikely to be obtained later, an interested party may, prior to initiating a legal proceeding or applying for arbitration, request the people's court in whose jurisdiction the evidence is located or the party against which the application is made or the competent court in charge of the case in question, to preserve the evidence."

[125] Effective as of 1 April 2002

[126] Please refer to Paragraph 3 of Article 23 of the Provisions on Evidence: "Where any law or interpretation provides for pre-trial evidence preservation, such provisions shall prevail."

improved (cases are classified during the filing stage into those that are applicable for regular procedure or summary procedure); the rules concerning the service of documents are improved, with a new form of services, namely services of documents to the domicile of the party concerned (i.e., where the person on which a litigation document is served refuses to accept such a document, and the competent grassroots administrative office or the employer of such a person refuses to sign the receipt of such a document, the service process shall be deemed as complete after the document is left at the domicile of such a person), and more convenient means of serving documents (such as by fax or email) are included; the term for the service of foreign-related litigation documents is shortened; the enforcement procedure is revised (new provisions are added that enforcement measures may be adopted upon the service of enforcement notice) and new provisions permitting competent people's court to sell off enforced items are added.

Fourth, the procedure for the prosecution's supervision over civil legal proceedings is improved. Through the current round of amendment, the form in which the prosecution supervises civil legal proceedings has been expanded from prosecutorial protest-based supervision to comprehensive supervision over the procedure and result of civil legal proceedings as well as the enforcement of rulings, as are embodied by the following: one, the coverage of supervision is expanded, where prosecution supervision is expanded from trial of civil cases to the entire process of civil proceedings, including supervision over illegal activities of adjudicative personnel in the trial procedures other than trial supervision procedure as well as civil enforcement activities; two, new ways in which supervision is carried out are added: the new law not only standardises and consolidates "prosecutorial protest", the traditional form of supervision, but also introduces a new form, namely, "prosecutorial advice"; three, means of supervision are enhanced and a new provision is introduced: "for the purpose of putting forward prosecutorial advice or protest as part of their legal supervisory duties, the competent people's procuratorates may consult parties to the case or any person or entity that is not a party to the case", which makes supervision more effective. Those provisions play a positive role in enhancing prosecutorial supervision, guaranteeing legal rights and promoting judicial fairness. Furthermore, the amended law also straightens out the order of self-correction by the court and prosecutorial supervision. Prior to the 2012 amendment of the Civil Procedural Law, some litigants, in wanting to protect their rights and interests, submit their application concurrently to the court and the prosecutor's office. This two-pronged approach resulted in disorder in the trial supervision procedure and a waste of the country's limited judicial resources. In view of this, the current round of amendment gives prominence to self-correction by the court; if the party insists on applying to the prosecution after the self-correction is made by the court, then the prosecution will get involved. Through this arrangement, the order between internal and external supervision is more reasonable.

Fifth, the improvement made to the pre-trial mediation system is conducive to the coordination and connection between mediation and litigation. Mediation is viewed as an important heritage of traditional Chinese legal culture and an important feature of its traditional legal system. Historically, non-official mediation and official mediation existed side by side and were actually complementary, forming a sophisticated and diversified dispute solution and settlement mechanism. This time-honoured tradition of solving disputes through non-litigation and the rapidly expanding need for mediation have greatly spurred the development of mediation and arbitration. As a result, there has emerged a diversified dispute solution system integrating both litigation and non-litigation dispute-solving measures, which has played an effective and indispensable role in solving civil disputes in China, whose number has been rocketing in recent decades. After the establishment of "the greater mediation" system that combines the people's mediation, administrative mediation and judicial mediation, this integrated approach to mediation has demonstrated great vitality in meeting the needs of the public in local judicial practice. With regard to people's mediation, by the end of 2011 there were 811,000 people's mediation organisations, employing as many as 4,336,000 mediators. These mediation organisations intervened in a total of 8,935,000 disputes in 2011 and successfully solved 96.9% of them.[127]

In 2010, a regulatory document promulgated by the Supreme People's Court, entitled Opinions on Further Implementing the Principles of "Priority to Mediation and Integration of Mediation and Litigation", clearly stipulated that mediation should be given priority in judicial practice. Under the amended Civil Procedural Law, "where a civil dispute referred to a competent people's court by the parties thereto is eligible for mediation, the mediation procedure shall be commenced, except for where the parties reject mediation". Given the fact that China is facing a rapid increase in the number of civil disputes, the local and immediate solution of disputes through mediation is the best way to solve disputes in a timely manner and to promote social harmony and stability. As a matter of fact, the extra-litigation dispute-solving mechanism is "in competition" with the litigation system. If the extra-litigation dispute-solving mechanism is more cost-effective than the litigation system or otherwise more convenient to achieve the objectives of the parties, such parties, if they are sensible, would opt to choose the former to solve disputes. On the other hand, the courts, faced with such competition, would

---

[127] Qi Shujie and Zhou Yiyan, Judicial Reform and Approach to Justice: After the Amendment of the Civil Procedural Law. Journal of Heilongjiang Administrative Cadre Institute of Politics and Law, 2013(1)

strive to improve the quality of their services so as to prevent a loss of revenue in the form of litigation costs, which is conducive to the protection of the litigation rights of litigants.

Sixth, proceedings initiated by a third party to alter or cancel the ruling for another case are confirmed.[128] Such third-party-initiated proceedings are a legal procedure through which a third party to an existing case lodges a complaint to the court to cancel or alter an effective ruling to protect its rights and interests, if such a ruling (whether it be a judgment or mediation award) infringes on the legal rights and interests of the third party. Before the latest amendment, the Civil Procedural Law prescribed three forms of protection for the third party: first, involvement of the third party in litigation, and on the basis of whether it has a separate recourse right, a third party may initiate a separate proceeding if it has such a recourse right, and the court may combine the new legal proceeding and the existing legal proceeding into one; if the third party does not have a separate resource right, the court will notify the third party to participate in the existing legal proceeding, the third party may also get involved in the legal proceeding on its own initiative. However, whether it has a separate recourse right or not, it is often unlikely that such a third party is aware of the existing legal proceeding, especially in cases where the plaintiff infringes upon the rights and interests of the third party through vicious collaboration or false admission, which will place the third party at greater disadvantages.

The second form is third-party objection to enforcement. Although this form of remedy was added back in 2007, the third party would still do nothing if its rights or interests were damaged by a civil judgment that modifies a civil legal relationship between parties or a civil judgment that determinates civil legal relationship between parties, or a civil judgment that orders a party to under-

---

[128] According to Article 56 of the Civil Procedural Law amended in 2012: "Where a third party believes that it has a separate recourse right against the object of litigation between parties in another case, such a third party shall have the right to initiate a legal proceeding against such object of litigation. Where the third party does not have a separate resource right against such object of litigation but is nonetheless legally interested in the outcome of the case, such a third party may apply to participate in the litigation, or be notified by the competent people's court to participate in the litigation. A third party to a case who, according to the ruling by the competent people's court for the case, is to assume civil liability shall have the rights and obligations pertinent to a party to the case. Where the third party in the preceding paragraphs does not participate in the case due to causes not attributable to the third party itself but believes on the ground of valid evidence that the ruling, judgement or mediation award (which has taken legal effect) for the case is wrong, whether wholly or partly, and may therefore infringe on its civil rights and interests, the third party may, within six months after the day when it becomes aware of or is reasonably assumed to have become aware of the damages to its civil rights and interests, bring a lawsuit to the people's court that makes such ruling, judgment or award. The people's court, if it finds the claims of the third party valid, shall either alter or cancel the ruling, judgment or award; if the claims of the third party are not valid, the people's court shall reject such claims."

take civil obligations and is yet to enter the enforcement procedure. The third form is third-party application for retrial during the enforcement of the original ruling, judgement or award. However, this form only applies when the enforcement procedure has started, and is subject to the precondition of objection to enforcement. Therefore, the third party cannot have access to remedy if the enforcement procedure is yet to commence. All in all, third-party protection under China's Civil Procedural Law before 2012 was flawed. In view of this, the third-party-initiated cancellation was confirmed and introduced through the latest round of amendment. This newly added form, aimed at cancelling or altering effective rulings that have been proved to be defective, is capable of providing remedy to a third party who is not involved in an existing legal proceeding, and is based on the same or similar legal values and function as the trial supervision procedure.

Seventh, considerable modifications were made to provisions concerning arbitration in the current round of amendment, which is likely to have a notable impact on the development of arbitration in China. Through the amendment, two qualification conditions for the annulment of court rulings were deleted: "where the main items of evidence based on which matters of facts are verified are insufficient" and "it is proved that the application of law is incorrect". In their place are two new conditions: "where the evidence based on which the ruling is made is forged" and "the opponent party conceals from the arbitration body evidence that is sufficient to affect the fairness of ruling". Thus, the inconsistency between the conditions for "annulment of court ruling" and "application for cancelling of arbitration awards", against which arbitration sector insiders had appealed for years, was finally settled through the latest amendment to civil procedural law. Further, the amended civil procedural law also includes some pioneering alteration to such aspects of arbitration as property preservation, evidence preservation and vicious arbitration. Therefore, the latest amendment to the law is believed to provide a boost for the arbitration sector. According to some senior lawyers, modifications made to arbitration-related provisions through the latest amendment will facilitate innovation in public administration and judicial democracy in China, provide institutional support for solving social problems and maintaining social harmony and stability through diversified means, and promote the development of and competitiveness of Chinese arbitration agencies in international business dispute resolution.[129]

The latest amendment to the civil procedural law not only improves on exist-

---

[129] The Arbitration Sector Stands to Benefit from Civil Procedural Law Overhaul, Faren Magazine, 2013(1)

ing rules and systems, but also introduces new systems. However, in spite of the many highlights, there are also some problems, which are primarily manifested by the expansion of the power of judges.

As a means to solve disputes over private rights, civil legal proceedings must give priority to the parties' right of disposition. Since its inception, the Civil Procedural Law of China has adopted the principle of disposition as one of the fundamental principles of civil legal proceedings. The reform of the adjudicative model, which began in the mid-1990s, is also aimed at reducing the power of the court, bringing the initiative of the parties into fuller play and uncovering facts through in-court adversarial process between the parties. This reformed model has won the recognition and acceptance of the Chinese public. However, the newly amended Civil Procedural Law seems to backtrack on the reform. Most obviously, Paragraph 2 of Article 65 of the amended Civil Procedural Law stipulates that, "the competent people's court shall, on the basis of the claims of the parties to a case as well as the actual circumstances of the case, specify the evidence that the parties should produce as well as the time limit before which such evidence must be produced". This newly added provision grants[130] the court with excessive power in two aspects, which may give rise to new problems in judicial practice. First, the provision that it is the people's court that specifies the evidence that the parties need to furnish is inconsistent with the fundamental principle of "whichever party makes a claim shall produce evidence for that evidence", and may even in the scenario where the judge controls the legal proceeding and the parties fully rely on the judge, which contravenes the inherent rules of contemporary civil litigation. Second, the provision that the time limit for the production of evidence is specified by the court completely negates the initiative that parties have in setting the timeframe for evidence production, and may therefore result in abuse of power on the part of the court and hence undermines judicial justice. According to the Legislative Affairs Committee under the National People's Congress, one of the reasons why the people's court is designated to set a time limit for evidence production is that, "seen from the context of China's judicial practice, it is not feasible for the parties to a case to negotiate and set a time limit for evidence production, because they rarely reach a consensus on such a time limit". However, it is the parties to the case that are the most aware of whether it is difficult to produce evidence or not, and hence it is unreasonable that the option for the parties to decide among themselves on the time limit is completely excluded. In addition,

---

[130] The Arbitration Sector Stands to Benefit from Civil Procedural Law Overhaul, Faren Magazine, 2013(1)

Civil Law Office of the Legislative Affairs Commission of the Standing Committee of the National People's Congress, Interpretation and Application of the Civil Procedural Law of the People's Republic of China, Beijing: People's Court Press, 2012, page 103

it remains to be verified whether expanding the discretion of judges will result in more uncertainty or corruption, given the fact that China's judicial system is yet to become truly independent of the country's administrative system.

Chapter 5

From the planned economy to the mechanism of market and regulation
— Evolution of China's economic law over the past decade

The practice of China's reform and opening up in the last 36 years has proven that the introduction of a market economy has been necessary for the country to boost productivity, escape from the stagnation of a planned economy and realise rapid development. However, research in modern economics indicates that pure market regulation can have negative effects, such as blindness and hysteresis. So the government needs to regulate the market. Economic law briefly refers to the legal norms introduced by the government to manage the economy and adjust market relations through methods such as government regulation with the aim of maintaining the overall interests of society. These legal norms are used by the government to intervene, manage, regulate and balance economic activities from the perspective of the coordinated development of the economy and society.

Economic law plays an important role in a market economy. It provides the basis and guarantee for macro regulation and control, and the effective means to balance the interests of members of society, which can help to maintain market order. Economic law, on the one hand, encourages and protects legal competition, which can promote the rational flow of social resources and realise the optimal configuration of resources. On the other hand, it forbids and fights against unfair competition to prevent the destruction of competition rules. Economic law works together with relevant legal branches such as civil law, criminal law and administrative law to regulate the market and build a sophisticated legal environment for the development of China's market economy.

On 11 December 2001, China joined the World Trade Organization (WTO), which marked the country's further participation in economic globalisation. Motivated by this event, China still needs more consideration from domestic and international markets in order to improve and develop its legal construction. In the years since it joined the WTO, China's economy has undergone dramatic changes. In tandem, China's economic law system has gradually adapted to the requirements of WTO rules and international conventions, which provides a driving force to promote trade and maintain competition order.

From the Planned Economy to the Mechanism of Market and Regulation

In order to deepen the reform of the foreign trade system, develop the national economy and implement the trade-related rules of the WTO, China has developed and amended normative documents in areas such as foreign trade, finance and competition:

1. In order to join the WTO, China amended many trade laws and regulations in 2001. In 2004, it passed amendments to the foreign trade law and developed rules for the implementation of trade protection measures such as anti-dumping and countervailing, and safeguarded measures. From 2008 to 2010, China again amended its laws on intellectual property.

2. In order to further open its financial markets, improve financial regulation, protect the financial industry according to law and improve the international competitiveness of China's financial institutions, China has amended the Law of Commercial Banks, and enacted the Regulation on Foreign Financial Institutions, Regulations on Foreign Banks and the Foreign Exchange Law.

3. In order to maintain fair competition and develop the national economy, China has enacted the Antitrust Law and amended the Anti-Unfair Competition Law, and introduced a series of subordinate regulations, rules and juridical explanations.

4. In order to continue to promote tax system reform and improve the tax collection and management system, China has developed a number of laws and regulations, such as the Individual Income Tax Law, Enterprise Income Tax Law, Provisional Regulations on Value Added Tax, Provisional Regulations on Business Tax and Provisional Regulations on Consumption Tax.

Thus it can be seen that, since joining the WTO, China has begun to learn and adapt more of the rules of the international economy and trade to develop and amend a series of normative documents about economic law, which has initiated the process of monitoring global developments from China. With its ever-deepening participation in the global economy, China has found that it has been necessary to amend economic laws and regulations in line with the practical conditions of the current domestic economy, which then starts a process of introspection. The parallel and continuous interaction between these two processes reflects the transformation of China's economic regulation principle from the planned economy to one governed by markets and regulation. It has effectively promoted the development of China's economic law and has had a wide-ranging and important impact on the improvement of China's economic law system.

Trade law

In the early days after it became the 143rd member of the WTO, China's original foreign trade law system could not completely meet the requirements of the global trade body's rules. Since then, it has adjusted its legal system, removing laws and regulations that conflict with WTO rules, amending several foreign trade regulations and enacting a batch of foreign trade regulations that meet the demand of the new situation.

In the field of foreign trade, China amended and passed the latest Foreign Trade Law on 6 April 2004. It abolished the content that does not conform to the purpose of promoting foreign trade and added provisions that correspond with WTO rules. It has also amended trade safety guarantee regulations, such as the Regulations of Anti-Dumping and Anti-Subsidy and Regulations on Safeguards.

International trade law

Newly amended in 2004, the Foreign Trade Law is actually the process by which China has started to integrate WTO rules in its major laws on foreign trade.

In 2004, the Foreign Trade Law was amended in the following main aspects.

First, the legislation fully reflects the basic principles of the WTO.

The first principle concerns trade liberalisation. The WTO requires all of its members to remove or limit tariff and non-tariff barriers in international trade, improve accessibility to domestic markets and promote free competition. Keeping the promises it made upon joining the WTO, China has encouraged foreign trade, maintained fair and free trade order, and actively participated in regional economic integration. But considering the importance of economic stability, China must implement a progressive liberalisation process. For one thing, China must keep its promises when joining international treaties. Moreover, it should comply with the regulations of domestic laws and administrative regulations to gradually open its domestic market.

The second principle is non-discrimination. WTO rules allow certain restrictive measures to be implemented by the contracting parties. But there should be no discrimination on the other contracting parties during implementation. In China's Foreign Trade Law, this principle was realised by giving the other contracting parties most-favoured nation status and national status.

The third principle is transparency. The WTO requires that the regulatory bodies of member countries must publicise formally implemented and trade-related laws, regulations, rules, policies and international trade agreements. When joining the WTO, the Chinese government promised to remove internal files when managing foreign trade. It means that the government will only enforce publicised laws, regulations, rules and policies. The new Foreign Trade Law also emphasises the obligation of public notice in the two chapters of foreign trade order and foreign trade investigation. In Article 54, it also states that the national competent authorities of foreign trade must develop the public information service system about foreign trade to provide information to foreign trade operators and the other people in society.

Second, limitations on the qualification of foreign trade operators and foreign trade management rights have been relaxed.

WTO rules require member countries to give foreign citizens and companies national treatment and allow them to conduct foreign trade. If China still followed the old regulations to forbid natural persons from conducting foreign trade, it would lead to internal discrimination whereby foreign citizens are allowed to conduct foreign trade but Chinese citizens are not. So, in order to treat domestic and foreign entities equally and promote the development of foreign trade, China has expanded the scope of foreign trade operators to any legal person, other organisation or individual that has handled industrial and commercial registration or other formalities for business operation and is engaged in foreign trade business activities according to the provisions of the present law and other relevant laws and administrative regulations in the newly amended Foreign Trade Law.

In joining the WTO, China has promised to remove the restriction on the approval of foreign trade rights and open foreign trade rights in goods and technology within three years of joining the organisation. Under the old foreign trade regulations, foreign trade operators active in the import and export of goods and technology needed to satisfy certain requirements and secure permission from competent authorities on foreign trade in the State Council. This provision does not meet the requirements of international agreements. In the new Foreign Trade Law, it states that China allows the free export and import of goods and technology, unless it is otherwise prescribed by any law or regulation. It also changes foreign trade rights from examination and approval system to filing system.

Third, China has added some chapters to safeguard national interest in line with WTO rules.

To conform to WTO clauses, China has supplemented and perfected its Foreign Trade Law to develop a mechanism in to deal with emergency and abnormal conditions in foreign trade and safeguard the country's interests. By continuously monitoring abnormal conditions in the import and export of goods and technology, and international service trade, China can analyse the impact on domestic industries and publish warning information in a timely manner that serves decision-making in the State Council, along with relevant departments of government, industries and enterprises.

China has enjoyed member rights after joining the WTO. Domestic laws have introduced new regulations on the implementation mechanism and procedure when enjoying this right. In order to prevent other member countries from abusing trade remedy means, and reasonably protecting the interest of domestic industries and maintain fair competition in the market, the Foreign Trade Law has added the 7th Chapter about foreign trade investigation. The Commerce Ministry is authorised to investigate the impact on domestic industries and their competitiveness from the related goods trade, the import and export of technology and service trade, and the impact from trade barriers set by trade partner countries, and take remedial measures in line with the investigation results. These provisions provide a fundamental quantitative analysis framework and evaluation procedure for China in foreign negotiations and discussion, signing multilateral and bilateral agreements, and initiating foreign investigation and trade remedy measures, which can help balance the impact on domestic industry and employment from changes in the international economy.

The Foreign Trade Law has also added a new chapter about foreign trade remedy measures, which countries use to defend their foreign trade and thereby improve enthusiasm for foreign trade laws. The Foreign Trade Law clearly states trade remedy measures such as anti-dumping, anti-subsidy, safeguard measures, emergency safeguard measures in services and anti-circumvention. In order to coordinate with the provisions about foreign trade remedy measures in the Foreign Trade Law, the State Council of China also amended the Regulations of Anti-dumping of PRC and the Regulations of Anti-subsidy of PRC, which has effectively remedied the weakness of provisions about remedial measures in China's original foreign trade laws. Anti-dumping, anti-subsidy and safeguard measure are the three major trade remedy measures stated by the WTO, and they are legal trade barriers. (a) Anti-dumping comprises counter measures taken when foreign goods are sold in the domestic market at a price lower than the normal level. If dumping has been confirmed after investigation to cause substantial damage to or cause the threat to substantially damage domestic industries, or cause substantial barriers to develop relevant industries in the domestic market, an additional tax will be imposed on foreign goods in addition to the general import tax, which will make them unable to be sold cheaply. Alternatively, the exporter will be required to make a price promise to eliminate the threat to domestic industries. (b) Anti-subsidy refers to opposing the governments or any public institutions of exporting countries to provide preferential measures in funds or finance to make their goods more competitive in the international market than unsubsidised similar products. Facing subsidies provided by exporting countries, victimised countries can impose countervailing duties or take provisional measures. (c) Safeguard measures refer to the temporary relief of member countries from the obligations prescribed in WTO agreements when their imports increase sharply and cause serious damage or threat of serious damage to their domestic industries.

Legal disputes cases in foreign trade

Each year since it joined the WTO, China has been involved in investigations about anti-dumping and countervailing, as well as safeguard measures. With an increasing trade surplus, China has also been the target of an increasing number of investigations. Statistical data from China's Ministry of Commerce indicate that China has suffered the most anti-dumping investigations in 18 consecutive years and the most anti-subsidy investigations in eight successive years[131]. In 2013 alone, China was involved in 89 trade remedy investigation cases initiated by 19 countries or regions worth a total of US$3.619bn[132]. In recent years, trade remedy investigations facing China have covered several important industrial sectors, including steel and stainless steel products[133]. Australia initiated an anti-dumping investigation of China's galvanised sheet and aluminium-zinc sheet sectors, while the EU started an anti-dumping investigation of its photovoltaic industry[134]. Other countries have also taken juridical and retaliatory measures relating to China's foreign trade. For example, the US Department of Commerce ruled that there were dumping subsidies in China's tyre exports to the US[135]. The International Trade Commission of the US approved retaliatory tariffs on high pressure steel cylinders im-

---

[131] Zhou Rui and Li Xiaoyu, chinanews. com, 16 January 2014

[132] Ministry of Commerce of the People's Republic of China.
http://www.mofcom.gov.cn/article/hyxx/jidian/201403/20140300532263.shtml

[133] He Min, Phoenix Net, quoted from chinanews. com.
http://finance.ifeng.com/news/industry/20130218/7671461.shtml

[134] China Information Net of Industry Economy
http://www.cinic.org.cn/site951/nypd/2012-09-17/591633.shtml

[135] ifeng.com, http://auto.ifeng.com/roll/20120320/758027.shtml

ported from China. The Eurasian Economic Commission imposed anti-dumping duties on China-made cast iron bathtubs[136]. Although China has gradually eliminated a great number of export subsidies in order to meet its WTO commitments, many preferential policies for exporters remain[137]. So, China is vulnerable to anti-dumping, countervailing and other investigations at a time when the global economy is sluggish and trade protectionism is rising after the financial crisis.

However, China has accumulated great experience in dealing with the anti-dumping and countervailing investigations from foreign countries over recent years. Through cooperation between government and enterprises, and by fully using the Foreign Trade Law and the trade rules of international agreements, China has safeguarded its interests in many anti-dumping, countervailing and specific safeguard cases. Successful cases in the early days include the anti-dumping accusation levelled at Chinese ball-bearing exports to the US in 2002[138]. The Mechanical Basic Parts branch of China Mechanical and Electrical Products Chamber of Commerce organised China's leading bearing manufacturers to actively respond to the investigation and answered the suit of the United States International Trade Commission, which forced the commission to rule on 3 April 2003 that there was no damage or threat of damage to America's bearing industry from China's ball bearing exporters to the US. This decision was supported by the verdict of the US Court of International Trade on 16 September 2004. Thanks to this verdict, China was not affected in 2005 when the US Department of Commerce announced that it would continue to impose anti-dumping duties on ball bearings. Another successful case was the United States International Trade Commission's decision in April 2012 not to impose anti-dumping and countervailing duties on steel wheels imported from China[139]. The value of this trade continued to increase during the financial crisis, from US$80.4m in 2010 to US$84.2m in 2011. This made China's steel wheel exporters become a scapegoat for America's weak economy. The US Department of Commerce initiated the anti-dumping and countervailing investigations on China's steel wheels and made the affirmative final awards on 19 March 2012. It affirmed the dumping acts by China's manufacturers or exporters of steel wheels when selling products in the US, and the dumping margin was be-

---

[136] China's industrial security guide net,
http://www.acs.gov.cn/sites/aqzn/aqjxnr.jsp?contentId=2677517230055

[137] China Net.
http://www.china.com.cn/international/txt/2012-12/27/content_27530855.htm

[138] http://www.chinaacc.com/new/253/263/2006/2/ma23711155190226002161160.htm

[139] http://www.baidu.com/link?url=GM90EC9nW2XGllyRiC61qyppGsM4BmsRr11ZdBjQ8JbJbKa1dN2Z-DxqYoR322yGOFdzphUpaj-7PdZDYnYpmbubBDNpkoQTuYk2_rUQRKS

tween 45% and 193.5%. These products also received subsidies from 25.66% to 38.3%. So, anti-dumping and countervailing duties were imposed on steel tyres exported from China to the US. But due to the unremitting efforts of China's steel tyre exporters and industry associations, the situation was reversed. The International Trade Commission of the United States finally decided that the steel tyres imported from China would not pose a substantial damage or threat to American industry and the Commerce Department would not require customs to impose anti-dumping and countervailing duties on these products.

The increase in foreign trade disputes has persuaded the Chinese government and enterprises to place greater emphasis on the legal system of foreign trade. With the continuous improvement of China's foreign trade legislation and the gradual accumulation of expertise in international trade law, China will be better able to protect its own interests when facing anti-dumping and countervailing investigations from foreign countries.

With the improvement of its foreign trade legal construction, China is better placed to cope with anti-dumping, countervailing and safeguard measures investigations, and protect the interests of the export enterprises. It has also gained the ability to be more proactive and to fight dumping and subsidies from other countries more effectively, which can help to protect the interests of Chinese manufacturers and maintain the fairness of the domestic market and the order of international trade. According to the provisions of the Anti-dumping Regulation and Countervailing Regulation, there are two approaches to initiate anti-dumping and countervailing investigations. The first one is for an application to be made by China's domestic industries or their representatives to the Ministry of Commerce, formerly known as the former Ministry of Foreign Trade and Economic Cooperation. The second approach is for an active investigation initiated by the Ministry of Commerce, which is quite rare in practice; most investigations are initiated by aggrieved enterprises.

The first anti-dumping and countervailing investigation case initiated by China against another country was the one proposed by Wuhan Iron and Steel (Group) Corp and Baoshan Iron and Steel Group representing China a domestic oriented silicon steel industry to the Ministry of Commerce. They asked the ministry to start an anti-dumping and countervailing investigation for oriented silicon steel imported from the US, and an anti-dumping investigation for oriented silicon steel imported from Russia.[140] After a legal investigation and evidence collection process that took nearly six months, the Ministry of Commerce concluded on 10

---

[140] http://business.sohu.com/20090605/n264351885.shtml

September 2009 that the US and Russia had dumped silicon steel in China and that America's silicon steel industry had also benefited from domestic subsidies, and that provisional anti-dumping and countervailing duties would be imposed on silicon steel imported from the US and Russia. Later, the Ministry of Commerce also initiated anti-dumping and countervailing investigations on American-made sedans and off-road vehicles with an engine size of 2 litres and above in line with an application proposed by the China Automotive Industry Association representing domestic industries, and affirmed dumping of between 2% and 21.5%, and subsidies between 0% and 12.9%. A more recent anti-dumping and countervailing investigation involved China's domestic wine industry in June 2013. China believed that wines originating from the EU were the subject of unfair trade acts such as dumping and subsidies, which had damaged the domestic wine industry. The industry asked the Ministry of Commerce to start an anti-dumping and countervailing investigation.

In recent years, China has more actively coped with dumping and subsidies following the principle of only opposing unfair international trade. So, the application of anti-dumping and countervailing measures has been strictly limited by laws and regulations. Investigatory bodies have always tried to avoid the misuse of trade remedy measures, and make sure that their primary purpose is to restrain unfair competition and to maintain a fair trading environment.

China has become more expert in applying WTO rules and domestic foreign trade laws to protect its own interests while at the same time coping with anti-dumping and countervailing investigations in foreign markets, or when facing dumping and subsidy acts from importing countries in the domestic market. The legal construction of foreign trade has made a great contribution in effectively protecting the international export market explored by Chinese firms, and protecting the legal interests of domestic manufacturers and operators. It is the positive and effective method to maintain a free, open and fair international trade environment, and adjust trade relations between different countries when both the Chinese government and its enterprises can use the rules to better cope with trade conflicts.

Competition laws

Anti-monopoly law

The anti-monopoly law, also known as the antitrust law, refers to the legal system of opposing monopolies and protecting competition. It is one of the basic economic legal systems in a mature market economy. China had no independent anti-Monopoly law in the past and it only had scattered anti-monopoly provisions in the anti-unfair competition law. In order to perfect China's market economy legal system, the standing committee of the 10th People's Congress of China passed the Anti-monopoly Law of People's Republic of China on 30 August 2007 at its 29th meeting. This law took effect on 1 August 2008. After that, the Supreme People's Court introduced the Provisions of the Supreme People's Court on Several Issues concerning the Application of Law in the Trial of Civil Dispute Cases Arising from Monopolistic Conduct (or the judicial interpretation for anti-monopoly) on 8 May 2012. It has been implemented since 1 June 2012. These two legal norms are the major legal basis applied in the anti-monopoly area. They have provided the legal protection to prevent and stop monopolistic behaviour, protect fair competition in the market and improve the overall efficiency of economic operation.

The Anti-Monopoly Law has made the following contributions:

First, it states three types of monopolistic behaviour: monopoly agreements reached between business operators, the abuse of dominant market position by business operators and the concentration of business operators that may have the effect of eliminating or restricting competition. The concentration of business operators must be examined to strictly forbid monopolistic behaviour that can limit and exclude competition. Business operators with dominant market positions are required not to abuse their dominant position to eliminate or restrict competition. But considering the practical situation that there will be no competitiveness in a single weak enterprise, the Anti-Monopoly Law states that business operators may get together according to the law to expand the scale of their business operations through voluntary association. China is not against enterprises becoming bigger and stronger, but it wants to prevent monopolies arising from over-concentration. For industries that highly important to the national economy or national security, greater emphasis is placed on the improvement of controlling forces. If foreign capital mergers and acquisitions occur in an area of national security, an examination of national security will be specially conducted.

Second, although it is needed to improve control over important industries, the Anti-Monopoly Law forbids large state-owned enterprises from harming consumer interests by taking advantage of their controlling position, and clearly forbids the abuse of administrative power to limit competition. The Anti-Monopoly Law has not only regulated economic monopolies where business operators try to prevent competition by taking advantage of their monopoly position, but also emphasised the regulations on administrative monopolies in the forms of industrial monopoly and regional protectionism. Administrative monopoly refers to the acts that administrative organisations, affiliated departments of administrative organisations and organisations in public administration abuse their administrative power to illegally intervene in normal operating activities and limit competition. It includes the specific behaviour of intervening in normal market competition, such as designating the purchase of products made by certain operators, hindering the free inter-regional flow of products by setting up regional barriers, and rejecting and limiting non-local operators from participating in bidding or setting up branch offices in local markets. The Anti-Monopoly Law has also stated in principle that local policies developed by governments cannot eliminate and restrict competition.

Third, the Anti-Monopoly Law established the Anti-Monopoly Commission to separate regulatory from law enforcement bodies, and define the roles of each regulatory body in anti-monopoly area. Article 9 of the Anti-Monopoly Law clearly states that the State Council shall establish an Anti-Monopoly Commission that is responsible for organising, coordinating and guiding anti-monopoly work. The Anti-Monopoly Law enforcement agency has the right to investigate any suspicious monopolistic conduct and can take measures such as inquiring about the bank accounts of business operators, and seize and detain relevant evidence.

The first judicial anti-monopoly interpretation issued by the Supreme People's Court was made on 8 May 2012. The interpretation stated that, in two situations where a monopoly has caused direct losses and the clauses have violated the provisions of the Anti-Monopoly Law, the parties involved can directly file a lawsuit without need of administrative identification as a first step. When it comes to presenting evidence, considering the complexity in proving anti-monopoly behaviour, the judicial interpretation stated that the burden of proof is reversed in certain circumstances in favour of the plaintiff. It also introduced a system of punitive compensation to improve regulation and law enforcement.

With the enactment of the Anti-Monopoly Law and the judicial interpretation, China finally established the legal basis and operational norms needed to crack down on monopolistic activities. Anti-monopoly work has entered the legal arena and the methods used to allocate resources have evolved from governmental administrative orders to the market competition mechanism.

Anti-Unfair Competition Law

The Anti-Unfair Competition Law has great significance in protecting the interests of legal market participants, cracking down on illegal market economic behaviour, regulating the order of the socialist market economy, and advocating fair and orderly competition. In order to encourage and protect fair competition, prevent unfair competition and guarantee the sound development of the socialist market economy, China enacted and passed the Anti-Unfair Competition Law of the People's Republic of China (or the Anti-Unfair Competition Law) in 1993. On 30

September 2006, the Judicial Committee of the Supreme People's Court adopted the Interpretation of the Supreme People's Court on Some Issues Concerning the Application of Law in the Trial of Civil Cases Involving Unfair Competition at its 1412th meeting and it came into force on 1 February 2007. Having been implemented for nearly 20 years, the Anti-Unfair Competition Law was included by the Standing Committee of the 10th National People's Congress in the 2011 legislative programme, and there will be significant amendments to this law. With changes to economic conditions and the requirements of social development, China has also enacted laws and regulations such as the Auction Law and the Advertising Law to regulate unfair competition behaviour in different areas.

The Anti-Unfair Competition Law forbids operators from carrying out deceptive transactions through forging, counterfeiting and copying trademarks. It also forbids acts of commercial bribery for business opportunities. This law forbids behaviour such as false advertising, improper premium sales and violations of commercial secrets. The judicial interpretation introduced in 2007 defines the specific content of such behaviour and illustrates special situations. First, for using a well-known product's unique name, it defines a "well-known product" as one having certain market popularity within the territory of China and is known by the public. The scope of protection is limited to the territory where the product is well-known, but the case of malicious use is limited by this. Second, the judicial interpretation illustrates some special types of false promotion, such as promoting products in a biased or contrasting manner, or using ambiguity or other misleading methods in promotion. In order to evaluate whether the general public has been misled, the judicial interpretation requires the people's court to ascertain false or misleading promotion in the light of daily life experiences, the general attention of the public concerned, the fact that has been misunderstood, as well as the reality of promotional objects. Third, the judicial interpretation stipulates the specific identification of the constitutive requirements for the violation of commercial secrets. Commercial secrets should be unknown to the public, and should meet the twin conditions of not being commonly known and difficult to obtain. Business secrets should comprise practical information that has potential commercial value, and can be used for enhancing the competitive advantage of the obligee. The obligee should take proper business secrets protection measures that are suitable for specific circumstances.

The Anti-Unfair Competition Law has effectively regulated market competition behaviour. It forms the basis to punish illegal acts such as violating commercial secrets and counterfeiting well-known trademarks, which used to be rampant in China. This behaviour has been contained as a result, a remarkable achievement in the past 10 years after the enactment of the Anti-Unfair Competition Law. However, provisions of this law have included part of the content that should be regulated by the Anti-Monopoly Law, such as administrative monopoly and predatory pricing. Administrative monopoly relies on the authority of administrative agencies, while predatory pricing will damage competition only when an organisation in a monopolised market position maliciously forces down prices. Such behaviour cannot occur between equal business subjects, and instead they should be regulated by the Anti-Monopoly Law and are expected to be eliminated in future amendments.

Anti-Unfair Competition Law cases

After the enactment of the Anti-Unfair Competition Law in 2008, many anti-unfair competition cases have been submitted for review by operators. The most notable was the proposed acquisition of Huiyuan Juice by Coca-Cola that was forbidden by the Anti-Monopoly Bureau of China's Ministry of Commerce in accordance with the law. As the first acquisition case that did not pass an anti-monopoly investigation, this case has attracted great public attention, and made people more aware of the order and culture of competition, which promotes the development of China's anti-monopoly law.

On 3 September 2008, Coca-Cola made an offer to Huiyuan to purchase all of its shares for a sum of US$2.4bn, and submitted application materials to the Ministry of Commerce about acquiring the company. For Coca-Cola, the acquisition would give it direct ownership of canned juice production lines and selling networks, which would help it quickly enter a market in China that was growing rapidly. For Huiyuan, Coca-Cola offered a price that it could not reject, with US$2.4bn being nearly three times its market value. This huge premium would provide Huiyuan with significant funds and relieve the pressures it was facing due to sharply increasing costs. Both Coca-Cola and Huiyuan were satisfied with the acquisition terms. However, the Ministry of Commerce must consider the impact of an acquisition on China's beverage market as a whole. So, it examined the concentration of undertakings from aspects such as market share, its dominance on the market, the market concentration status, its impacts on market entry and technological progress, its impact on consumers and other operators and its impact on national economic development.

After 30 days of preliminary examination, the Ministry of Commerce decided to extend the examination due to the complexity and size of the proposed deal. After 90 days of comprehensive assessment, the Ministry of Commerce made the following judgement about the impact on competitiveness. Three negative influences would arise from Coca-Cola's acquisition of Huiyuan[141]. (a) Coca-Cola would

---

[141] Announcement No. 22 [2009] of the Ministry of Commerce

have the ability to transmit its ascendancy in the carbonated soft drink market to the fruit juice market, which would eliminate and restrict competition for existing fruit juice beverage enterprises, and then harm the legal right of beverage consumers. (b) Brand is the key factor influencing effective competition in the beverage market. After the proposed acquisition, Coca-Cola would increase its control of the fruit juice market through its two famous fruit juice brands, Minute Maid and Huiyuan. Combined with its existing ascendancy in the carbonated soft drinks market, the concentration of manufacturers would obviously increase the barriers for potential competitors to enter the fruit juice market. (c) It would squeeze China's domestic medium- and small-sized fruit juice enterprises, which could restrain the involvement of domestic enterprises in the fruit juice market and their ability to innovate. This would result in a negative influence on effective competition in China's fruit juice market and go against the sustained and healthy development of the industry.

Operators involved in proposed mergers or acquisitions can propose remedial measures to reduce the negative influence of a concentration in production, which can help them to secure permission from the Ministry of Commerce. Before the Coca-Cola case, InBev's acquisition of Anheuser-Busch Companies Inc (AB Company) (Announcement No.95, 2008 of the Ministry of Commerce) involved a promise not to increase the equity share of the parties concerned in other large-scale beer enterprises, whether through direct or indirect means. As a consequence, InBev received Ministry of Commerce permission, with certain restrictions and conditions. These restrictions and conditions included: AB Company not being allowed to increase its existing 27% equity stake in Qingdao Beer; InBev not being allowed to increase its existing 28.56% equity stake in Pearl River Beer; and a ban on the future holding of shares in China Resources Snow Breweries (China) and Beijing Yanjing Brewery. Soon after the case of Coca-Cola, Mitsubishi Rayon proposed an acquisition of Lucite (Announcement No.28, 2009 of the Ministry of Commerce), which involved a pledge not to acquire and build new plants in five years, and to remove part of its production capacity. Mitsubishi Rayon finally received Ministry of Commerce's permission, with restrictions and conditions. In this case, the Ministry of Commerce followed the rule that required Coca-Cola to provide practical solutions to the problems found in the examination. However, the initial solutions and the revised ones proposed by Coca-Cola were not accepted by the Ministry of Commerce after the assessment, since it was considered that they would not effectively reduce the negative influence arising from a concentration of production. The Ministry of Commerce made a final decision on 18 March 2009 that this proposed acquisition would eliminate and restrict competition, and would have a negative influence on effective competition in China's fruit juice market and the healthy development of the fruit juice industry. There was insufficient evidence to prove that the positive effect of this acquisition outweighed the negative effect, or that it accorded with the interests of the public. In addition, Coca-Cola did not propose practical solutions to reduce the negative influence.

The case of Coca-Cola's thwarted acquisition of Huiyuan strictly followed the regulations of China's law in procedure, and satisfied open and transparent principles. But there are still disputes on how to identify the negative influence of restricting and preventing competition in relevant markets resulting from a proposed acquisition. For example, it is still unclear what criteria should be used for different markets. More cases are needed to accurately distinguish those situations that should allow a concentration of production, those that should not, and those where restrictive conditions should apply. Coca-Cola did not propose practical and effective solutions to reduce a monopoly, which resulted in the embargo of its proposed acquisition. But debates about whether the government should amend acquisition terms on behalf of the enterprises have also been raised in social circles in the cases where the concentration was approved due to additional restrictive conditions. The fundamental objective of anti-monopoly legislation is to maintain sufficient competition in the market and protect consumer interests. Although the voice of enterprises and various departments can be heard in anti-monopoly investigation hearings and seminars, there is no channel for consumers to express their opinions. Working out how to better represent consumers in order to safeguard their rights and interests is the future direction of China's competition law.

Banking law

China started its financial system reform in 1993. Two years later, a number of banking and financial laws were enacted. Rule of law is quite important for the financial industry, since only the rule of law can fundamentally guarantee financial security, and crack down on financial corruption and address external financial order disturbance, which can fundamentally guard against financial risk and promote the development and prosperity of financial markets. In order to perfect the socialist market economic system, China has gradually deepened its financial reform, amended its Commercial Banking Law, and enacted and detailed the Foreign-funded Banking Law since the turn of the century.

Commercial banking law

Commercial banks are the legal bodies of enterprises that operate the business of absorbing public funds, making loans, handling settlements, and so on. China's existing Commercial Banking Law was one deliberated and passed at the 13th Session of the Standing Committee of the Eighth National People's Congress on 10 May 1995, amended at the Sixth Session of the Standing Committee of the 10th National People's Congress on 27 December 2003, and carried into effect in

2004. It's worth noting the following aspects about the newly revised Commercial Banking Law.

First, adapting to the demands of financial supervision system reform, the Commercial Banking Law has clearly stated that the China Banking Regulatory Commission (CBRC) should perform the responsibility of banking supervision.

In order to distinguish the responsibilities of the People's Bank of China and the State Council's banking regulatory authority (CBRC), and implement the concept of separate operation and separate supervision, the revised Commercial Banking Law states that the CBRC will supervise the businesses of commercial banks such as buying and selling foreign exchange on their own account or as agents, and buying and selling government bonds or issuing, buying and selling financial bonds. Foreign exchange settlement and selling, and the payment of deposit reserve funds will be supervised by People's Bank of China in accordance with the law.

Second, the Commercial Banking Law has stated prudential supervisory rules in line with international standards.

The newly revised Commercial Banking Law emphasises secure business principles for commercial banks. In terms of effectiveness, safety and liquidity, this law stresses that safety is the most important factor. Commercial banks should also meet other prudential supervisory requirements according to this law. Banking is an industry with high risks and high profits. Financial laws are the operating instructions that the banking industry must follow. Referring to the Core Principles for Effective Banking Supervision developed by Basel Committee on Banking Supervision, the Commercial Banking Law has developed China's prudential supervision indicators, including capital sufficiency and ratios for deposits and loans, and current assets and liabilities. They meet the latest international prudential supervisory requirements and are the unbridgeable credit rules for banks.

As stipulated in the internationally recognised Basel III agreement, the newly revised Commercial Banking Law states that the commercial banks' rate of capital sufficiency shall be no less than 8%, the proportion of the balance of loans to deposits shall not exceed 75%, the proportion of the balance of circulating assets and circulating liabilities shall not be lower than 25%, the ratio of the balance of loans to the same borrower and the balance of capital of commercial banks shall not exceed 10%. These provisions can guarantee the sound operation of commercial banks and control risks to an acceptable level.

Third, the newly revised Commercial Banking Law has adapted to the modern development of commercial banks.

(a) The newly revised Commercial Banking Law has expanded the business scope of commercial banks by allowing them to handle the acceptance and discount of negotiable instruments, buy and sell government bonds or financial bonds, and engage in the business of bank cards. Commercial banks can also undertake foreign exchange settlement and selling businesses after being approved by the People's Bank of China, which has expanded their business scope. The time restriction on making inter-bank borrowing or lending has also been removed.

(b) The newly revised Commercial Banking Law has increased the autonomy of commercial banks and it frees them from the compulsion to make policy-based loans. Before it was amended, the Commercial Banking Law stated that: "solely State-owned commercial banks should issue loans to special projects that have been approved by the State Council. The State Council will adopt corresponding measures to make up for the losses of the banks because of issuing the loans." However, commercial banks are market operators and compelling them to issue loans and requiring the government to bear any losses will harm the autonomy and independence of commercial banks, which does not give rise to fair competition. So, in accepting that commercial banks should bear responsibility for their own profits and losses, the revised Commercial Banking Law has removed the provision that means they cannot adapt to the market economy environment.

(c) The newly revised Commercial Banking Law has also left space for the mixed operations of commercial banks in future. Although China is now implementing a policy of "separate operation and separate supervision", mixed operation is an established trend in other parts of the world. In order to leave room for the new business of commercial banks and improve their comprehensive strength, the revised Commercial Banking Law does not completely forbid behaviour such as engaging in trust investment and stock businesses, investing in real estate other than for its own use, or making investment in non-banking financial institutions and enterprises. They will be determined in line with the regulations of the state.

Foreign-funded banking law

On 20 December 2001, the State Council of China promulgated the Regulations of the People's Republic of China on the Administration of Foreign-Funded Financial Institutions, which used to play the major legal role in supervising foreign financial institutions. In order to adapt to the demands of opening to the outside world and economic development, strengthening and perfecting the supervision and administration of foreign-funded banks, and promoting the steady operation of the banking industry, the State Council formally enacted the Regulation of the People's Republic of China on the Administration of Foreign-funded Banks, and abolished the Regulations on the Administration of Foreign-Funded Financial Institutions promulgated in 2001.

First, the Rmb business has been fully opened to foreign-funded banks. As a condition of its accession to the WTO, China has removed the restrictions in geography and clients. And after the enactment of the Administration Regulation, there would be no difference in business scope between foreign-funded banks and domestic Chinese banks. In the Administration Regulation, foreign-funded banks are stated to have 13 financial businesses in their business scope, including absorbing public funds, issuing different term loans and handling acceptance and discount of negotiable instruments. They can also operate foreign exchange settlement and sale businesses after being approved by the People's Bank of China, which is completely the same as for domestic banks.

China has kept its promises made when entering the WTO to give national treatment to foreign-funded banks, and has fully opened its financial business. After the enactment of the Administration Regulation, foreign-funded banks can operate business in any Chinese city. They can also provide services to both enterprises and individuals, and in terms of business scope, they can conduct foreign currency and Rmb business. Before the introduction of the Administration Regulation, there were 430 foreign-funded banks and more than 270 representative offices, among which only 20 had been approved to conduct Rmb business. China has gradually opened its financial market after entering the WTO to guarantee fair competition among domestic and foreign-funded banks, as well as among foreign-funded banks.

Second, foreign-funded banks are allowed to freely choose their own form of business and are encouraged to get registered locally in China in order to become independent legal entities.

Considering the operational nature of foreign-funded banks, it is quite improper to compulsively require them to set up institutions with legal person status. So the Administration Regulation now allows foreign-funded banks to freely choose to establish wholly foreign-funded banks, Sino-foreign joint-venture banks, or just subsidiary banks or representative offices, whatever suits their particular needs. While they are operating, foreign-funded banks can also change their business form to apply to become legal person banks registered locally. China has adopted different rules and supervision methods in market entry for foreign-funded banks with different business forms. The Administration Regulation states that foreign-funded legal person banks can handle Rmb wholesale and retail business. Foreign-funded non-legal person banks can only operate Rmb wholesale business, which means they can only absorb deposits of more than Rmb1m.

This accords with the basic spirit of China's promises made when entering the WTO, which are to allow foreign-funded banks to freely choose their business forms, open Rmb businesses to foreign-funded banks and create a fair competition environment for both domestic and foreign-funded banks. It also accords with the principle of prudence allowed by the WTO to open different business scopes to foreign-funded banks with different business forms, since it is hard for the host country to control risk from the head office of foreign-funded banks and it is impossible for the host country to take supervision measures directly on foreign-funded banks which are not independent legal persons. So, in order to protect the rights and interests of depositors, and maintain financial stability, China has introduced prudential supervision of foreign-funded banks appropriate to their different business forms.

The Administration Regulation introduced in 2001 has given more freedom to the operation of foreign-funded banks. In 2006, the CBRC released the Detailed Rules for the Implementation of the Regulation of the People's Republic of China on the Administration of Foreign-funded Banks to detail and explain the principle provisions of the Regulation on the Administration of Foreign-funded Banks. It has provided the operation methods for foreign-funded banks, and stipulated the grace period for loan-to-deposit ratio, of which there is widespread concern.

The Implementation Detailed Rules have added specific operational provisions for matters such as establishment and registration, business scope, qualification management, supervision management, termination and liquidation, which has improved the contents of risk supervision and prudential supervision, and specifically defined the conditions and operation procedures for foreign-funded banks to establish, change business form and operate Rmb business. When foreign-funded banks are established, they are required to meet prudential requirements, have a sound reputation and performance, and perfect internal control and accounting systems. Foreign-funded banks are encouraged to change their business form to wholly foreign-funded banks, and they are allowed to keep a subsidiary bank to handle wholesale business. When foreign-funded banks operate Rmb business for the first time, they should meet the requirements such as having been open for at least three years and been profitable for two consecutive years.

The Implementation Detailed Rules also stated a certain grace period for meeting the required asset-liability ratio. The Commercial Banking Law states that: commercial banks within the territory of China must have a capital sufficiency rate of no less than 8%, the proportion of the balance of loan to the balance of deposit shall not exceed 75%, the proportion of the balance of circulating assets and the balance of circulating liabilities shall not be lower than 25%, the ratio of the balance of loans to the same borrower and the balance of capital of the commercial bank shall not exceed 10%. After transforming to become domestic legal person banks, foreign-funded banks will enjoy national treatment, and they also need to follow stability indicator requirements detailed in China's Banking Law. However, for most foreign-funded banks, high risk and high profit are their preferred operation models, which results in a great difference with the stability indicator. This is especially true for the indicator about the proportion of the balance of loans to the balance of deposits, which has reached as high as 200% in some foreign-funded banks. Considering the practical situation of foreign-funded banks, the Implementation Detailed Rules has provided a certain grace period for wholly foreign-funded banks and Sino-foreign joint venture banks to manage the asset-liability ratio. They were required to meet the requirements before 31 December 2011.

Tax law

The overall direction of the development of China's tax system is to establish a system in which turnover tax and income tax have equal importance. Turnover tax can be used to guarantee the efficiency of tax collection and provide a steady revenue source for the country. It can also function as an important tool to regulate income. Over time, the original tax laws and regulations cannot meet the demands of a modern market economy. So, China greatly reformed its tax system in 2008. Several major tax laws and regulations have been amended with the aim of building a more effective and fairer economic regulation and tax law system, which can effectively safeguard citizens' economic rights.

Income tax

Income tax sets the natural person and legal person as the objects of taxation, and can be distinguished as individual income tax and enterprise income tax. Individual income tax law refers to the legal norm enacted by the state to adjust the rights and obligations relationship between the collection and payment of individual income tax. Enterprise income tax law is the legal norm enacted by the state to adjust the rights and obligations relationship between the collection and payment of enterprise income tax.

1. Individual income tax law

The basic norm currently applied in individual income tax is the Individual Income Tax Law of the People's Republic of China. It has been amended six times after being enacted in 1980 and the latest amendment passed the deliberation of the Standing Committee of the National People's Congress on 30 June 2011. The 2005 amendment stated that taxpayers with an annual income of more than

Rmb12,000 are obliged to file their own declaration of income, and withholding agents are obliged to pay the tax for all taxpayers and in full amount. It also increased the deduction standard for wages and salaries by increasing the pre-tax deducted expense standard from Rmb800 to Rmb1,600 every month. In the 2007 amendment, the State Council was authorised to adjust individual income tax to the income of savings deposit interest. Actually, the individual income tax to the income of savings deposit interest was levied at the reduced tax rate of 15% from 15 August 2007 to 9 October 2008, but was suspended thereafter. At the end of 2007, the Individual Income Tax Law was amended again to increase the deduction standard of wages and salary income from Rmb1,600 to Rmb2,000 per month. This trend was also continued in the 2011 amendment.

The 2011 amendment to the Individual Income Tax Law is the one that made the largest number of amendments. First, it increased the deduction standard of wages and salaries. This standard is determined by referring to the costs of a residents' basic life, which means it changes according to practical factors such as inflation and economic development. The amendment of 2011 updated the deduction standard from Rmb2,000 to Rmb 3,500 per month, and this change has exceeded the total amount of previous changes. Second, it adjusted and optimised the tax rate structure of wages and salary income tax. The nine-grade progressive rating system was reduced to seven bracket rates. The application range of some grade rates has also been expanded, too, which helps to solve the problem of overly narrow income brackets in the lower tax rates and an excessively rapid progression of tax rates. The tax burden has also been smoothed, which prevents an unreasonable fluctuation of tax due to changes on taxable income. This amendment has decreased the rate of the lowest grade from 5% to 3% and expanded the coverage of the tax rate grades of 3% and 10%, which can effectively reduce the tax burdens of medium- and low-income people. It has also expanded the application scope of the highest tax rate of 45% by including it within the scope of the original 40% tax rate, which can force people with high incomes to pay more tax and thereby realise one of the functions of tax, to adjust income. Third, this amendment has optimised the tax payment service. Coordinating with other tax categories, the declaration time for individual income tax has been extended from 10 days to 15 days to help taxpayers with their tax declarations.

2. Corporate income tax law

The Enterprise Income Tax Law of the People's Republic of China was enacted in 2007 to replace the Income Tax Law for Enterprises with Foreign Investment and Foreign Enterprises enacted in 1991 and the Provisional Regulations on Enterprises Income Tax enacted in 1993. Before the enactment of the Enterprise

Income Tax Law, in order to invite investment and promote regional development, China provided foreign-funded enterprises with various preferential tax measures, including a low tax rate, plus deductions, etc., which resulted in a lighter tax burden on foreign-funded enterprises than domestic enterprises. This system did not comply with the demands of China's entry to the WTO. The Enterprise Income Tax Law has unified the tax burden of domestic and foreign-funded enterprises. It has also unified the tax burden of state-owned and private enterprises with the aim of creating a fairer competitive environment. So, in the newly enacted Enterprise Income Tax Law, all enterprises, irrespective of the source of their capital and ownership, uniformly pay tax in line with the Enterprise Income Tax Law. Their tax rates have also been unified. Except for "small-profit" enterprises that enjoy a tax rate of 20% and important high-tech enterprises necessary to be supported by the state that enjoy a preferential tax rate of 15%, all other enterprises pay a flat tax rate of 25%. This law has also unified the deductible amount before tax and tax preferential measures, and strengthened measures in anti-tax avoidance. The Enterprise Income Tax Law fully implements the principle of tax equity, which can help reduce the distortion effect on market competition from tax and promote fair competition among different types of enterprises in the market.

On 28 November 2007, the Regulation on the Implementation of the Enterprise Income Tax Law of the People's Republic of China was adopted by the State Council at the 197th executive meeting. This regulation stipulated the calculation method of taxable income in a fair, objective and reasonable way. First, it stated the accrual system as the basic principle in calculating taxable income. This principle is similar to the accrual basis of the accounting standard. If the rights and duties occur in the current term, all activities should be recorded in the current term, no matter whether funds have been received or paid. However, there are differences between tax law and accounting standard. If the legal and valid vouchers have not been received, the related expenses will not be deducted in the current term even if they occur in the same term. Second, the Implementation Regulation has classified incomes as taxable, tax exempt and tax-free. The specific time and condition for income recognition have been stipulated according to the different sources and types of incomes. Third, this regulation has stated that pre-tax deductions must be determined according to the three principles of actual incurrence, direct correlation and reasonable expense. The principle of actual incurrence requires that only the expenses that had taken place and had received a payment document can be deducted pre-tax. According to the principle of direct correlation, deductible expenses must directly correlate with income. The principle of reasonability requires that expenses must accord with the common practice of production and operation activities, which means they must be necessary and normal expenses.

Turnover tax

Turnover tax includes tax categories such as value-added tax, business tax and consumption tax. In order to lighten the tax burden, and expand tax bases and clean tax preferential policies by tax system reform and policy adjustment, China implemented a turnover tax reform in 2008 and amended the major turnover tax-related laws and regulations. It has amended the Interim Regulation of the People's Republic of China on Value Added Tax, the Interim Regulation of the People's Republic of China on Consumption Tax and the Interim Regulation of the People's Republic of China on Business Tax. They have been in force since 1 January 2009. Detailed rules for the implementation of these three interim regulations have been enacted and implemented since the same time.

1. Value-added tax

Value-added tax targets the added value realised by entities and individuals engaged in the sale of goods, supply of processing, repair and replacement services, and the import of goods. The Value-Added Tax Interim Regulation of 2008 made three main changes. First, it introduced structural tax reduction to realise fair taxation and lighten the burden of taxpayers. In order to balance the tax burden between small-scale taxpayers and general taxpayers, this regulation decreases the tax rate for small-scale taxpayers. There is no longer any tax rate difference between industrial and commercial small-scale taxpayers, with the rate decreased to 3% for both of them. The regulation has also expanded the number of deductible items. It states that, when purchasing the fixed assets of machinery equipment, the input tax can be deducted from the output tax, which can help to lighten the burden of enterprises. Second, the Value Added Tax Interim Regulation clearly states the procedure for the collection and payment of tax to facilitate the declaration of taxpayers. In order to shorten the waiting time in declaration and ease the pressure from centralised tax declaration, the regulation has extended the time limit for tax declaration from 10 days to 15 days. Third, the Value Added Tax Interim Regulation has regulated the collection and payment system of tax to prevent tax evasion and fraud. The regulation has legalised current value added tax policies. It has included the provisions of detailed implementation rules of value added tax about the identification standard of general taxpayers, the deduction standard of the freight of agricultural products and the exclusion of equipment imported in the trade of processing with supplied materials, the assembly of provided parts and compensation trade, from value-added tax exemption into the regulation. It has also regulated that the withholding VAT of consumption goods for personal use that have not been technically improved by enterprises and can easily be misconstrued as personal consumption cannot be deducted. While lightening the tax burden and rationalising the tax payment procedure, the regulation has also improved the collection and payment system to effectively prevent tax evasion and fraud.

2. Business tax

Business tax is targeted at the turnover received by entities and individuals engaged in providing taxable services, the transfer of intangible assets or the sale of immovable assets within the territory of the People's Republic of China. The main law currently applied in business tax is the Interim Regulation of the People's Republic of China on Business Tax enacted on 13 December 1993, and amended and adopted at the 34th executive meeting of the State Council on 5 November 2008. In 2011, after being approved by the State Council, the Ministry of Finance and the State Administration of Taxation[142] jointly issued the Pilot Plan for Levying Value Added Tax in Lieu of Business Tax[143]. China began to try to levy value added tax in industries such as transportation, construction, post and telecommunications, modern services, culture and sports, real estate sales, intangible assets transfer, finance and insurance and service industries that used to be levied with business tax. At the same time, tax rates have been decreased. On the basis of the existing 17% standard rate and 13% low rate, two new grades have been added: an 11% tax rate applicable to the transportation and construction industries, and a 6% rate applicable to modern service industries. This change can reduce the original business tax burden, solve the repetitive taxing problem that was criticised for years and help to perfect the tax system structure. It can also promote industry convergence and optimise investment structure. This tax change will be expanded to a larger area of China if the pilot plan is successful in Shanghai. The State Council had increased the number of the pilot areas to 10 from 1 August 2012 to the end of that year. The range of the tax change from business tax to value added tax has expanded to the whole country. Since 1 January 2014, the railway transportation and postal service industries have been included in the pilot, which means that the entire transportation industry is now included in this tax change. The telecommunica-

---

[142] See the website of China's State Administration of Taxation,
http://www.chinatax.gov.cn/n2226/n2271/n2272/c121778/content.html

[143] See the website of Ministry of Finance of the People's Republic of China,
http://www.mof.gov.cn/xinwenlianbo/xinjiangcaizhengxinxilianbo/201405/t20140505_1075060.html

tions industry also has been included in the pilot scope of this tax change since 1 June 2014[144].

The tax switch from business tax to value added tax is an important reform. Designed to reduce structural tax, it can help to solve the repetitive taxing problem, which involves certain items being subject to more than one tax. But structural tax reduction does not mean only reduction and no addition. It should include both, which will inevitably alter the tax burden of taxpayers. Various obstacles have occurred in the pilot plan[145]. China still needs to work through the problem of how to implement the change from business tax to value added tax

3. Consumption tax

Consumption tax is the general term for various tax categories relating to the turnover of consumer goods. While value added tax targets all kinds of goods, consumption tax is aimed at specific consumer goods in order to adjust product structure, lead consumption behaviour and add financial income. The current consumption tax legal norm in China is the Interim Regulation of the People's Republic of China on Consumption Tax amended and adopted at the 34th executive meeting of the State Council on 5 November 2008. The amended interim regulation mainly emphasises the following aspects. First, it has expanded the scope of taxpayers. Before the amendment, consumption tax was only collected from entities and individuals engaged in the production, the subcontracting for processing or the importation of items referred to as "taxable consumer goods" in accordance with the provision of this regulation within the territory of the People's Republic of China. The new interim regulation has added other entities and individuals that sell consumption goods as prescribed in this regulation, and as determined by the State Council. This means that, for certain consumer goods, they will be levied tax in the wholesale and retail processes. Second, the tax categories and tax rates have also been greatly changed. The new interim regulation has increased the tax to 14 categories and each category has been further divided into detailed categories. Based on the simple quota calculation and flat rate calculation, this new interim regulation has added the composite method for tax calculation. For example, the tax rate for grain liquors should include both the 25% rate in relation to the price and Rmb0.5 tax for every 500g in weight. Third, in order to accord with the change of value added tax, the collection of consumption tax has been adjusted, such as adding a season as the tax

---

[144] Zeng Kanghua, the head of the Finance Department of the Finance Institute of the Central University of Finance and Economics, a digest from Xiao Kang, 10 October 2012

[145] No.00010 [2011] Final trail of Intermediate People's Court of Bengbu

payment period and extending the responding period for tax declaration to 15 days.

Cases about tax disputes

Legal disputes in tax fields are mainly about tax collection management and tax penalties.

Disputes about tax collection management typically involve situations in which taxpayers think the tax amount approved by the administrative department charging taxation is wrong, the jurisdiction of administrative department is disputable and the tax collection method is unsatisfied. For example, in the illegal administrative collection dispute case between Li Hongbin et al and Longzihu district branch bureau of Bengbu local taxation bureau[146], the dispute resulted from the taxpayers not accepting the tax amount approved by the tax authorities. The two taxpayers, Li Hongbin and Zhang Hong, entered a house transaction with the value of the house sale contract put at Rmb324,000. The administrative departments in charge of real estate transactions confirmed the house's transaction value at Rmb340,000, which was also stated on the real estate tax deed. The plaintiff confirmed this price by signing the affirmative documents of transaction price in the municipal real estate exchange house. The stub form of the real estate tax deed also confirmed that the plaintiff had paid the tax based on the transaction price valued by the real estate exchange house. The most important thing is that the municipal real estate exchange house has the legal authority to confirm the transaction price of real estate. So it was legal for the tax department to collect tax based on the price of Rmb340,000 confirmed by the department.

The case of Wu Wenqi suing the National Taxation Bureau of Hongkou district in Shanghai[147] in 2011 is mainly about what information can be disclosed during the tax collection process. Wu Wenqi, the plaintiff, applied to the National Taxation Bureau of Hongkou district to disclose information about (a) a copy of the application form about tax change from Shen Tai Housing Demolition Company for the period from 2 August 2002 to 31 December 2004, and (b) the contents of tax registration documents of this company over the same period. The National Taxation Bureau of Hongkou district replied on the day of the application. It considered that the second type of information belonged to the government and it disclosed this information to the applicant in accordance with the law. But in the

---

[146] No.33 [2011] First trail of Intermediate People's Court of Hongkou district
[147] No.41 [2010] Final trail of Intermediate People's Court of Xiamen District

first type of information, it contained business secrets such as the financial seal, enterprise seal and phone number. Individual seals are personal property and Shen Tai Company did not agree to provide this information. So the bureau made the decision not to disclose this information. The plaintiff thought that the legal representative of Shen Tai on the disclosed tax registration documents was not the same as the one on the materials he received himself. The disclosed information was false and the information applied could not be classified as a business secret and should therefore be disclosed. So the plaintiff filed a lawsuit to the court. The court thought that the two types of information applied by the plaintiff were all involved in tax administration and were in the authority of the tax administration departments. The National Taxation Bureau of Hongkou district had faithfully disclosed the second type of information in response to the application of the plaintiff. With regard to the first type of information, the court ruled that company's phone number, finance seal, enterprise seal and individual seal were functional through publicity and should not be regarded as a trade secret or person secret. So the court withdrew the response made by the National Taxation Bureau of Hongkou district that the first type of information applied by the plaintiff included business secrets and personal privacy. This case has played a positive role in guaranteeing the citizens' right to know and supervise, and improve the transparency and credibility of the government's work.

Tax penalty cases are mainly disputes involving the identification of tax evasion and fraud, and the penalties for illegal tax. A dispute between Xiamen Zhiyisihai Import & Export and the National Taxation Bureau of Siming district in Xiamen of Fujian province was about the identification of tax evasion and fraud. Zhiyisihai, as the plaintiff, recorded some sales income as deferred revenue and did not recognise the income in 2005. In 2008, National Taxation Bureau of Siming district, the defendant, considered that Zhiyisihai had constituted tax evasion and punished it accordingly. But the plaintiff held that the reason for its delayed tax declaration was that it did not want to affirm its status as general taxpayer and did not agree to apply for and use the value added tax special invoice. Both the courts decided that Zhiyisihai had made fraudulent tax returns by selling equipment for a huge profit, trying to not recognise the sales income by financial processing, and not declaring this sales income in the related tax return documents in the following four years. The payment of value added tax can be divided into income with invoice and income without invoice. So there was no causal relationship between the lack of general taxpayer status, the inability to issue the invoice for output tax, and Zhiyisihai's failure in its tax returns. So the behaviour of Zhiyisihai did constitute tax evasion and the penalty made by the National Taxation Bureau of Siming district was upheld by the courts.

The legal norms in the financial sector such as tax law and banking law have shown the following development tendencies over the last 10 years. (a) They treat domestic and foreign subjects equally. First, according to the requirements of the WTO, China cannot discriminate against foreign-funded enterprises and should give them national treatment. So, China has gradually opened some areas that used to be forbidden to foreign-funded enterprises. For example, in the field of Rmb business, qualified foreign-funded banks enjoy the same operational scope as domestic banks. Second, equal treatment between domestic and foreign-funded enterprises requires China not to discriminate against domestic enterprises. In order to use foreign funds to develop the economy, China used to offer supernational treatment to foreign-funded enterprises. For example, their income tax burden was lighter than for domestic enterprises. But in order to implement the fair and equality principle, the new financial laws and regulations have removed provisions about special treatment for the foreign-funded enterprises. (b) They have kept pace with the times and referred to international advanced experience to develop rules suitable for China's national conditions. For example, in the field of financial supervision, China has always sought the most advanced rules in the world. It has learnt from the Basel Agreement to adjust domestic financial laws and regulations. China has stipulated the supervision requirements of macro prudence and the specific requirement on capital adequacy ratio. These measures are even stricter than Basel Agreement, and China has been working hard to regulate its financial markets. But China also considers the huge differences that exist between banks and their business fields. Longer grace periods have been given to foreign-funded banks to meet their practical needs.

Product quality law

China's Product Quality Law was enacted in 1993, based on the absorption of the experience of foreign countries' product liability legislation. It also broke through the narrow range of product liability by combining product liability with supervision. In the last 20 years, the Outline of Quality Improvement enacted by the State Council in 1996 proposed to fundamentally improve the overall quality of China's major industries. In the criminal law amendment of 1997, a provision about the crime of manufacturing and selling shoddy commodities was added, which can increase the punishment for this crime. The State Council enacted the Regulation about the Several Questions in Further Improving Product Quality Work in 1999, which further stated the direction of the problems of product quality.

In 2000, the amendment to the Product Quality Law was passed. The new amendment has greatly changed the provisions about the supervision of product quality and the associated penalties. The amended law has more content, a stronger operability and clearer rights and obligations of subjects. Generally speaking, the current Product Quality Law has integrated product liability with the supervision and administration on product quality. It has further defined the duties of governments at all levels in product quality work. This law has built the constraint mechanism for enterprises' product quality. Producers and sellers are required to establish and perfect, and strictly implement, an internal product quality management system. It has improved the methods in administrative enforcement of law, especially in the area of imposing penalties on the manufacture and sale of illegal products. While giving the product quality watchdog and social intermediaries such as product quality inspection organisations and certification bodies the right to supervise and evaluate quality, this law has also added provisions about bearing relevant legal liability and preventing the abuse of power. China's lawmakers and jurisprudential circle are rethinking the deficiencies in China's product quality legislation when facing a diversified commodity market and frequently emerging product quality incidents in recent years, ranging from the Sanlu milk powder incident to the shocking story about the use of out-of-date meat by Shanghai Fuxi Company, which was a supplier to foreign fast food companies such as McDonald's, KFC and Pizza Hut. A combined legislation model has been applied to China's product liability and product quality supervision systems. But in the laws, two third of the provisions are about administrative penalties and product quality supervision and management. There is no specific law regarding product liability and we can only find relevant provisions through the Food Safety Law and General Principles of the Civil Law. The confusion that exists in the initial design of this type of legislative system has increased the difficulty in investigating liability. When considering future legislation, China can refer to product liability law enacted in countries such as Japan and Germany. The legislative system can be perfected by combining related laws and regulations such as the Consumer Protection Law and Tort Liability Law. In addition, China needs to build an effective investigatory system for governments' responsibility and supervision as well as a system for the public that can encourage efforts from society to guarantee quality safety and further improve the practical operational effect of this law.

Law of the PRC on protection of consumer rights and interests

When a commodity economy is underdeveloped, consumers and operators have the same legal status. Laws can give them equal protection. However, with new developments in society and technology, producers, sellers and consumers have drifted apart, leading to an unequal status between operators and consumers. On the one hand, relying on their strong economic and technological strength, operators will not hesitate to take steps to harm the interests of consumers to seek profit. On the other hand, facing an increasing number of products, numerous advertisements and fast-changing technology, consumers inevitably lose some decision-making capacity compared with operators. They have gradually become the weak group in market transactions. In practice, equal protection in civil law provides the basis for one-sided protection on the part of operators. Based on this fact, the Law on Protection of Consumer Rights and Interests emerged at the right moment to seek practical equality between consumers and operators, and safeguard the normal transaction order.

Legislation on consumer rights and interests protection started quite late in China. There is a close relation between its emergence and the worldwide consumer protection movement. The condition of consumer rights and interests protection legislation has become an important symbol in evaluating a country's social and civil development, and the maturity level of legal construction. The Law of the People's Republic of China on Protection of Consumer Rights and Interests implemented on 1 January 1994 states that consumers have nine rights: the rights of safety, being informed, choice, fair trade, claim, association, information, being respected and supervision. It has introduced the provision of punitive damages, which can effectively improve the protection of consumers' rights and interests. By digesting and absorbing the experiences of foreign countries, combined with China's national condition, China's legislative body has formed consumer rights and interests protection as composed of laws and regulations such as the Law on Protection of Consumer Rights and Interests, Product Quality Law, Food Safety Law, Anti-Unfair Competition Law and Tort Liability Law. In particular, the newly amended Law on Protection of Consumer Rights and Interests implemented in March 2014 provides clear regulations on pressing issues in the protection of consumer rights and interests. For example, this newly amended law has introduced the principle of the rebuttal burden of the proof for some durable products or decorative and other services, and given consumers the right to return goods without reason, which is widely known as the right of rescission. This law has added the information disclosure system in off-site shopping models such as online shopping to protect the consumers' right of being informed. Personal information protection is also covered by this law. This law has also stated that the Consumer's Association can play a role in public welfare lawsuits, which can be applied in situations where the rights and interests of a group of consumers have been harmed. In order to improve punishment, this law has changed the multiples of punitive compensation from two times to three times, but has also set the minimum amount of compensation. The amendment of consumer rights and interests protection law has adapted to the changes in China's consumption structure and patterns, and absorbed the legislative achievements of developed countries such as the cooling-off period and the system of returning goods without reason. It is a legislative milestone for consumer protection and it better supports the implementation of other economic laws.

Over the past 10 years, the economic laws of China have been in the process of integrating with the world and evolving based on the country's own circumstances. For one thing, deeply influenced by joining the WTO, China's economic construction has kept up with the world, and its domestic laws have been adjusted to meet the demands of WTO agreements. Much advanced international experience has also been introduced to improve China's economic legislation. And, having gone through the experience of amending domestic laws by learning from the world, China's economic laws have returned to focus on the practical situation at home. Outdated laws and regulations have been amended to solve the problems faced by China in its development, and new ones have been added to adapt to the changing situation. China's economic rule of law has seen progress and setbacks over the past 10 years. But having accumulated a lot of experience, the Chinese government and Chinese enterprises have become law conscious, which can become a driving force for the future development of the economic rule of law.

Chapter 6

A balance between "administrative efficiency" and "administration power control"
— Development of China's administrative laws over the past decade

Overview

The Constitution is the fundamental law of a country. It is also a cornerstone of public law and the parent law of a nation, as it regulates fundamental social relations, determines the fundamental rights of citizens, and forms basic system and principles of the country. Known as the "mini-constitution", the administrative law is concerned with how to implement the norms of basic public law prescribed by the Constitution, how to impose constraints and regulations on administrative power described by Thomas Hobbes, an Enlightenment thinker, as the beast of national public authority, and how to protect citizens' rights from being violated while carrying out effective social management.

In China, feudal concepts and ruling modes such as "the divine right of kings" have had a far-reaching impact over the past 2,000 years, and people tend to fear public authority. But with the development of society, especially after the reform and opening up initiated by Deng Xiaoping in 1978, Chinese people increasingly value the rights of citizens and recognise that public authority should be intended for protecting the rights of citizens. But public authority tends to be expansionary, and if it is unchecked, civil rights may often be infringed.

Chinese people have universally come to realise that the most effective way to limit public authority is to establish a society ruled by law, so that the government can exercise its public authority within the limits prescribed by law. The exercise of administrative powers by administrative organs must be authorised and constrained by relevant administrative laws and regulations through strict enforcement so as to keep society running in a fair, equitable and orderly manner. The exercise of public authority must properly resolve the relationship between the power of administrations and the legitimate interests of citizens and organisations, which will organically and reasonably unify the interests among state, community and individuals.

China's economy has changed radically over the past decade, and it has inspired people to better regulate administrative power in order to promote sustainable economic development and secure citizens' rights. The government has also recognised the need to build a law-based government for social development, for which administrations should shift to become service-oriented rather than original governance-oriented as originally conceived.

On this basis, China's administrative law has made considerable progress over the past decade, reflecting the balance between "administrative efficiency principle" and "administration power control principle" in terms of government management. In order to regulate the exercise of public authority and safeguard the fundamental rights of citizens, China has promulgated a number of administrative laws and regulations, such as Administrative Licence Law of the People's Republic of China, Civil Servant Law of the People's Republic of China, Regulation of the People's Republic of China on the Disclosure of Government Information, Administrative Compulsion Law of the People's Republic of China and Regulation on the Expropriation of Buildings on State-owned Land and Compensation, and revised existing administrative laws and regulations such as Administrative Supervision Law of the People's Republic of China amended on 26 June 2010.

Administrative Licence Law of the PRC in 2003

Administrative licence refers to the acts that administrative organisations permit, upon examination based on the law, the citizens, legal persons or other organisations to engage in special activities when they file such an application.[149] Administrative licence is concerned whether citizens, legal persons or other organisations may engage in certain activities. Thus, the development of an administrative licence law is of great significance in regulating the acts of administrative organisations and protecting the legitimate rights and interests of citizens and legal persons.

Promulgation and main contents of the Administrative Licence Law

Before the reform and opening up of China, excessive administrative examination and approval procedures under the old-fashioned social governance model of a planned economy caused excessive intervention from administrative organisa-

---

[149] As set forth in Article 2 of the Administrative Licence Law: "The term "administrative licence" mentioned in this law refers to the acts that administrative organisations permit, upon examination according to law, the citizens, legal persons or other organisation to engage in special activities according to their applications."

tions in economic activities, which was not conducive to economic development. After the reform and opening up, the Chinese government realised the significance of simplifying administrative examination and approval procedures. In order to regulate the establishment and implementation of administrative licence, protect the legitimate rights and interests of citizens, legal persons and other organisations, safeguard public interests and social order, and ensure and supervise the effective implementation of administration management, on 27 August 2003, the Administrative License Law of the People's Republic of China was adopted by the Fourth Session of the Standing Committee of the 11th National People's Congress. This law came into force on 1 July 2004.

The Administrative Licence Law consists of eight chapters, with 83 articles. It prescribes procedural contents such as "how to establish an administrative licence, who should implement an administrative licence, how to implement an administrative licence, how to monitor an administrative licence, and the liabilities for violating an administrative licence". This law also regulates other contents, such as "how to apply for an administrative licence, how to accept an administrative licence, how to review an administrative licence application, how to make an administrative licensing decision, and how to request modification and extension for an administrative licence".

Pursuant to the Administrative Licence Law, the circumstances under which an administrative licence may be established fall into five categories: (a) special activities that directly bear on state security, public security, macro-economic control, ecological environment protection, and those that directly relate to human health, safety of life and property, which shall be approved according to legal requirements; (b) the development and utilisation of limited natural resources, allocation of public resources and the market entry of special trades that directly concern public interests, which shall be entitled with special rights; (c) vocations and trades that provide public services and directly relate to public interests, which require qualification of special credit, conditions or skills; (d) important equipment, facilities, products, articles that directly concern public security, human health, the safety of life and property, which shall be examined and approved by means of inspection, testing, and quarantine according to technical standards or criteria; (e) the establishment of enterprises or other institutions, that need to determine subject qualification; and (f) other matters, for which administrative licence may be established in accordance with the laws and regulations.[150]

The Administrative Licence Law also provides that, even if a circumstance falls into one of the above categories, an administrative licence may not be a necessity

---

[150] See Article 12 of the Administrative Licence Law

if: (a) it can be decided by citizens, legal persons or other institutions themselves; (b) it can be regulated effectively by the market competition mechanism; (c) it may be subject to self-discipline management of trade organisations or intermediary institutions; and (d) it can be solved by administrative organs by means of subsequent supervision or through other administrative methods.[151] As a result, a reasonable space has been left for follow-up reform of China's administration mode.

Great significance of the Administrative Licence Law

1. Clarify the standards and principles of establishing an administrative licence

In accordance with the provisions of the Administrative Licence Law, the establishment and implementation of an administrative licence must tally with legal authority, scope and procedures, and should abide by the principle of publicity, fairness and impartiality. The relevant regulations of an administrative licence shall be announced to the public; those undisclosed shall not be the basis for the implementation of the administrative licence. The implementation of an administrative licence and the results thereof, except for those that concern state secrets, commercial secrets or individual privacy, shall be disclosed. Applicants who meet the legal conditions and standards are entitled to obtain equal right under an administrative licence, and administrative organisations shall not discriminate against any of them.

2. For the vagueness existing in the authority of administrative licence in practice, clarify the establishing authority and establishing the subject of an administrative licence

At first, this law provides that an administrative licence may be established by means of law. Where there is no governing law, an administrative licence may be established by means of administrative regulations. Where necessary, the State Council may adopt the form of releasing decisions to establish an administrative licence. After implementation, except for matters under temporary administrative licence, the State Council shall propose to the National People's Congress and its Standing Committee to formulate laws, or formulate administrative regulations by itself.

Second, as provided in this law, if there is yet no governing law or administrative regulation, an administrative licence may be established by means of local regulations for any matter; if there is no governing law, administrative regulation

---

[151] See Article 13 of the Administrative Licence Law

or local regulation, but it is really necessary to immediately establish an administrative licence to conduct administrative management, a temporary administrative licence may be established by means of a regulation of the people's government of a province, autonomous region or municipality directly under the central government. If it is necessary to keep on implementing the administrative licence after a year, the people's congress and its standing committee at the same level shall be proposed to formulate a local regulation.

Third, this Law restricts the scope of an administrative licence established by local laws and regulations, and excludes any administrative licence determined by the state about qualifications of citizens, legal persons or other institutions; no administrative licence or pre-administrative licence may be established for the establishment and registration of enterprises or other institutions. The administrative licence established thereby shall not hinder individuals or enterprises of other regions from dealing in production and business and providing services in one region; nor shall it restrict the products of other regions from entering into a market of the local region. This will put an end the practice of local governments providing an "umbrella" for local protectionism in these aspects, so as to maintain market competition order featuring fairness and openness.

3. Standardise the procedures of establishing an administrative licence and determine the hearing system of an administrative licence

Where an administrative licence is planned to be established by means of drafting a law or regulation, or a regulation of the people's government of a province, autonomous region or municipality directly under the central government, the drafting entity shall consult opinions through hearing and argumentation, and shall give explanations to the law- or regulation-making organ about the necessity to establish the administrative licence, the potential effects on the economy and society, and the opinions heard and adopted. Furthermore, for a hearing as provided for the implementation of an administrative licence in any law, regulation or rule, or for any other licensing matters of great importance to public interest that the administrative organisation considers it necessary to hold a hearing, the administrative organisation shall announce it to the public and hold a hearing. For hearing matters directly related to the applicant and interested parties, the administrative organisations are obliged to inform them of, and organise, the hearing.

4. Centralise administrative licences and reduce the costs of applying for and operating an administrative licence

According to this law, the people's government of a province, autonomous region or municipality directly under the central government that is empowered by the State Council may decide to have an administrative organisation exercising other administrative organisations' power of administrative licence. Where it is necessary to handle an administrative licence through several interior institutions of an administrative organisation, this administrative organisation shall identify one institution to accept all applications for the administrative licence and serve all decisions about the administrative licence. Meanwhile, where an administrative licence is handled by more than two institutions according to the law, it can be handled uniformly, jointly or collectively. This solves the problem that an approval has to be sent between different departments; and it also plays a positive role in further reducing the establishment of administrative institutions and promoting the reform of administrative institutions.

5. Affirm the principle of legitimate expectation in the field of administrative licence for the first time, and establish the compensation mechanism for civil rights damages

The principle of legitimate expectation requires the government to comply with the principle of good faith and not to arbitrarily change administrative acts already in force; otherwise, the losses caused to the counterpart of the administrative act shall be compensated. The Administrative Licence Law of the People's Republic of China provides that administrative organisations shall not change an effective administrative licence without permission. Only where any of the laws, regulations and rules that the administrative licence is based on is amended or abolished, or the objective circumstances that the administrative licence rests on change greatly, in order to meet the demands of public interests, the administrative organ may modify or withdraw the effective administrative licence. Damage caused to the property of citizens, legal persons or other institutions accordingly shall be compensated for by the administrative organ in accordance with the law. Where an administrative organ impairs the legitimate rights and interests of the parties concerned due to its illegal implementation of an administrative licence, it shall make compensations in accordance with the compensation law of the state.

6. For the phenomenon of preferring approval to supervision in practice, specifically regulate the regulatory responsibility of administrative organisations

One of the primary functions of an administrative licence is to control risk, but in practice, all administrative licences with risk control are conditional, that is, to strengthen supervision and inspection on whether the licensee operates as required upon the issuance of an administrative licence. As our existing supervision mechanisms are not perfect, and the issuing authority does not impose adequate supervision on accidents or grants an approval but fails to supervise it, it follows that the problem cannot be fundamentally solved. The administrative licence law stipulates that the implementation rights of an administrative licence shall be extended to the supervision of the activities of the licensee, following the principle that "those who grant an approval shall be responsible for supervision" and specifying the provisions on the acts of supervision. By strengthening the supervision of an administrative licence and the responsibilities for its implementation, the current phenomenon of preferring approval to supervision may be changed. Supervisory responsibilities are also clarified within administrative authorities, where the upper administrative organisations shall strengthen supervision and inspection over lower administrative organs in the implementation of the administrative licence, and shall get the illegal acts right in a timely manner.

7. Make clear that an administration licence obtained in accordance with the law shall not be transferred except for those that may be transferred in light of legal conditions

This provision is very necessary. Special qualifications shall be imposed on the object of an administrative licence, and its authority may only be approved by a special agency, with its rights and qualifications being bundled together; therefore it is not transferable as a general rule. Only certain administrative licences legally obtained can be transferred, but such transfers must be explicitly provided by laws and regulations. If no strict restrictions are imposed on the transfer of an administrative licence, it may provide a chance to illegally deal a licence and commit to other criminal behaviour, leading to economic and social disorder.

8. A licensee obtaining an administrative licence through illegal means shall be subject to legal sanctions

As prescribed in this law, when applying for an administrative licence, an applicant shall faithfully submit relevant materials to the administrative organisation, report the actual information, and shall be liable for the authenticity of the substantial contents of the application materials. Where an applicant for an administrative licence conceals any relevant information or provides false materials, the administrative organisation shall not accept its application or shall not grant it such a licence, and shall give it a warning; if such an application for an administrative licence directly concerns public security, human health or safety of life and property, the applicant shall not re-apply for this administrative licence within a year. A licensee that has obtained an administrative licence by illegal means of cheating or offering bribes shall be given an administrative punishment by the administrative organisation in accordance with the law; if the administrative licence directly concerns public security, human health or safety of life and property, the applicant shall not re-apply for it within three years; if the licensee's violation constitutes any crime, he shall be subject to criminal liabilities in accordance with the law.

This law also provides legal consequences and legal liabilities for those concerning an administrative licence to conduct illegal operations. Where the functionaries of the administrative organ decide to approve an administrative licence as the result of abusing their power and neglecting their duties, or a decision on approving an administrative licence is made due to the decision-makers' excess of their statutory power, or an applicant who doesn't meet the applying qualification or the statutory conditions is approved of an administrative licence, then the decision-making administrative organisation or its upper administrative organisation may annul an administrative licence according to the request of the interested party or according to its functions. Nevertheless, where the annulment of an administrative licence in accordance with relevant provisions may seriously impair the public interest, it shall not be annulled. Administrative sanctions shall be imposed on persons directly responsible for the case; and if the case constitutes a crime, criminal responsibility shall be investigated according to the law.

Through strict liability regime and disciplinary mechanisms, theoretically it can effectively constrain the acts of administrative licence applicants and contractors. Of course, it is bound to take a long time from the birth of a law to giving full play to its control and constraint functions, in which there will be many twists and turns. Therefore, for China, a developing country without a history and tradition of governance by law, it will be a long and difficult process to achieve effective control and restrain government power.

The first administrative licence case relating to a ministerial department after the implementation of the Administrative Licence Law

In China's first administrative licence case relating to a ministerial department after the implementation of the Administrative Licence Law, the administrative act that the Trademark Office of the State Administration for Industry & Commerce (SAIC Trademark Office) rejected a law firm in Nanjing to engage in trademark agency services is regarded as lacking in legal basis. On 14 March 2003, a lawyer of Nanjing Zhishi Law Firm, as an agent, submitted an application for trademark registration to SAIC Trademark Office. The trademark office decided to reject this application as it believed the law firm was not a valid trademark agency. In a subsequent administrative review, SAIC upheld the decision of the Trademark Office. On 29 October 2003, Nanjing Zhishi Law Firm filed administrative proceedings to Beijing First Intermediate People's Court in terms of the trademark office's administrative decision. Finally, the court maintained that there was no law prohibiting a lawyer engaging in trademark business as the State Council had cancelled two administrative approval items, "Trademark Agency Approval" and "Trademark Agent Qualification Approval". Therefore it declared invalid the decision by the SAIC to not allow Nanjing Zhishi to engage in trademark agency.[152] The failure of the trademark office in the first instance showed that China will be shifting from "administrative state" to "limited government", that is, government operations should be carried out under the premise of regulatory restrictions.

The promulgation and implementation of the Administrative Licence Law marked a change in the Chinese government from an "authority-based government" to a "responsible government", which draws the basic outline of a law-based government. It has important significance in regulating government behaviour, promoting the administrative process according to the law, preventing and controlling corruption and safeguarding citizens' rights.

Civil Servant Law of the PRC in 2005

In order to meet the needs of modern social governance, improve administrative efficiency and strengthen scientific and democratic personnel management, China's civil service system has been developed in response to the in-depth development of economic system reform and in support of political reform.

Provisional Regulations on State Civil Servants and its Supporting Regulations

In August 1993, the State Council promulgated the Provisional Regulations on State Civil Servants. Since then, the State Council has gradually developed dozens of supporting regulations in the course of implementing the Provisional Regulations, thus forming a set of regulation-based systems, and initially establishing a civil service system with Chinese characteristics.

The promulgation and implementation of the Provisional Regulations has played an important role in establishing China's civil service system, but years of practice shows that it is far from enough by itself to constrain and regulate the acts of civil servants, and it is also difficult to correct various deviations and mistakes that have occurred, especially for China, which has a long history of "rule of man" and a weak rule of law. It is even more important to strengthen the legal construction of the civil service system. The national civil service system should have its basic legal status, but the Provisional Regulations on State Civil Servants has not

---

[152] See Beijing Youth Daily 23 July 2007

been raised to a law enacted by the National People's Congress or the Standing Committee of the National People's Congress. Therefore, the introduction of the Civil Servant Law of the People's Republic of China was inevitable.

Development of civil service system after the introduction of the Civil Servant Law

On 27 April 2005, the 15th Session of the Standing Committee of the 15th National People's Congress adopted the Civil Servant Law of the People's Republic of China, which has been developed and formulated on the basis of the Provisional Regulations on State Civil Servants, reflecting the continuity and stability of the system and showing greater improvements. Compared with the Provisional Regulations on State Civil Servants, the development of the civil service system after the introduction of the Civil Servant Law is shown in the following aspects:

i) **Raise the legislative level** The Civil Servant Law is a law adopted by the NPC Standing Committee, while the Provisional Regulations on State Civil Servants is an administrative regulation reviewed and adopted by the Standing Committee of the State Council. Therefore, the legislative level of the Civil Servant Law is higher than the Provisional Regulations on State Civil Servants.

ii) **Adjust the scope of civil services** The scope of civil services provided in the Provisional Regulations on State Civil Servants is the staff working in state administrative organisations except logistics workers. The Civil Servant Law has adjusted the scope of civil services. Article 2 states: "The term "civil servants" refers to those personnel who perform public duties according to law and have been included into the state administrative staffing and whose wages and welfare are borne by the state public finance." This means a civil servant shall perform public duties according to law, be included into the state administrative staffing and enjoy the wages and welfare borne by state public finance. In accordance with this provision, in addition to state administrative organisations, personnel serving in CPC authorities, NPC authorities and CPPCC authorities, judicial organisations, procuratorial organisations and democratic institutions are civil servants as long as they tally with the above three conditions.

iii) **Increase the requirements that civil servants shall meet** Pursuant to Article 11 of the Civil Servant Law, a civil servant shall meet the following requirements: (1) being a national of the People's Republic of China; (2) reaching the full age of 18; (3) upholding the Constitution of the People's Republic of China; (4) having good ethics; (5) being in a proper health state to perform his functions and duties normally; (6) having the educational level and working capacity as required by the post; and (7) any other requirement as prescribed by law. There are no such requirements in the Provisional Regulations on State Civil Servants.

iv) **Further improve the classification management system for civil servants** Although Article 8 of the Provisional Regulations on State Civil Servants provides that "state administrative organisations shall implement a job classification system", no further classification has been made for the job requirements of civil servants. However, the Civil Servant Law has made clear provisions on the classification management system of civil servants, as provided in Article 14: "The state adopts a classified system for civil servant posts. Civil servant posts shall, according to the nature, features and necessity of administration of civil servant posts, be classified into categories such as comprehensive administrators, technological professionals and administrative law enforcers. The State Council may, according to the present law, add any other category of posts for those with positional peculiarities and in need of separate administration." Meanwhile, provisions are also made concerning the setting of duties for different civil service jobs.

v) **Impose restrictive provisions for the hiring of civil servants** The Provisional Regulations on State Civil Servants provides the requirements of applying for state civil servants, but does not specify who may not be employed as a civil servant. However, the Civil Servant Law has made it clear that those having been given a criminal punishment, having been removed from public office, or under any other circumstance as prescribed by law under which one shouldn't be employed as a civil servant shall not be employed as a civil servant.

vi) **Add the relevant provision of the employment system through selection** Pursuant to the Provisional Regulations on State Civil Servants, the system of appointment shall be adopted for the posts of state civil servants, and the system of employment shall be adopted for certain posts. According to the Civil Servant Law, the system of employment through selection and the system of employment through appointment shall be adopted for the posts of civil servants.

vii) **Add the systems of competing for posts and open selection** The Civil Servant Law has absorbed the recent reforms to the way cadres and government personnel are appointed, stating that, "Where there is any vacancy of a leading post lower than the chief at the department and bureau level in an organisation, the candidate may be decided through competitive bidding within the said organisation or within staff members thereof", and "The systems of public announcement before assuming the post and probation shall be adopted in the promotion of a civil servant to a leading post according to the relevant provisions".

viii) **Further improve the disciplinary system** The Civil Servant Law adds a disciplinary provision on civil servants, i.e. "being absent from work or in the event of a business trip or leave, failing to return upon expiration of the leave or trip without any justifiable reason". The Civil Servant Law also specifies how to deal with cases in which a civil servant, in the performance of official duties, believes that there is something wrong with the decision or order of his superior. To be specific: "Where a civil servant, in the performance of official duties, deems that there is something wrong in the decision or order of his superior, he may make a suggestion on correcting or cancelling the said decision or order. Where the superior refuses to change the decision or order, or requires immediate performance, the civil servant concerned shall carry out the decision or order. The superior shall be held responsible for the consequences of the performance of duties and the civil servant shall not be subject to any liability. However, where a civil servant carries out any decision or order that is obviously illegal, he shall be subject to the corresponding liabilities according to law."

ix) **Further improve the wage system** (i) The Provisional Regulations on State Civil Servants provides that the post-rank salary system shall be adopted for state civil servants, while the Civil Servant Law stipulates that a uniform wage system of the state that combines posts and ranks together shall apply to civil servants. (ii) The Provisional Regulations on State Civil Servants specifies that the salary of a state civil servant mainly consists of post wage, rank allowance, basic wage and wage for seniority"; "state civil servants enjoy a regional allowance and other allowances in accordance with national regulations". The Civil Servant Law provides that the wage of a civil servant shall include basic pay, allowances, subsidies and bonuses; a civil servant may enjoy allowances such as regional additional allowances, difficult and outlying region allowances and subsidies appropriate to particular jobs according to the provisions of the state; a civil servant may enjoy subsidies or allowances in housing and medicine according to the provisions of the state. (iii) provides that the wage of a state civil servant shall be roughly at the same level with the wage of a corporate employee at an equal post. The Civil Servant Law stipulates that the wage level of a civil servant shall be in line with the national economic development and conform to the social progress.

x) **Make provision for the resignation of civil servants holding a leading post**
As prescribed in the Civil Servant Law, if a civil servant who holds a leading post needs to resign due to a work change in accordance with the provisions of law, the formalities of resignation should be followed. A civil servant who holds a leading post may resign that post on his own initiative due to his personal reasons or any other reason. Where a senior member of staff causes any serious damage or social impact due to severe mistakes in his work or breach of duty or bears the leading liabilities for any serious accident, he shall take the blame and resign that post. Where any leading member of staff takes the blame and resigns his post or is no longer suitable for that post but fails to hand in his resignation, he shall be ordered to resign. There is no such a provision in the Provisional Regulations on State Civil Servants.

xi) **Modify the content related to the early retirement of civil servants** The Provisional Regulations on State Civil Servants provides that, if a civil servant has worked for 30 years, he or she may apply for retirement in advance and may retire upon the approval of the organisation in charge of appointments and dismissals; if a male civil servant has worked for 20 years and is aged 55, or 50 in the case of a female civil servant who has worked for 20 years, he or she is also eligible for early retirement. The Civil Servant Law prescribes that a civil servant can retire in advance upon the application for retirement on his own initiative and the approval of the organisation in charge of appointment and dismissal where he/she has worked for 30 years, or he/she has worked for 20 years and is less than five years from retirement as prescribed by the state, or other circumstances where the law provides eligible.

xii) **Further improve the appeal system for civil servants** (i) On the basis of the Provisional Regulations on State Civil Servants, the Civil Servant Law has added matters where a civil servant can apply to appeal regarding matters such as cancellation of employment, being removed from his post, his application for resignation or retirement in advance being rejected, failing to decide or deduct his wage, or if he is unhappy with his welfare or insurance treatment according to relevant provisions. Thus the scope of matters concerning an appeal has been expanded. (ii) There is no provision in the Provisional Regulations on State Civil Servants or the Interim Provisions on Appeal and Accusation for State Civil Servants (Ren He Pei Fa [1995] No. 91) where a civil servant can re-lodge an appeal to a higher authority if he is unhappy with the decision made by the authority dealing with the appeal, while the Civil Servant Law adds such a provision, namely: "Where anyone is unhappy with the punishment for his appeal made by an organisation below provincial level, he may appeal again to the counterpart at a level higher."

xiii) **Make specific provisions on appointment for posts** Although the Provisional Regulations on State Civil Servants provides the employment system through appointment is adopted for certain posts, it has not been implemented, while the Civil Servant Law makes specific provisions on the appointment for posts in the chapter "Employment": (i) specifying the scope of posts adopting the appointment system, i.e. highly specialised posts and posts with supplementary features; (ii) specifying the ways an appointment is made, i.e. to conduct an open invitation for employment with reference to the procedure for civil servant examination and recruitment, or to make an appointment through a the direct selection of those who satisfy the requirements; (iii) specifying the approaches of management, i.e. the implementation of the employment contract management; and (iv) specifying the solution to any dispute arising out of the employment contract between a civil servant through employment and the employment organisation, i.e. to lodge a suit to the people's court within 15 days of the day when the dispute arises.

The introduction of the Civil Servant Law has filled a gap in China's legal system, and provided a fundamental legal basis for perfecting the civil service system and building a high-quality team of civil servants. Furthermore, a high-quality civil service system will improve the rule of law in administration agencies and the protection of citizens' rights.

Regulation of the PRC on the Disclosure of Government Information in 2007

Open government information means state administrative organisations or organisations authorised and entrusted in accordance with laws, regulations and rules, in the process of exercising state administrative functions, make available government information to all society or a particular individual or organisation making such an application pursuant to law through legal forms and procedures. Administrative disclosure is an important part of modern democracy.

Promulgation and main contents of the Regulation of the PRC on the Disclosure of Government Information

On 24 April 2007, the promulgation of the Regulation of the People's Republic of China on the Disclosure of Government Information placed China's open government information on a legal basis. As the rules featuring inflexible constraints, the promulgation of the Regulation on the Disclosure of Government Information is important for promoting the legalisation and standardisation of open government information and guaranteeing citizens' rights to information.

When disclosing government information, administrative agencies shall observe the principles of justice, fairness and convenience to the people. Administrative agencies shall disclose government information promptly and accurately, establish and improve a coordination mechanism for government information disclosure to ensure the government information released is accurate and consistent.

Administrative agencies should disclose, on their own initiative, government information that satisfies any one of the following basic criteria: 1) information that involves the vital interests of citizens, legal persons or other organisations; 2) information that needs to be extensively known or participated in by the general public; 3) information that shows the structure, function and working procedures of the administrative agency; and 4) other information that should be disclosed on the administrative agency's own initiative according to laws, regulations and relevant state provisions.[153]

Citizens, legal persons or other organisations may, based on the special needs of such matters as their own production, livelihood and scientific and technological research, also file requests to departments of the State Council, local people's governments at all levels and departments under local people's governments at county level and above to obtain relevant government information.

Administrative agencies may not disclose government information that involves state secrets, commercial secrets or individual privacy. However, government information involving commercial secrets or individual privacy may be disclosed by administrative agencies with the consent of the right-holder(s) or if administrative agencies believe that non-disclosure might have a major impact on the public interest.

Government information to be disclosed on administrative agencies' own initiative should be disclosed by means of government gazettes, government websites, press conferences, as well as through newspapers and other publications, radio, television and other methods that make it convenient for the public to be informed.

If citizens, legal persons or other organizations believe an administrative agency has failed to fulfil its obligations in respect of open government information in accordance with the law, they may report it to the administrative agency at a higher level, the supervision agency or the department in charge of open government information. The agency that receives the report should investigate and handle it.

If citizens, legal persons or other organisations believe a specific administrative action of an administrative agency in its open government information work has infringed their lawful rights and interests, they may, in accordance with the law, apply for administrative reconsideration or file an administrative lawsuit.

Importance of the Regulation of the PRC on the Disclosure of Government Information

1. Implement constitutional concept and safeguard human rights

"Respect for and protection of human rights" has been written in the Constitution

---

[153] See Article 9 of the Regulation of the People's Republic of China on the Disclosure of Government Information

of the People's Republic of China. The Constitution clearly stipulates that all powers of the People's Republic of China belong to the people. The people administer state affairs and manage economic and cultural undertakings and social affairs through various channels and in various ways in accordance with the provisions of law. As the subject performing administrative power, the power of administrative agencies at all levels can only be derived from the people, and must ultimately be returned to the people. The people have the right to know the truth of, participate in, express their opinions about and supervise the contents, procedures and processes of the government exercising power. This right is not only a right entitled by the Constitution to the people being the masters of the country, but also an important manifestation of the people's democratic rights.

The right to information is a fundamental right that citizens exercise in accordance with the provisions of the Constitution. Only when administrative agencies make available the public information they have obtained on their own initiative will the people's right to information be able to be realised. The Regulation on the Disclosure of Government Information not only provides administrative agencies' open information system and scope, but also prescribes the obligation of administrative agencies to positively disclose government information on their own initiative and citizens have the right to apply for open government information, which has provided a legal basis for citizens to realise the right to information entitled by the Constitution. The Regulation on the Disclosure of Government Information has an important role in safeguarding the citizens' right to information, and further promoting the exercise of rights to participate, express and supervise. As "network information" plays an increasingly important role in contemporary society, it is even more important to safeguard the right to information for the effectiveness of social management and social harmony and stability.

2. Conducive to establishing a credible government ruled by law

Since the market economy has given rise to the idea of administrative services, the transparency of administration needs to be further improved. Government information that is disclosed by administrative agency is conducive to changing the ideas and work styles under the long-term planned economy, and breaking the "mystery" of administration. Administrative information exchanges can greatly reduce the blindness of public behaviour, relieve public distrust in administrative agencies, form good social conduct and social order, and enhance the self-consciousness of the public to accept administration and perform administrative obligations. Meanwhile, disclosing administrative information can create a new way for citizens to engage directly in the management of national affairs, which helps administrative counterparts make the necessary preparations in advance and work with administrative subjects to perform duties, thus protecting the

A Balance Between "Administrative Efficiency" and "Administration Power Control"

legal interests of administrative counterparts and improving administrative efficiency.

The open government information system established in accordance with the Regulation on the Disclosure of Government Information has provided the institutional basis and practical guarantee for citizens to engage in democratic participation, democratic decision-making and democratic supervision, leading to the establishment of government by law. By taking disclosure as the principle and non-disclosure as the exception, open government information has stepped out on the institutionalised legal path. Moreover, the Regulation on the Disclosure of Government Information has also made detailed provisions on the procedures of open government information, thus standardising the legalisation of open information in terms of procedures. The Regulation on the Disclosure of Government Information has also provided the applicant with three kinds of relief channels -- appeal, administrative reconsideration and administrative litigation -- and made specific provisions on supervision and accountability in the process of information disclosure, thus reflecting the principle of the rule of law: "A right without remedy is not right." Therefore, the open administrative information system presented in the Regulation on the Disclosure of Government Information is the need to establish a transparent, service-oriented and credible government.

3. Conducive to strengthening power supervision and anti-corruption

Power is inherently corrosive and transformative. Practical experience shows that the most obvious characteristic of all corrupt practices lies in the secrecy of its behaviour. Non-disclosure of administrative acts provides a chance for the corrupted to engage in secret dealing. Secret operations are susceptible to corruption, while open administration is the best antidote, which has become the consensus of countries ruled by law. Realising information disclosure and making government acts public can help to put an end to trading power for money, and prevent government officials extorting or accepting bribes with their authorities or abusing the authority for personal gain so as to promote the construction of a clean and honest administration. At the same time, open administrative information is also a prerequisite for the public to participate in anti-corruption, as full right to information can encourage enhance the public to participate in anti-corruption. The establishment of an open government information system has become a goal of all countries to fight against corruption.

A citizen succeeded in his claim against the Ministry of Railways based on the Regulations on the Disclosure of Government Information

On 31 October 2010, Yang Jinzhu spent Rmb301 on buying a second-class ticket for the D309 EMU train, and the ticket showed Seat 8, Carriage 8. On the evening of 1 November, Yang boarded the train from Beijing South Railway Station, and soon he found that Carriage 8 was a dining car. He felt that he had been treated unequally, so he wrote a letter to the Ministry of Railways requesting that it disclose on what basis the railway agency sells tickets relating to a dining car. He then mailed the Application Form for Open Government Information to the Ministry of Railways, but received no clear reply after 15 days, so he decided to take legal action.

On 12 July 2011, Yang Jinzhu received the first-instance decision. Beijing Intermediate Court held that the agency in charge of open government information should have given a reply within 15 working days since the day when the application was received in accordance with the Regulation of the People's Republic of China on the Disclosure of Government Information. However, in this case, Yang Jinzhu, the plaintiff, did not receive a reply within 15 days after the application was submitted, and the current evidence was not sufficient to prove that the Ministry of Railways had given any reply. Therefore, the court ordered the ministry to reply to the application dated 5 November 2010 by Yang Jinzhu within 15 days after the judgement took effect in accordance with the law.[154]

In short, the promulgation of the Regulation on the Disclosure of Government Information has established and improved China's open administrative information system from the perspective of legislation, which is required for social development as it can protect public interest, meet citizens' right to information and supervise administrative activities; furthermore, it can encourage administrative agencies to improve the transparency and efficiency of their work, and reduce the possibility of secret operations. But due to China's history and culture of putting government officials above the people, it will be a long and tortuous process for the government to achieve a transparent and open governance model, and in several important cases arousing general concern, repeated public requests for making administrative information public have received inadequate attention. This situation should be corrected and improved under the general trend of the internet era.

State Compensation Law of the PRC, revised in 2010 and 2012

State compensation refers to the compensation that shall be given to citizens, legal persons and other organisations for their personal or property rights

---

[154] See Chengdu Evening News 31 July 2011

being damaged by a state organisation and its staff when exercising their powers in accordance with the law. The obligations of state compensation shall be performed by the organisations under compensatory obligations. The introduction of the State Compensation Law is extremely important for China's legislative progress. Throughout China's history over thousands of years, this law has placed the state and its citizens on an equal position for the first time; as prescribed by the law, the state shall be liable for damages in cases where citizens' rights and interests are infringed, and citizens have the right to claim state compensation in such cases. The actual operation of this legal system can be seen as the real start of "rule of law" where the state respects and safeguards human rights and the people can control and restrict state power.

Promulgation and revision of the State Compensation Law

The State Compensation Law was adopted by the Seventh Session of the Standing Committee of the Eighth National People's Congress on 12 May 1994, and became effective on 1 January 1995. At the beginning of the legislature, people placed great expectations on this law, hoping it could minimise injustice. However, in the course of implementation, a number of problems gradually emerged, such as the doctrine of liability fixation for compensation, scope of compensation, compensation procedures, compensation standards and compensation expense payment. Therefore, there was growing demand for the amendment of the State Compensation Law. On 29 April 2010, the 14th Session of the Standing Committee of the 11th National People's Congress adopted the revised state compensation law.

Improvements of the State Compensation Law 2010 in state compensation system

The State Compensation Law 2010 amends and improves the prominent and urgent problems manifested in the implementation of the old State Compensation Law. It has played an important role in further safeguarding citizens' legitimate rights and interests. The major improvements of the State Compensation Law 2010 are as follows:

1. Improve compensation standard for damages

The State Compensation Law 2010 amends the relevant provisions on compensation for personal and property damage. In terms of compensation for personal damage, the State Compensation Law 2010 makes a new provision on expenses such as assistance expenses for items that help disabled people, living subsidies, disability compensation funds and living expenses necessary for the dependents of the disabled. In terms of compensation for property damage, the amount of compensation is increased. According to Article 36 of the State Compensation Law 2010, if a fine, recovery or confiscation of property has been imposed or any property has been illegally expropriated or requisitioned, such property shall be returned. If any property has been auctioned or otherwise sold, the income from the auction or sale shall be paid to the victim; if the income from the sale is obviously lower than the value of the property, a corresponding compensation shall be paid. If a paid fine, or recovered or confiscated money is refunded, or the freeze on a deposit or remittance is lifted, interest calculated at the bank deposit rate over the same period shall be paid.

2. Specify compensation for mental damage

As the compensation for mental damage is not mentioned in the old State Compensation Law, a number of applications for compensation for mental damage are often rejected. Provisions on compensation for mental damages are added in Article 35 of the State Compensation Law 2010: "If any infringement as mentioned in Articles 3 and 17 of this Law inflicts any mental distress on the victim, the infringing organisation shall eliminate the effects of infringement for the victim, restore the victim's reputation and make an apology in line with the influence of the infringement. If serious repercussions arise, the infringing organisation shall pay a proper amount of compensation for the mental distress", which can provide a clear legal basis for mental damage compensation. This reflects China's current people-oriented concept of governance and highlights the law-based progress in respect of human rights protection. It also further standardises the legislative convergence of China's legal system, which is of great significance for building a harmonious society.

3. Improve the scope of compensation

The principle of illegal liability is reflected in the provisions of the old State Compensation Law, which states that state organisations and their staff need to pay compensation only when they infringe upon the legitimate rights and interests of citizens, legal persons and other organisations arising from the illegal performance of their authority. Thus, even though the behaviour of staff in a state organisation is inappropriate, compensation will not follow if there is no violation of the law. According to the old State Compensation Law, the state is liable for damages only if its acts are in violation of relevant laws and regulations, rather than depending upon whether the acts of state organisations and their staff have caused damage to citizens' rights and interests. Such a legal evaluation ignored the damaging consequences arising from acts, and is contrary to the purpose of state compensation legislation.

However, pursuant to Article 2 of the State Compensation Law 2010, if any state organisation or state functionary, in performing its/his functions, commits any infringement upon the legitimate rights and interests of a citizen, a legal person or any other organisation as prescribed in this Law, causing any damage, the victim shall be entitled to state compensation in accordance with this Law. Thus, the State Compensation Law 2010 establishes the principle of result-oriented liability that state organisations or state functionaries shall be liable for damages according to the law if they infringe upon the legitimate rights and interests of a citizen, a legal person or any other organisation in the course of performing their duties. In other words, it no longer matters whether their acts are legal or valid, as long as the rights of relevant personnel are infringed, they shall be liable for such damages. Compared with the old State Compensation Law, the principle of result-oriented liability established in the State Compensation Law 2010 is more reasonable. In addition, according to Paragraph 3 of Article 3 and Paragraph 4 of Article 15 of the old State Compensation Law, where violent acts such as battery or abetting others in battery causes bodily injury or the death of a citizen, the victim has the right to compensation, while Paragraph 3 of Article 3 of the State Compensation Law 2010 provides that the victim shall have the right to compensation "where bodily injury or death to a citizen is caused by battery, maltreatment, etc. or by instigating or conniving at battery, maltreatment, etc. by another person". Therefore, the scope of compensation also includes the situation where prisoners are physically injured by fellow inmates and prison officers turn a blind eye. This new provision of the State Compensation Law 2010 has played a positive role in restraining non-normal deaths in detention centres, and expanding the scope of compensation.

4. Simplify procedures of compensation and secure compensation request channels

The State Compensation Law 2010 cancels the confirmation process in criminal compensation, and clearly provides that a compensation claimant shall firstly apply for compensation to the organisation obligated to make compensation. An organisation obligated to make compensation shall, within two months upon receipt of an application, make a decision on whether to pay compensation. Where an organisation obligated to pay compensation fails to decide whether to do so within the prescribed time limit or the compensation claimant raises any objection, he may apply for reconsideration to the organisation at the next level above the organisation obligated to make compensation on a legal basis. If a compensation claimant refuses to accept the reconsideration decision, he may apply for a compensation decision to the compensation committee of the people's court, and a decision will be made by this committee. Such an application may be raised in an administrative compensation case or upon applying for administrative reconsideration or bringing an administrative lawsuit. In addition, the victim also has the right to claim for compensation against an organisation performing a criminal investigation, prosecution or trial functions, a detention centre or prison administrative organisation or any of its functionaries. These provisions have greatly simplified the procedures of state compensation and also significantly reduced the cost of the compensation claimant in safeguarding his rights and interests.

The old State Compensation Law states that: "An administrative counterpart, when applying for state compensation, shall firstly apply for compensation to the organisation obligated to make compensation, and can be compensated after being confirmed by the organisation obligated to make compensation." The State Compensation Law 2010 cancels the original confirmation process in both administrative compensation and criminal compensation, and allows the compensation claimant to directly apply for compensation. As a result, it can effectively prevent the organisation obligated to make compensation from finding a reason not to confirm or to delay confirmation, and different restrictions are also imposed on the organisation obligated to make compensation during different periods, thereby reducing the threshold for the compensation claimant to apply for state compensation, and increasing the efficiency of state compensation.

5. Determine the burden of proof between two sides

The old State Compensation Law makes no provision on the burden of proof regarding administrative compensation cases handled by the people's court or criminal compensation cases handled by the compensation committee of the people's court. In certain compensation cases, the compensation claimant and the organisation obligated to make compensation may separately persist in their own views, making it difficult for the court to make a decision as there is no provision on the burden of proof. The State Compensation Law 2010 explicitly provides that the compensation claimant and the organisation obligated to make compensation shall provide evidence for their respective claims; if a person in custody dies or loses his civil conduct capacity during the period of custody, the organisation obligated to make compensation shall provide evidence on whether there is a link between its action and the death or loss of civil conduct capacity of the person in custody.

6. Claimant finally received compensation for mental damage

In the first half of 2011, Huang Chengcheng, a citizen of Chongqing, was detained as he posted a status of "drinking tea" on the internet, leading to a loss of freedom for 641 days. In December 2012, Chongqing Municipal Detention Commission revoked the decision of detention against him on the grounds of "improper handling", which is the reason for most revoked detention decisions. On 5 July 2013, the People's Court of Bishan county made a decision on an administration compensation case. According to the judgement, Huang received Rmb116,000 in state compensation for the restriction of his personal freedom. He also received Rmb680,000 of compensation for mental damage. The court made a final decision that the compensation for mental damage to Huang should be Rmb18,000. If the State Compensation Law had not been amended, the compensation for mental damage to Huang Chengcheng would have been difficult to get support.

In summary, the implementation of the State Compensation Law 2010 has largely solved a number of problems arising from state compensation, such as the difficulty of identification, low compensation rates and IOUs for compensation, reflecting the functions of the law to protect human rights.

In 2012, slight modifications were made to the State Compensation Law, providing where a procuratorial authority, under certain circumstance, decides not to prosecute in a criminal case, state compensation may not be made.[155]

The Law of the People's Republic of China on Administrative Supervision (revised in 2010)

The key to building a government by law is to promote administration according to law, where regulating administrative power is an essential requirement. Administrative supervision is an important part of supervision and regulation on the operation of administrative power within the government. Adequately performing the functions of administrative supervision helps to supervise government agencies and their staff to exercise their powers and perform their duties pursuant to statutory authority and procedures, to prevent improper administration and illegal administration, which is important for regulating government power and safeguarding civil rights.

Promulgation and revision of the Administrative Supervision Law

The Law of the People's Republic of China on Administrative Supervision was adopted and implemented by the 25th Session of the Standing Committee of the 8th National People's Congress on 9 May 1997. As the basic law for regulating

---

[155] See Article 19 of the State Compensation Law

the work of administrative supervision, the Administrative Supervision Law has played an important role in strengthening the work of supervision, ensuring the smooth implementation of government decrees, maintaining administrative discipline, promoting clean government and improving administrative management and administrative efficiency. With the increasing speed of administration by law and the deepening of administrative reform, in order to enrich and improve the objectives, ways and procedures of administrative supervision, and the duties of supervisory organisations, and legalise and standardise the work of administrative supervision, it became necessary to amend the Administrative Supervision Law. On 25 June 2010, the 15th Session of the Standing Committee of the 11th National People's Congress adopted the Decision of the Standing Committee of the National People's Congress on Amending the Law of the People's Republic of China on Administrative Supervision, which went into effect on 1 October 2010.

Main changes and improvements to the Administrative Supervision Law

After summing up the practical experience of administrative supervision and learning lessons, the revised Administrative Supervision Law has strengthened the supervision on administrative power, further clarified the scope of supervised objects, imposed additional duties and obligations on supervisory organs and improved some regulations such as the reporting system. The main changes and improvements are reflected in the following aspects.

i) **Further clarify the scope of supervision objects** Supervision objects refer to the organisations and individuals under supervision of the supervisory organisation as prescribed in the Administrative Supervision Law. The Civil Servant Law, which took effect on 1 January 2006, renamed "state civil servant" as "civil servant" to expand the scope of civil servants to personnel working in CPC authorities, NPC authorities and CPPCC authorities, judicial organisations, procuratorial organisations and democratic institutions in addition to administrative organs. It has become a matter of great concern whether the scope of supervision objects needs to be expanded in accordance with the scope of civil servants established in the Civil Servant Law. As provided in Article 2 of the new Administrative Supervision Law, supervisory organs refer to those that exercise the supervision function on behalf of the people's governments, supervising the administrative organisations of the state and their public servants, and other persons appointed by administrative organisations of the state in accordance with this Law.

Furthermore, as prescribed in Article 50, this Law shall apply when supervisory organisations exercise supervision over organisations with a public affairs management function empowered by any law or regulation and their personnel provision of public services, and over organisations engaged in the management of public affairs upon the authorisation of administrative organisations of the state and their personnel provision of public services.

ii) **Improve the reporting system** The revised Administrative Supervision Law has improved the reporting system and strengthened the responsibilities of supervisory organisations: The supervisory organisation shall accept any reporting case and investigate it according to law. If the informant offers a tipoff in his (its) real name, he (it) shall be given a reply about how the complaint is being handled and other information. The supervisory organisation shall keep details of the informant confidential and protect the informant's lawful rights and interests. Specific measures shall be formulated by the State Council. In addition, in order to strengthen the protection of informants, the legal consequences arising from the disclosure of reporting information have also been clarified: Where any person divulges information, or information about the acceptance of a tipoff, or relevant information about any informant, he shall be given a sanction; if any crime is constituted, he shall be subject to criminal liabilities according to law. The provision of the revised Administrative Supervision Law on the reporting system is conducive to urging supervisory organisations to handle reporting matters in a more timely and responsible manner and strengthening the protection of informants, thus encouraging the masses to actively provide supervisory organisations with violation clues of administrative disciplines.[156]

iii) **Improve the management system of dispatched bodies** The revised Administrative Supervision Law stipulates that supervisory bodies or supervisors dispatched by supervisory organisations shall be responsible for and report their work to the said supervisory organisations. The supervisory organisation shall uniformly administer the supervisory bodies and supervisors dispatched by it and establish an exchange mechanism for the supervisors. This has improved the management system of dispatched bodies. The bodies dispatched by the supervisory organisation shall be responsible and report their work to the said supervisory organisation, highlighting the full authority and independent status needed to carry out the work. Practice has shown that, since the implementation of uniform management of dispatched bodies, the supervisory function has been strengthened and efforts of investigating cases have been intensified, with remarkable results achieved. The revised Administrative Supervision Law is to establish the results of the work in legal form and include the uniform management system of dispatched bodies in the law.

---

[156] See Article 6 of the Administrative Supervision Law

iv) **The revised Administrative Supervision Law has made necessary adjustments to the duties of supervisory organisations** According to the revised Administrative Supervision Law, a supervisory organisation shall supervise the law enforcement, cleanness and efficiency of the supervisory objects. It shall fulfil the relevant duties. Supervision on law enforcement involves inspecting the problems of the administrative organisations of the state that occur in the course of their work, observing and enforcing laws and regulations as well as decisions and decrees of the people's governments. Supervision on the cleanness refers to the supervisory acts that the supervisory organisations use to punish corrupt practices and strengthen the construction of clean government by investigating corruption, abuse of power and other illegal cases. Supervision on efficiency refers to the supervisory acts employed by the supervisory organisation to measure the performance of the supervision objects on their legal duties and administrative efficiency, effectiveness and efficacy and so on. This amendment has also imposed the duties of responsibility on the part of the supervisory organisation to make government affairs public and to correct improper acts: A supervisory organisation shall, under provisions of the State Council, organise, coordinate, inspect and direct work on the disclosure of government information and correct acts that harm the interests of the general public. Specifying the duties of correcting improper acts in the Administrative Supervision Law is conducive to promoting the supervisory organisation to carry out rectification work and earnestly safeguard the interests of the masses.

v) **The revised Administrative Supervision Law has also made adjustments and modifications to the authority of supervisory organisations** According to Article 22 of the revised Administrative Supervision Law, when handling a case in violation of administrative disciplines, the supervisory organisation may ask the relevant administrative departments or institutions to offer assistance. In other words, where the supervisory organ needs assistance from relevant administrative departments and agencies in the process of investigating a case involving matters within the duties of relevant administrative departments and agencies, such administrative departments and agencies shall offer assistance without exception. This modification provides two new circumstances where the supervisory organisation may make supervisory recommendations: (1) "Where the liable person is subject to the accountability handling, including ordering him to make a public apology, suspending his duties for inspection, him taking the blame and resigning, ordering him to resign, and removing him from his position"; and (2) where it is necessary to improve the system of clean and diligent government. Perfecting the system is the basic measure to prevent corruption at source. When the supervisory organisation finds the unit under supervision is lacking in regulations to maintain a clean and diligent system, making supervisory recommendations according to law may facilitate the unit under supervision to stop prevent a loophole in a timely manner and prevent the acts violating that violate administrative disciplines from happening again.

The revised Administrative Supervision Law also stipulates that a supervisory organisation shall disclose information about supervision work according to law.[157] With the implementation of the Regulation on Open Government Information, disclosure of relevant information according to law has become a legal obligation of the supervisory organisation. For example, the supervisory organisation is in duty bound to conduct special inspections and major case investigations drawing wide attention and involving the vital interests of people in such a way that the people can know about the work and accept the supervision of the supervisory organisation. In practice, supervisory organisations are also disclosing information about their supervisory work to the public by building websites, holding press conferences and by other means. In order to facilitate supervisory organisations at all levels to open information according to laws and regulations, it is necessary to make it clear in legislation.

Compared with the old Administrative Supervision Law, the revised Administrative Supervision Law can strengthen the supervision over public power, constrain the exercise of public power and better protect the rights of citizens.

Administrative Compulsion Law of the PRC in 2011

Practice has proved that administrative power is one of the state powers controlling the most public resources and having an extremely strong capacity to intervene in real society. Administrative enforcement power is one of the state powers with the greatest compulsion, control and risk, and is therefore a powerful tool to realise administrative objectives. Conferring and guaranteeing administrative organisations to exercise administrative compulsion power according to law can effectively and legally implement administrative enforcement acts in line with the needs of administrative practice. On the other hand, administrative compulsion may also have potential threat if applied inappropriately. Administrative compulsion may directly affect personal rights, property rights and other fundamental rights of citizens or social organisations, and false or improper implementation will lead to serious harm; ineffective control of administrative compulsion power may easily harm the rights and interests of citizens or social organisations, giving rise to counterproductive consequences.

---

[157] See Article 27 of the Administrative Supervision Law

Promulgation of the Administrative Compulsion Law

In terms of China's administrative compulsion practices over past years, due to the lack of unified and standardised administrative compulsion, administrative authorities have encountered a number of problems such as inadequate administrative compulsory measures, careless enforcement, failure to effectively curb illegal acts and infringement upon the legitimate rights and interests of citizens, legal persons and other organisations by abusing administrative compulsory measures, including unclear rights to enact administrative compulsion. The problems are also reflected in a wide range of administrative compulsory measures with different names but a lack of standards, unclear enforcement authorities, non-standard procedures and random administrative compulsion and so on. Therefore, more specific legislation is required to achieve the empowerment of administrative compulsion and the legalisation of the enforcement process.

On 30 June 2011, the 21st Session of the Standing Committee of the 11th National People's Congress examined and adopted the Administrative Compulsion Law of the People's Republic of China, which came into force on 1 January 2012. The announcement and implementation of the Administrative Compulsion Law was a major event in China's legal system, as it has great significance for securing and supervising the strictly legal administration of administrative authorities, safeguarding public interests and social order, and protecting citizens' legitimate rights and interests.

Main contents of the Administrative Compulsion Law

The Administrative Compulsion Law has made provisions that are more detailed relating to the administrative compulsory system, which is reflected in the following aspects:

i) **Clarify the setting system for administrative compulsion** In order to ensure the effective exercise of administrative power and accomplish administrative management objectives, compulsory powers must be granted; however, after they are granted, they may easily be abused and cause harm, so we need to be vigilant. Therefore, the types of administrative compulsion and setting system need to be clarified through legislation so as to prevent arbitrariness and the abuse of administrative compulsory powers. Consequently, adhering to the concept of a high threshold for administrative compulsory powers, the Administrative Compulsion Law provides administrative compulsory measures and administrative enforcement set by law. Only under very strict conditions can administrative regulations and local regulations set limited administrative compulsory measures, and no regulatory documents other than laws and regulations may set administrative compulsory measures.[158]

ii) **Clarify the system of administrative compulsory measures** In order to prevent arbitrary administration and regulate the exercise of powers, the Administrative Compulsion Law provides general procedures of administrative compulsory measures and special procedures including seizure, impoundment and freezing. This requires administrative authorities to strictly follow the procedures and requirements to take appropriate administrative compulsory measures according to law; otherwise they will assume administrative liability, criminal liability and compensatory liability.[159]

iii) **Clarify the compulsory enforcement system of administrative authorities** According to the implementation subjects of administrative enforcement, the Administrative Compulsion Law divides administrative enforcement into enforcement by administrative authorities and application to the people's court for enforcement. This continues the current compulsory enforcement mode of "focusing on the application to the people's court with the support of enforcement by administrative authorities" established in the Administrative Procedure Law of the People's Republic of China. The Administrative Compulsion Law provides general procedures of administrative enforcement and special procedures consisting of performance on behalf of the party concerned, pecuniary sanction for specific performance and direct enforcement, setting unified specifications for enforcement.[160]

iv) **Define the administrative compulsory acts as the liability system** Chapter VI of the Administrative Compulsion Law makes a centralised provision on the legal responsibilities of administrative authorities, people's courts and their staff as well as financial institutions with assistance obligations; the liability consists of administrative sanction, compensatory liability and criminal liability. However, the liability system prescribed in this chapter is narrow. This is because the ways to assume liabilities may vary, such as correction, cancellation and illegal confirmation in respect of administrative acts, as well as compensation for any damages that may arise. Therefore, the pursuit of illegal liabilities regarding administrative compulsion shall not only take the Administrative Compulsion Law as a basis, but also must refer to the Administrative Procedure Law, the State Compensation Law and other legal documents for comprehensive consideration.

---

[158] See Article 10 and Article 11 of the Administrative Supervision Law
[159] See Chapter III of the Administrative Compulsion Law
[160] See Chapter IV of the Administrative Compulsion Law

These institutional arrangements play an important role in effectively constraining administrative compulsory powers, and help to achieve the dialectical unity of upholding civil rights and public interest, respecting for individual freedom, maintaining public order, protecting citizens' rights and ensuring administrative efficiency.

Significance of the Administrative Compulsion Law for China's rule of law development

China has long experienced an imperfect administrative compulsory setting and implementation, and has faced constant demands for the promulgation of a unified administrative compulsion law. The promulgation of the Administrative Compulsion Law can be regarded as a landmark event in the development of China's administrative legislation.

i) **The promulgation of the Administrative Compulsion Law helps to protect civil rights** Pursuant to the Administrative Compulsion Law, civil rights and administrative efficiency are twin objectives of the law, and they should be given equal consideration. Therefore, the Administrative Compulsion Law emphasises the regulation of administrative compulsory powers and protection of civil rights while placing an emphasis on improving administrative efficiency. The Administrative Compulsion Law makes specific provisions on the procedures to implement compulsory measures to restrict personal freedom, defines the rights of citizens, clarifies the things or persons to be seized and detained, and specifies civilised law enforcement. These have greatly protected civil rights from being infringed in the course of setting and enforcing administrative compulsion.

ii) **The promulgation of the Administrative Compulsion Law has put an end to the lack of unified legislation in China's administrative compulsion** Before the Administrative Compulsion Law was enacted, regulations on administrative compulsion were widely scattered in different levels of legal documents such as laws, regulations and rules. Driven by the concepts of rule of law, democracy and service, the introduction of a unified administrative compulsion law has become an urgent need for China's law-based development. The promulgation of the Administrative Compulsion Law has put an end to the lack of unified legislation in China's administrative compulsion, and its compulsory principle system and compulsory institutional system have provided standards for administrative compulsion legislation and subsequent legislation, essentially forming a mechanism to contain administrative compulsory powers and safeguard the fundamental rights of citizens according to law.

iii) **The promulgation of the Administrative Compulsion Law has filled many**

gaps in China's administrative compulsion legislation The Administrative Compulsion Law has established the basic principles of administrative compulsion, scientifically defined the connotation and classification of administrative compulsion and systematically combed the measures and ways of administrative compulsion. Meanwhile, in terms of the physical content, this law provides the elements for exercising the powers to set administrative compulsion, giving more explicit applicable conditions to China's previous and applicable enforcement ways such as pecuniary sanction for specific performance and performance on behalf of the party concerned. In terms of procedural rules, this law provides the mechanism to solicit opinions and post evaluation for the setting of administrative compulsion, unifying the general procedures of administrative compulsion and setting the requirements for special procedures applicable to seizure, impoundment, performance on behalf of the party concerned, and pecuniary sanction for specific performance. In addition, this law has a positive implication for changing the previous situation of China's administrative compulsion legislation featuring "preferring substantially to procedure" and "preferring power granting to power controlling" and improving the systems of substantive law and procedural law.

iv) **The promulgation of the Administrative Compulsion Law will become the driving force to promote the building of a Chinese government ruled by law** Administration according to law and building a government ruled by law have become China's long-standing basic principles. As administrative compulsory power can severely infringe upon the rights and interests of others, if it fails to be included in the system of rule of law, and is allowed to go beyond the strict constraint and control of the law, it will be detrimental to the protection of fundamental rights of citizens, the building of a government ruled by law, and social harmony and stability. The promulgation of the Administrative Compulsion Law can ensure that administrative compulsory acts are conducted in a legitimate way and provide a legal guarantee for promoting the building of a government ruled by law.

The Regulation on the Expropriation of Buildings on State-owned Land and Compensation in 2011

The Regulation on the Dismantlement of Urban Houses was adopted at the 40th Standing Committee of the State Council on 6 June 2001, and went into effect on 1 November 2001. With the emergence of "stubborn owners", "corrupt officials" and "barbaric demolitions", vicious demolition incidents have taken place and caused widespread social impact all over the country, making it a necessity to modify the Regulation on the Dismantlement of Urban Houses. The Property Law, which took effect in 2007, clearly takes the public interest as a prerequisite for the expropriation of buildings on state-owned land, while the Regulation on the Dismantlement of Urban Houses shows no expropriation principle or spirit of public interests in general or in specific provisions. As there are apparent conflicts between the Regulation on the Dismantlement of Urban Houses and its upper law, the Property Law, the Property Law should be modified or repealed as soon as possible.

In order to strengthen and regulate the management of demolition activities, on 19 January 2011, the 141st Standing Committee of the State Council adopted the Regulation on the Expropriation of Buildings on State-owned Land and Compensation, which went into effect from the date of announcement. This new regulation consists of five chapters with 35 articles, namely General Provisions, Expropriation Decisions, Compensation, Legal Liability and Supplementary Provisions. The new regulation mainly provides the principles, scope of expropriation, compensatory subjects of expropriation, procedures of expropriation decision, principles and procedures of compensation, dispute resolution and legal liability. Compared with the original regulations, the new regulation has changed the concept from "demolition" to "expropriation", and strengthened the protection of citizens' property rights in many institutional designs and arrangements.

1) The scope of expropriation is strictly limited within the range of public interests According to the provision of Article 8 of the new regulation, the circumstances under which government can make a decision on the expropriation of houses on state-owned land are strictly limited to the five categories for "public interests' needs", namely: national defence and foreign affairs; construction of energy, transportation, water and other infrastructure; public utility services such as science and technology, education, culture, health, sports, environment and resource protection, disaster prevention and mitigation, protection of cultural relics, social welfare or municipal utilities; construction of a social security housing projects; and rebuilding of old urban areas where dilapidated buildings concentrate and with poor quality housing and infrastructure lags behind. State-owned land reserves, government office buildings, modern services, strategic emerging industries, commercial facilities and real estate development projects, which were implemented in the past throughout the country, are not included in the scope of expropriation.

2) The expropriation subject is changed from construction unit to the people's government at the city or county level According to the previous regulations, the project to be constructed is generally demolished by the construction unit or the land reserve centre under the land department. Article 4 of the new regulation explicitly provides that the people's government at the city or

county level shall be responsible for building expropriation and compensation within its administrative region, and the building expropriation department as determined by the people's government at city or country level shall organise and implement building expropriation and compensation within its administrative region. The building expropriation department may designate a non-profit entity to undertake specific work on building expropriation and compensation.

3) Expropriation procedures have changed greatly In accordance with the provisions of the original regulations, demolition can only be implemented after the construction unit, being the demolition unit, applies to the administrative department of building demolition at the city or county level for a demolition permit and issues a demolition notice and after a demolition compensation and resettlement agreement is signed between the demolition unit and the owner. In accordance with the provisions of the new regulation, all kinds of construction activities requiring expropriation of buildings within the scope of public interests shall first comply with the national economic and social development plan, overall land-use plan, urban and rural plan and other plans for special purposes. The construction of social security housing projects and the rebuilding of old urban areas shall be incorporated into the annual plan for national economic and social development at the city or county level. Second, the building expropriation department shall draft an expropriation and compensation plan and report it to the people's government at the city or county level. The people's government at the city or county level shall organise the relevant departments to demonstrate the expropriation and compensation plan, publish it for public opinion, make amendments, hold a hearing, make a social stability risk assessment and adopt it at the executive meeting of the government before making the expropriation decision. Third, the people's government at the city or county level shall announce the decision on expropriation to the public, and the building expropriation department shall organise surveys and registration of the ownership, location, use, construction area of buildings, assess the value of buildings and other losses and compensation and make compensation before implementing the demolition work.[161]

4) Compensation standards are more transparent and reasonable Article 17 of the new regulation clearly defines the scope of compensation for building expropriation shall include compensation for the value of the building expropriated, compensation for the relocation or temporary settlement resulting from the building expropriation, and compensation for the production or

---

[161] See Chapter II of the Regulation on the Expropriation of Buildings on State-owned Land and Compensation

business interruption losses resulting from the building expropriation. Article 19 states that, "the compensation for the value of the building expropriated shall not be less than the market price of real estate similar to the building expropriated on the date of announcement of the building expropriation decision". In order to ensure fair, reasonable and transparent compensation, the new regulation also specifies information about the selection of the assessment agency, monetary compensation or exchange of titles, priority to providing housing security by the government and household compensation that shall be made available to the owners.

5) The administrative compulsory demolition has been eliminated Pursuant to Article 27 of the new regulation, "compensation shall be made before relocation in building expropriation", and, "No entity or individual shall force an owner to relocate by means of violence or threat, by cutting off the supply of water, heating, gas or electricity or road passage in violation of the relevant provisions or by any other illegal means. Construction entities shall be prohibited from involvement in relocation activities." Where an owner does not apply for administrative reconsideration or file an administrative lawsuit within the statutory time limit and fails to relocate within the time limit as determined in the compensation decision, the people's government at city or county level that makes the building expropriation decision shall apply to the people's court for enforcement according to law, thereby eliminating the old approach that the administrative compulsory demolition was decided and implemented by the building expropriation department.

Conclusion

History has shown that unrestrained administrative power is bound to be abused and will inevitably lead to corruption. This is because any power has the potential to expand and corrode, and a person with power, when using power, will never stop until he reaches the limit. Thus, power can easily be abused, and will eventually lead to corruption. Only when the power is under the constraint of the law will we be able to control the expansion of power and prevent corruption; only in this way can power play a positive role in social development to inhibit its negative effects. The authority of the power holder derives from the people, and must be used to serve the people, maintain and safeguard national interests and the rights of the people. Any individual power holder will never be allowed to seek personal gains by means of the power of the people. The essence of abusing power to seek personal gain is to trample and violate the legitimate rights of the people. Therefore, the implementation of power must be within the limits prescribed by law, and must strictly be restricted and supervised by the law. Only when the law is under the constraint of the law will the breeding and spread of corruption be effectively prevented and will the legitimate rights of citizens be effectively protected.

In order to achieve the goal of building a socialist law-based country respecting for and protecting human rights at the constitutional level, China has experienced an unprecedentedly productive period of laws and regulations. The introduction of these laws and regulations has provided a legal basis for China's national governance and social life. By combing through China's main administrative laws and regulations during the past decade, it can be seen that one of the purposes of China's administrative legislative development is to impose constraints on public power, strengthen the protection of civil rights and seek a balance between civil rights and state power. With the aim of striking a reasonable balance between administrative power and civil rights, the administrative laws will play a crucial role in building a law-based society.

Running state affairs according to law originates in governance by law. China's administrative law development has made remarkable achievements, but still has a long way to go. It has become a major proposition to explore and figure out how to effectively implement the administrative legislative system and give full play to its deterrent effect, how to deal with the relationship between the government and the people, how to reasonably distribute functions and powers among different governmental departments, how to give full play to the mutual checks and balances of administrative departments in the distribution of functions and powers, and how to put an end to the "abuse of power" in the momentous campaign to fight against corruption fundamentally from the institutional level. The level of administrative law development will become one of the touchstones for China's democratic development. The author believes that the administrative law is destined to be one of the most important sector-based laws in China's law-based process, which will be continuously improved. While reflecting the principle of administrative efficiency for effective social management, it will manifest the principle of administration power control and build a stronger bridge between the Chinese government and the people.

Chapter 7

Towards a security system of human rights and social rights
— Changes in China's Labour and Social Security Law in recent years

China's labour law system

Overview of China's Labour Law

The Labour Law, China's first labour code, was adopted by the Standing Committee of the National People's Congress (NPCSC) on 5 July 1994. Before that, many labour regulations had been enacted, such as Provisional Regulations on Institution of Labour Contract System in State-Owned Enterprises, Interim Provisions on Handling the Labour Dispute of the State-owned Enterprise and Regulations on Settlement of Labour Disputes, but most of them were policy documents and administrative orders, deficient in legal regulation. Since then, various supporting administrative rules and regulations, local regulations, judicial interpretation and normative documents have been introduced, in order to establish a labour law system based on the Labour Law. As the basic law in this area, the Labour Law introduced in 1994 was considered a milestone. It has not only achieved the transformation from policy regulation to legal regulation, but also achieved the change from planned economy to market economy, with the introduction of the contract system between employees and employers to establish labour relations on an equal basis, implementation of two-way choice between employees and employers, and increasing the security of employees' individual rights.

China's labour law system can be divided into the following three parts:[162]

First, the law of labour and employment, which is mainly intended for regulating employment relations, namely employment relations or social relations in promoting employment processes between administrative organisations, labour service agencies, employers and employees. The law aims to safeguard employee rights, facilitate the promotion of employment by macro-control measures and build a fair employment environment to oppose discrimination in employment.

---

[162] See Lin Jia, Labour Law and Social Security Law (Second Edition), China Renmin University Press, May 2011, 2nd edition, p. 29

Specifically, it consists of the Employment Promotion Act, the Vocational Training Act, the Employment Services Act and the Employment Management Act and so on. The Employment Promotion Act adopted at the 29th Session of the 10th NPCSC on 30 August 2007, is the representative in this regard. In addition, the Chinese government also strives to improve the employment environment and carry out employment regulation through a variety of employment policies, including fiscal, monetary, industrial, investment and manpower.

Second, the law of moderating labour relations, which is mainly intended for regulating the operation of labour relations, covers labour relations between enterprises and employees (e.g. labour contract law and labour rules), relations between employees and relevant social groups (e.g. trade union law, collective contract law and the law of democratic management of employees) as well as state intervention laws (e.g. wage law, labour protection law, working hour, rest and leave laws). On 29 June 2007, the 28th Session of the 10th NPCSC adopted the Labour Contract Law of the People's Republic of China; on 3 September 2008, the 25th Executive Meeting of the State Council adopted the Regulation on the Implementation of the Labour Contract Law of the People's Republic of China; on 28 December 2012, the 30th Session of the 11th NPCSC adopted the Decision of the Standing Committee of the National People's Congress on Amending the Labour Contract Law of the People's Republic of China; and the Trade Union Law of the People's Republic of China was adopted in 1992 and amended in 2001, all of which are the representatives of China's laws in this regard.

Third, the law of labour security, which is mainly intended for regulating the realisation and relief of the parties' interests and rights in labour relations, consists of the law of handling labour disputes and the law of labour inspection as well as social insurance law closely related to employees in social security laws. In this regard, the 31st Session of the 10th NPCSC adopted the Labour Dispute Mediation and Arbitration Law of the People's Republic of China on 29 December 2007, and the Supreme People's Court also issued a series of interpretations of the law applicable to hearing labour disputes to further improve China's settlement mechanism on labour disputes.

Over the past decade, China's labour laws have made great progress and development in these three areas. First, the system of labour law has improved and around various provisions of the Labour Law, a range of laws and regulations covering labour contracts, occupational safety, labour arbitration, labour inspection and social insurance have been formulated to form a labour law system based on the Labour Law, making the laws and regulations governing labour relations increasingly standardised and unified. Second, the process of developing from nothing to being further refined for the Labour Contract Law has epoch-making significance for the protection of the rights of employees, and defining rights and obligations between employees and employers in contractual forms and giving tendentious protection to employees through contractual terms are not only the embodiment of the modern employment relationship, but also are conducive to simplifying legal relations and improving the efficiency of dispute handling. Third, for the purpose of dispute handling, the principle of beneficence has been further clarified through judicial interpretation and other forms: if labour contracts, employers' internal regulations and employers' unilateral commitment are inconsistent with the labour law, the agreement or provisions favourable for employees should apply; any unclear meaning should be interpreted in favour of employees; at the same time, limiting employers' litigious rights and protecting the employees' right relief will not be hampered by the employers' abuse of litigious rights, thus achieving the legislative goal of protecting employees as much as possible.

Labour contract law

1. The "Black Brick Kiln incident" resulting in the adoption of the Labour Contract Law

Many people will never forget the "Shanxi Black Brick Kiln incident" in 2007. On 5 June that year, an article entitled "The Path of Villainous 'Black Men'! More than 400 Fathers Whose Children Were Sold to Shanxi Black Brick Kilns are Crying for Help", was posted on Dahe BBS. In this article, fathers of the children claimed the children were abducted by traffickers and sold to Shanxi black brick kilns for a price of Rmb500 each. The post described the inhuman treatment that workers in black brick kilns were suffering and the heinous acts committed by the kiln owners. But because these black brick kilns were based in the mountains, and the kiln owners were "well-informed", and because public security authorities and the government turned a blind eye, it was difficult to rescue these children. The helpless fathers only managed to rescue 40 children. Like a tossed stone creating a thousand ripples, this post aroused widespread concern among internet users. Many called for help for these poor fathers and their children, struggling on the edge of death, and to punish the sinister black kiln owners who disregarded human life for money.

The "Black Brick Kiln" case aroused great concern in the State Council. Soon afterwards, Shanxi province established a leadership group to "fight against the black brick kiln owners and rescue the abducted migrant workers". Spot checks were carried out in several major cities and 80 migrant workers were rescued. During this entire process, a series of deficiencies in local governments and law enforcement agencies were exposed, including negligence and being unresponsive to illegal production and illegal employment. Those liable were put under investigation or given other sanctions.

The case had great influence at that time. On 24 June 2007, NPCSC members strongly criticised the practice of "black brick kilns" in Shanxi province while reviewing a draft of the labour contract law, and proposed to adopt the Labour Contract Law as soon as possible. The implementation of this law and other relevant laws would protect the legitimate rights and interests of workers and prevent the occurrence of similar incidents in future. At that time, CCTV broadcast a story, "The Birth of the Labour Contract Law - The Black Brick Kiln Case Facilitated Its Adoption[163]", explaining that the unanimous adoption of the Labour Contract Law was closely related to the "black brick kiln" incident in Shanxi province. Even those who had participated in the drafting said:[164] "An unexpected incident has suddenly accelerated the introduction of the Labour Contract Law. If the incident did not happen, the law may have to be discussed for some time." Controversy frequently arose during the drafting of the Labour Contract Law. The black brick kiln incident greatly stimulated legislative authority, and many members believed that such wrongdoing must be punished, thus pushing forward the adoption of the law. On 28 June 2007, the controversial Labour Contract Law was adopted almost unanimously.[165]

2. Significance for promulgating the Labour Contract Law

The promulgation of the Labour Contract Law originated out of practical need. But more important, the previous labour law was defective. The Labour Law in 1995 explicitly stated that a labour contract is the agreement to establish a relationship between employees and employers and defines both parties' rights and obligations, and that establishing labour relations should involve entering into a labour contract[166]. Its provisions on the labour contract were very simple and mostly principle-based, and the provisions on the regulating range of labour relations were relatively narrow, so that some labour relations that should have been regulated by the labour contract law could only be interpreted as labour relations. The new Labour Contract Law, consisting of eight chapters and 98 articles, has been amended to address these issues and came up with a detailed description for the conclusion, performance and change, cancellation and termination of labour contracts as well as other special circumstances such as collective contracts, labour dispatch and part-time employment. The new Labour Contract Law further specified the supervision, inspection and corresponding legal responsibilities for breach of contracts and systematically combing through and integrating China's

---

[163] "Economy Time", 27 December 2007

[164] According to Zhang Shicheng, Deputy Director of the Administration Office of the Legislative Affairs Commission of the NPCSC, who was involved in the drafting of the labour contract law

[165] Among 146 attendees, 145 voted in favour and one abstained from voting

[166] See Article 16.1 of the Labour Law

labour contract legislation, which has been one of the most important labour laws in recent years.

The labour contract law is independently legislated, making labour contracts distinct from civil contracts in the general sense; although both are derived from the contractual relationship of civil law, as the workers provide their own labour rather than a general commodity exchange, the protection that the contract law provides for the contracting parties is often far from enough. For the purpose of the labour contract law, legal mandatory provisions and worker-favoured intervention imposed on working hours, wages and benefits, rest and vacations, social security, labour protection, dispute resolution and other contents can help protect the interests of disadvantaged workers and better balance the rights and obligations of employees and employers. As China is in the process of industrialisation, urbanisation and rapid economic structural adjustment, the labour system is subject to profound change. As it moves from an "iron rice bowl" to a "contractual" system, the legitimate rights and interests of workers are often infringed; for example, there have been widespread instances of low labour contracting rates, short-term labour contracts and the infringement by employers on the legitimate rights and interests of employees by taking advantage of their strong position. Therefore, the labour contract relationship has been placed into a stricter legal framework, and the emergence of the labour contract law has a more urgent significance.

In contrast to the Labour Law (1995), although the Labour Contract Law has made more detailed provisions, interpretations of certain provisions are still divergent and vague, and contradictions and problems have also been encountered in the implementation. In this regard, the State Council has made three inquiries from 26 central departments, units, provinces and cities, and sought advice from the community through the website of Legislative Affairs Office (http://www.chinalaw.gov.cn). The Regulation on the Implementation of the Labour Contract Law of the People's Republic of China was finalised after several revisions, and was introduced as important supporting regulations of the Labour Contract Law on 18 September 2008, explicitly providing the original ambiguity in labour contracts without a fixed period, labour dispatch and other specific penalties.

3. Legislative improvements to the Labour Contract Law

The Labour Contract Law was officially put into effect on 1 January 2008. The improvements of the new law are as follows:

First, further expand the applicability of labour contracts to adapt to the needs of economic development.

With the deepening of China's reform and opening up and the rise of emerging economies, employment subjects are also showing new features in various forms. The employers mentioned in the Labour Law (1995) were limited to "all businesses and individual economic organisations in the territory of the People's Republic of China"[167], on the basis of which the Labour Contract Law adds "non-governmental non-profit units"[168], thus expanding the applicability of the labour contract law. The Regulation on the Implementation of the Labour Contract Law further includes partnerships and foundations such as accounting firms and law firms in the scope of employers, and provides that branches of the employer that have obtained a business licence or certificate of registration in accordance with the law can sign labour contracts with workers, thus clarifying its legal status as an employer. Therefore, the applicability of China's labour contract law is continuously expanding. The specific applicable scopes are described as follows:

Businesses China's business type is quite complicated, consisting of the types of business classified by ownership under the planned economic system (such as state-owned enterprises, collective enterprises, private enterprises and foreign-invested enterprises) and those classified by the form of contribution and responsibility under the market economy environment (such as companies, contractual enterprises and personally-owned enterprises). Given the current coexistence of two types of classification, "business" can be considered as a very macroscopic concept, including a variety of economic units engaged in production, distribution or service activities with independent economic accounting.

Individual economic organisations Article 26 of the General Principles of Civil Law of the People's Republic of China refers to "individual businesses" run by individual citizens who have been lawfully registered and approved to engage in industrial or commercial operation in corporate forms within the sphere permitted by law.

Non-governmental non-profit units The Provisional Regulations for the Registration Administration of Non-governmental Non-profit Units refer to enterprise institutions, societies and other social forces as well as social organisations established with non-state-owned assets by individual citizens for non-profit social services. They are mainly distributed in science, education, social welfare and other fields, such as private hospitals, schools, libraries and museums.

---

[167] See Article 2 of the Labour Law
[168] See Article 2 of the Labour Contract Law

Other organisations These include accounting firms, law firms and other partnerships and foundations mentioned in the Regulation on the Implementation of the Labour Contract Law.

Government agencies, institutions and social organisations With the deepening of reform, the employment forms of government agencies have also changed. Government agencies, institutions and social organisations that recruit employees by signing contracts and carrying out employment systems on a trial basis should also sign labour contracts, meaning they are also applicable to the Labour Contract Law.

By contrast, China's civil servants, staff of institutions and social organisations adopting the civil service system, rural workers (except workers of township and village enterprises, migrant workers and farmers engaged in business), work-study students and servicemen do not fall within the jurisdiction of the Labour Contract Law. Their rights and obligations between employment subjects should be regulated by other applicable laws.

Second, the new law clarifies the classification of labour contracts and highlights the protection of labour contracts without a fixed period.

As set forth in Article 12 of the Labour Contract Law, labour contracts are classified into labour contracts with a fixed period, without a fixed period and with a period to complete the prescribed work. This second category, labour contracts without a fixed period, is reflected in legal form for the first time to effectively protect the labour rights of workers after their prime years. In addition to the provision that the worker and employer can sign a labour contract without a fixed period through negotiation, Article 14 of the Labour Contract Law further provides for situations where the employer must sign a labour contract without a fixed period, including: the worker has worked for an uninterrupted term of 10 years for the employer; the worker has worked for an uninterrupted term of 10 years for the employer and he/she has reached the age which is less than 10 years up to the statutory retirement age when the employer initially performs the labour contract system or when a restructuring state-owned enterprise renew the labour contract; or the labour contract is to be renewed after the labour contract with a fixed period has been concluded twice successively. Meanwhile, according to Article 82 of the Labour Contract Law, if the employer illegally refuses to sign a labour contract without a fixed period with the worker, he/she will be subject to punitive measures such as double-wage payment, giving workers strong legal protection.

There are essential differences between labour contracts without a fixed period and "lifelong work" under China's planned economy system. In the context of a labour contract without a fixed period, if the employee has committed to acts that the employer may terminate the labour contract under the Labour Contract Law,[169] the employer may still terminate the labour contract, thus reducing pressure on the employer to ensure the operational efficiency of enterprises.

Third, the new law further clarifies issues concerning the establishment of labour relations and the signing of contracts, and enforces the signing of a written labour contract.

As set forth in Article 7 of the Labour Contract Law: "An employer establishes labour relations with a worker as of the date of starting to use the worker", so as to legally solve issues relating to the establishment of labour relations and the signing of a labour contract. In circumstances where the worker is employed without the signing of a labour contract, the establishment of labour relations will not be affected (i.e., generally known as "factual labour relations"); for a labour contract that has been signed before employment, labour relations will also be established upon employment.

The legal consequences of not signing written labour contracts are provided in the Labour Contract Law and the Regulation on the Implementation of the Labour Contract Law. One month from the date of employment is given as a grace period; if it exceeds one month, the employer may be subject to serious adverse consequences such as double wages and being deemed to go without fixed-term labour contracts, so as to persuade the employer to sign written labour contracts with workers.

Fourth, the new law further restricts employers from charging penalties and denying the effect of "imparity clause".

With the further deepening of China's economic reform, the mobility of enterprise staff has gradually improved. In order to maintain personnel stability and limit employee turnover, a number of employers insert stringent penalty clauses in labour contracts with their employees; once an employee leaves office or breaks the rules of the company, he or she will face a huge financial loss. Before the introduction of the labour contract law, arbitration authorities and courts tended to recognise the validity of such high penalties. For example, in a well-known case, a chef called Wu Lin left Tanfu Cuisine Restaurant. According to the agreement signed between Tanfu Cuisine and Wu Lin, a consultant of the company, "within the period of employment, except for force majeure, Wu Lin shall not leave office

---

[169] See Articles 39, 40 of the Labour Contract Law

during the employment period without good cause; otherwise the company has the rights to hold Wu Lin responsible for violation and economic loss of Rmb5m". Wu Lin resigned within the contract term in 2004, and the employer then filed an application for labour arbitration to Chengdu Labour Dispute Arbitration Committee, including a penalty of Rmb2.5m. The request was supported by Chengdu Labour Dispute Arbitration Committee, the People's Court of Qingyang district and Chengdu Intermediate People's Court.[170]

But in reality, when an employer signs a labour contract with workers, the workers are often in a relatively weak position, and are forced to accept the terms of the contract. Therefore, it is especially important to give workers legal protection. Consequently, the Labour Contract Law expressly prescribes that, except in the following two situations, the employer shall not hold employees responsible for penalties:

In the first situation, according to Article 22 of the Labour Contract Law, where an employer pays special training expenses exclusively for a worker, as well as special technical training, it may conclude an agreement with the worker concerning the service period. Where any worker is in violation of the service period stipulation, he/she shall pay the employer a penalty for breach of contract as stipulated. The amount of penalty for breach of contract shall not be in excess of the training fees as provided by the employer. The penalty for breach of contract that the worker pays as required by the employer shall be no more than the training expenses caused in the service period unperformed.

In the second situation, according to Article 23 of the Labour Contract Law, with respect to a worker who is obliged keep secrets, the employer may stipulate limitation of competition clauses with the worker in the labour contract or in the confidentiality agreement and stipulate that economic compensation shall be given to the worker within the period of limitation of competition in terms of months after the labour contract is discharged or terminated. Where the worker is in violation of the stipulation on limitation of competition, he/she shall pay a penalty for breach of contract to the employer.

Of course, the above limitations on penalty do not preclude the company's right to claim damages for losses caused by the worker to the company, but the amount of damages claimed should be consistent with the actual loss, rather than the amount agreed upon in advance. Therefore, after the Labour Contract Law was introduced, the high penalty in the case above has become invalid as it violates

---

[170] See Wei Haozheng, A Review of the Top 10 Cases of Labour Disputes in 2005 (II), Human Resources, 2006, 7th Issue

the mandatory provisions of the law, as the arbitrary tribunal and the court will make a judgement more favourable to workers.

Fifth, the new law further clarifies specific situations to terminate a labour contract between a worker and his/her employer and the corresponding amount of compensation.

In order to prevent the employer from abusing the right of termination to damage the interests of workers, and also to take account of the employer's need to make sure that work continues, the Labour Law (1995) has provided certain circumstances to terminate the labour contracts between the employer and the worker, to which the Labour Contract Law has made further extensions in order meet prevailing needs. Under the Labour Contract Law, in addition to terminating the labour contract by consensus, both the worker and the employer have the right to unilaterally terminate the contract under certain conditions. Specifically:

1) A worker's unilateral right to terminate the contract. According to Articles 37 and 38 of the Labour Contract Law, a worker may terminate the labour contract if:

a) He/she informs the employer in written form 30 days in advance or three days in advance during the probation period;

b) Terminating the contract at any time: the employer fails to provide labour protection or work conditions as stipulated in the labour contract, fails to pay the full amount of remuneration in a timely manner or fails to pay social security premiums for workers according to law; and the bylaws thereof are inconsistent with any law or regulation and impair the rights and interests of the workers, and so on;

c) Terminating the contract immediately: Where any worker is forced to work by violence, by threat or by illegally limiting his/her personal freedom, or is forced to perform dangerous operations that may endanger his/her personal safety under illicitly commands or forces of the employer.

2) Employer's unilateral right to terminate the contract. The Labour Contract Law does not entitle the employer to unconditionally terminate a labour contract by giving advance notice, unlike workers. According to Articles 36, 39, 40 and 41 of the Labour Contract Law and Article 19 of the Regulation on the Implementation of the Labour Contract Law, the circumstances where the employer may terminate a labour contract are limited to 14 kinds of situation, such as: upon unanimity through consultation between the employer and the worker; the worker has demonstrably not satisfied the recruitment

requirements during the probation period; the worker is in serious violation of the bylaws of the employer.[171] Any termination of the labour contract by the employer except for the above reasons shall be deemed illegal. In such cases, workers may require the employer to continue performing the labour contract, or pay double compensation in accordance with the financial compensation standard.

In addition, according to the provisions of the Labour Contract Law, where the employee terminates a labour contract at any time and does so immediately, and where the employer terminates the labour contract for reasons other than the employee's fault,[172] the employer shall pay economic compensations to the employee according to the number of years he has worked for the employer

---

[171] See Article 19 of the Regulation on the Implementation of the Labour Contract Law: Under any of the following circumstances, an employer may, according to the conditions and procedures prescribed in the Labour Contract Law, dissolve a labour contract with a fixed term, a labour contract without a fixed term or a labour contract that sets the completion of a specific task as the term of the contract concluded with an employee:
(1) the employer and the employee so agree;
(2) the employee is proved to have failed to meet the employment conditions during probation;
(3) the employee seriously violates the rules and procedures set up by the employer;
(4) the employee seriously neglects his/her duties or engages in malpractice for personal gain and has caused severe damages to the employer;
(5) the employee simultaneously enters an employment relationship with any other employer and thus seriously affects his/her completion of the tasks assigned by the employer, or the employee refuses to correct after the employer has pointed out the problem;
(6) the employee, by means of deception or coercion or by taking advantage of the employer's difficulties, forces the employer to conclude or change the labour contract against the employer's true will;
(7) the employee is under investigation for criminal liabilities;
(8) the employee is sick or is injured for a non-work-related reason and cannot resume his/her original position after the expiration of the prescribed time period for medical treatment, nor can he/she assume any other position arranged by the employer;
(9) the employee is incompetent in his/her position or remains so after training or having been assigned to another position;
(10) the objective situation on which the conclusion of the employment contract is based has changed considerably, which makes it impossible to perform the employment contract, and no agreement on changing the contents of the employment contract has been reached after negotiations between the employer and the employee;
(11) the employer is being restructured according to the Enterprise Bankruptcy Law;
(12) the employer encounters serious difficulties in production and business operations;
(13) the employer changes its products, makes important technological renovations, or adjusts the way of business operations, and it is still necessary to lay off some employees after modifying the labour contract;
[172] According to Article 46 of the Labour Contract Law, in the case of any of the following circumstances, employers shall make an economic compensation to the workers:
(1) any worker discharges the labour contract according to Article 38 of this Law;

at the rate of one month's salary for each full year he worked. Economic compensation is the special system designed by the labour contract law, fully reflecting the inclined protection of the rights and interests of employees and playing a dual role in regard to compensation for labour contribution and social security.

4. Deficiencies of the Labour Contract Law

According to Professor Zheng Shangyuan[173], a scholar specialising in China's labour law, the development stage of a country's industry and the level of economic and social development are correlated with research on labour law, and higher levels of economic and social development and well-developed industries will show a higher level of labour law research, and vice versa. The introduction of the Labour Contract Law cannot go beyond the realities of China, and the formation of a rational system cannot be achieved overnight, but will instead take a long time. The rationality of the current system still needs to be improved. The deficiencies of the Labour Contract Law are mainly reflected in the following aspects: (1) the periods of labour contracts need to be further classified, and the functions and applicability of contracts with different periods should be further defined. Currently, there is still a great deal of confusion surrounding the contract period. (2) The classification of labour contract which are labour contracts with a fixed period, without a fixed period and with a period to complete the prescribed work is quite distinctive; however it is not well supported by logic and legal theory. Great efforts still need to be made for the labour contract period system to be built so as to restrict unruliness and cultivate rationality. (3) There is a huge loophole in the part-time employment and labour dispatch regulations, and great efforts need to be made to close this loophole. (4) Legislation should be initiated for collective contracts (collective bargaining agreement), thereby leaving more room for the Labour Contract Law.

---

(2) any employer intends to discharge the labour contract with the workers according to Article 36 of this Law and reaches consensus with the workers through consultations;
(3) the employer discharges the labour contract pursuant to Article 40 of this Law;
(4) the employer discharges the labour contract subject to the first Paragraph of Article 41 of this Law;
(5) the labour contract is a contract with a fixed period, which is terminated in accordance with Paragraph (1) of Article 44 of this Law, except that the worker disagrees to renew the contract even though the conditions offered by the employer are the same as or better than those stipulated in the current contract;
(6) The labour contract is terminated in accordance with subparagraphs (4) and (5) of Article 44 of this Law; or
(7) Other circumstances as prescribed by laws and administrative regulations.

[173] Professor of Law School, Tsinghua University

China's labour dispatch system

Labour dispatch refers to a form of employment where labour relations are established between a labour dispatch service provider and a worker to be dispatched, and the worker is dispatched to the employer and works under the command and supervision of the employer. The separation between employment and use of the worker is its most essential characteristic. In this form of employment, the employer can set up and adjust positions in a more flexible manner, while also avoiding statutory obligations such as paying social insurance and housing funds for employees. Therefore, it is welcomed and adopted by a number of companies. Since the Labour Contract Law was promulgated, there has been a substantial increase in the number of labour dispatch service providers, and the size of labour dispatch has also expanded rapidly. Many employers have used dispatched workers for a long period, and even consider labour dispatch as their main employment channel. The legitimate rights and interests of dispatched workers are often not effectively protected, and problems such as unequal wages are increasingly prominent; therefore, on 28 December 2012, the 30th Session of the 11th Standing Committee of the National People's Congress adopted the Decision of the Standing Committee of the National People's Congress on Amending the Labour Contract Law of the People's Republic of China to make specialised provisions on labour dispatch.

The development of labour dispatch should follow the way of market-oriented reform, and fill any vacancies in the labour market. The prominent feature of labour dispatch is to provide temporary, substituted and assistant work. This falls within typical non-normal employment patterns, so labour dispatch cannot be abused in every industry.[174] With the introduction of the Labour Contract Law, mandatory requirements have been imposed on the signing of labour contracts without a fixed period. In order to circumvent the legal requirements to sign labour contracts without a fixed period with employees under certain conditions, many Chinese companies have begun to use a number of dispatched employees, and in some instances companies' main employees are hired from labour dispatch. Many dispatched employees cannot be fairly rewarded in line with their work, or their health and safety rights cannot be equally assured. The reasons are as follows: first, the provisions of the Labour Contract Law for labour dispatch are only superficially stringent. For example, as set forth in Paragraph 1 of Article 58 of the Labour Contract Law, a labour contract between a labour dispatch service provider and a worker to be dispatched shall indicate issues such as the entity to which the worker will be dispatched, the dispatched term and post; Paragraph

---

[174] Zheng Shangyuan, Frontier of Labour Law and Social Security Law, Tsinghua University Press, January 2011 edition

2 of this Article also stressed that the labour dispatch contract shall have a fixed period of more than two years, during periods when there is no work for the workers, relevant remunerations shall be paid to such workers by labour dispatch service providers on a monthly basis at the minimum salary as prescribed by the people's government of the region where the labour dispatch service provider is situated. Such mandatory legal provisions reflect the intentions of legislators to protect workers. However, administrative agencies were not directly involved in the initial occurrence of labour dispatch, since it is a characteristic of market behaviour; moreover, due to administrative departments' ignorance of and even direct engagement in labour dispatch, a variety of dispatching actions sprang up and in some of the cases the rights of the workers are greatly violated. Therefore, the absence of administrative supervision has, to a certain extent, given rise to the widespread existence of labour dispatch.

The problems connected with labour dispatch have caused widespread concern in the community. On 28 December 2012, CPCSC adopted the Decision of the Standing Committee of the National People's Congress on Amending the Labour Contract Law of the People's Republic of China, where the provisions on "equal pay for equal work" and "temporary, assistant or substituted" positions in labour dispatch were further refined, including:

1. Clarify that labour-contracting employment is China's basic employment, and labour dispatch is strictly limited to temporary, assistant or substituted posts, of which temporary post means a job involving a period of less than six months, assistant post means a non-primary business job, and substituted post means a job that can be substituted by other workers as the employer's full-time worker is unable to work due to studying on day release or on vacation for a certain period.

2. Raise the threshold of establishment of labour dispatch service providers, of which the registered capital has been raised from Rmb500,000 originally prescribed in the Labour Contract Law to Rmb2m, and the provider is required to legally apply for administrative licensing to the labour administrative department.

3. Further clarify the concept of "equal pay for equal work", and require the labour dispatch service provider to sign a labour contract with the worker to be dispatched and enter into a labour dispatch agreement with the employer, both of which shall state or agree to the labour remuneration paid to the worker to be dispatched and it shall comply with the requirements of "equal pay for equal work".

4. Intensify the penalties for corresponding violations. Any operations of labour dispatch services without administrative licensing shall be revoked by the labour administrative department, confiscating the illegal income and imposing a fine;

any labour dispatch service provider or employer violating the provisions of the labour contract law shall be subject to penalties, and the fine amount was appropriately increased (from Rmb1,000-5,000 per person to Rmb5,000-10,000 per person); the administrative licensing of labour dispatch may be revoked.

These amendments came into effect on 1 July 2013. Correspondingly, on 19 April 2013, the Ministry of Human Resources and Social Security promulgated the Administrative Measures for Labour Dispatch Licensing (Draft for Comments), which consists of five chapters with 35 articles, providing the conditions to apply for administrative licences of labour dispatch services, and refining the materials that shall be submitted for the application of operating labour dispatch services, including: the application of labour dispatch operating licences, business licence or Prior Approval of the Name of Enterprise, articles of association, capital verification report or financial audit report, proof of business premises, office facilities and equipment, identity certificate of legal representative and relevant qualification certificates of the staff as well as labour dispatch management system. After its formal introduction, the qualification management of labour dispatch will be further standardised.

The author believes that the above-mentioned judicial interpretation is highly desirable for the definition of "temporary, assistant and substituted posts" and the qualification admittance. However, strengthening supervision on practitioners is also needed to regulate the labour dispatch market. The labour market is not a free market, and workers are not cabbages in a farmers' market. Such a market must be regulated by the labour administrative department. Otherwise, it would be difficult to restrain illegal dispatch, anonymous dispatch and other improper dispatches. Therefore, practitioner supervision is irreplaceable in respect of document filing, business exit, and prohibited acts and so on.

China's social security law

Overview

After the founding of New China, the Chinese government established a series of social security systems. For example, the Regulations on Labour Insurance (1951) initially established an occupational social insurance system covering endowment, work-related injury, medical care, maternity and unemployment. After the economic reform and opening up, the social security system underwent reform and all-round restructuring. The Provisional Regulations on Institution Of Labour Contract System In State-Owned Enterprises (1986) stipulated that the endowment funds of workers through the labour contract system were wholly planned by society, officially initiating the social security reform, and the

Provisional Regulations on Unemployment Insurance for Staff and Workers of State-owned Enterprises issued in the same year established an unemployment insurance system for the first time, which further safeguarded the reform and workers of state-owned enterprises. After that, the Labour Law (1995) specially provided "social insurance and welfare" to legally introduce social insurance for enterprise workers as a mandatory requirement. The Decision of the State Council on Establishing the Urban Employees' Basic Medical Insurance System (1998) provided that all urban employers must participate in basic medical insurance; the Regulations on Unemployment Insurance (1999) extended the coverage of unemployment insurance to urban enterprises, institutions and their employees; the Provisional Measures for the Maternity Insurance for Enterprise Employees (1994) required enterprises to implement a maternity insurance system for staff; the Regulation on Work-Related Injury Insurances (2003) provided that all kinds of enterprises and individually-owned businesses that hire employees should participate in work-related injury insurance. Thus, the social insurance system covering endowment, work-related injury, medical care, maternity and unemployment has steadily improved.

Today, China's social insurance system is composed mainly of the following five types of social insurance:

1. Basic endowment insurance — jointly paid by employers and employees. An individual participating in basic endowment insurance shall receive a monthly basic endowment provided that he/she has contributed premiums for a cumulative period of 15 years or more when he/she reaches the statutory retirement age. The amount of endowment depends on many factors, including: the payment amount, payment term, current local average wage (adjusted annually) and average life expectancy.

2. Basic medical insurance — jointly paid by employers and employees. Certain (part or all of) medical expenses of employees are paid by the basic medical insurance fund.

3. Work-related injury insurance — only paid by employers. Premiums depend on the incidence of work-related injuries in different industries. Wages and other costs incurred from work-related injury are paid by a work-related injury insurance fund or employers.

4. Unemployment insurance — jointly paid by employers and employees. Where an individual pays unemployment insurance for a certain period, he/she may enjoy unemployment insurance benefits upon unemployment. The maximum period of receiving unemployment insurance benefits does not exceed 24 months.

5. Maternity insurance — paid by employers. The maternity insurance fund is intended for the payment of a certain amount of wages during maternity leave and for related medical costs.

Over the past decade, the Chinese government has paid more and more attention to social security by aiming to build a socialist harmonious society. First, social security coverage has been increasingly expanded, covering rural residents, migrant workers, urban non-employed residents and other "marginalised groups"; for example, the Decision on Perfecting Enterprise Employees' Basic Endowment Insurance System (2005) further expanded the endowment insurance coverage and reformed the ways of calculating and releasing the endowment; Opinions of the State Council on Addressing Migrant Worker Issues (2006) proposed to actively and steadily solve issues about social security of migrant workers; the Notice of the State Council on Establishing the Rural Minimum Living Standard Security System across the Country (2007) proposed to establish the subsistence allowances system in rural areas; the Guiding Opinions of the State Council about the Pilot Urban Resident Basic Medical Insurance (2007) expanded the coverage of basic medical insurance to all non-employed urban residents. Second, the level of social security legislation has been raised, changing from departmental and local regulations to centralised deployment; for example, the Social Insurance Law adopted on 28 October 2010 was the first time that China had promulgated national unified provisions on the five social security funds, which also provided a legal framework for the management of the social insurance system.

China's social insurance law

In 2006, a group of senior officials headed by Cheng Liangyu, former Politburo Member and Secretary of Shanghai Municipal Party Committee, and Zhu Junyi, former Director of Shanghai Municipal Administration of Labour and Social Security, were alleged to have misappropriated a huge amount of social security funds, leading to great concern about the regulatory regime of social security funds and even the entire social security system. In this context, the Chinese government has strengthened the institutional building of social insurance, and eventually adopted the Social Insurance Law (Draft) on 28 October 2010. After four years of review, the Social Insurance Law was finally promulgated and became effective on 1 July 2011. The law covers endowment, medical care, unemployment, work-related injury, maternity and many other social security measures, strengthening the supervision over social insurance and social security funds, enriching and improving China's social security system and becoming a milestone for China's social security legislation. Its main contents are as follows:

1. Interpret the five social insurance systems in legal form for the first time.

Before the introduction of the Social Insurance Law, in addition to administrative regulations such as the Regulations on Unemployment Insurance and the Regulations on Work-related Injury Insurance issued by the State Council, some policy documents regarding endowment, health care, maternity and insurance have also been introduced, showing a low level of legislation and enforcement. However, the Social Insurance Law was "legally" promulgated by the NPC Standing Committee, so it was enacted at a higher level than all previous relevant laws and regulations, making it a framework document in China's social security legislation. Its Chapters II to VI have further defined the contents of the five social insurance systems to comprehensively guide the implementation of every social security system.

2. Further expand social insurance coverage. According to Article 3 of the Social Insurance Law, the social insurance system shall adhere to the guidelines of "wide coverage, basic protection, multi-level and sustainability". Privately-owned businesses without employees, non-full-time employees who have not participated in the basic endowment insurance of their employers or other flexible employees may participate in the basic endowment insurance system and the premium of basic endowment insurance shall be paid by the respective individuals; in addition, migrant workers, farmers and foreigners who have been employed in the territory of the People's Republic of China may participate in the social insurance system with reference to the provisions of the law, further expanding social security coverage. Furthermore, in situations where employees cannot receive the basic endowment when they reach the statutory retirement age with a cumulative payment period of less than 15 years, pursuant to the Social Insurance Law, such people are allowed to continue paying premiums until the completion of 15 years, after which they may receive their basic endowment on a monthly basis. Alternatively, they can have it transferred to the new rural social endowment insurance or social endowment insurance for urban residents so as to enjoy endowment benefits in accordance with the relevant provisions of the State Council, which has lifted the concerns of those paying social insurance premiums at an older age, and included them in the coverage of social insurance.

3. The operation of a social security fund is more convenient. In terms of the transfer of social security records, with a vast expanse of territory, China has not fully realised the reimbursement of medical expenses in different places. Employers and employees in China who pay social security premiums will often face problems such as the transfer of medical relations and settlement of medical expenses in different places after they move to a different place for work, especially for employees living in a different place after retirement and migrant workers who are frequently on the move. The Social Insurance Law clearly provides that

social insurance administration and healthcare administration departments shall establish the system for the settlement of expenses for medical treatment that is not received locally. For individuals working across different regions, their basic medical insurance records shall be transferred with them, and the payment period is calculated on a cumulative basis in order to ensure that the insured enjoy basic medical insurance benefits. The Law also expressly states that the basic pension insurance records of individuals who work across regions shall also be transferred with them, and the payment period is calculated on a cumulative basis to give employees greater freedom in their employment. In terms of the payment of social security funds, the application processes were cumbersome, often making it difficult to solve the urgent needs of employees; in response, the Social Insurance Law establishes the principle of paying in advance from the social security fund, and pursuant to the law, medical costs that should be paid by a third party may be paid in advance from the basic medical insurance fund if the third party fails to pay or if it cannot be identified. Medical costs arising from work-related injuries shall be paid by the employer in instances where the employer fails to legally pay work-related injury insurance premiums; if the employer fails to pay, it shall be paid in advance from the work-related injury insurance fund; any work-related injury caused by a third party may also be paid in advance from the work-related injury insurance fund where the third party fails to pay medical costs or a third party cannot be identified. In terms of the processes, the principle of paying in advance from social security funds has ensured that employees can receive timely assistance in a more convenient way.

4. Define enforcement measures and intensify the penalties for deferred payment. As social insurance is compulsory, the employer must pay the social insurance premiums in full in a timely manner pursuant to the statutory standards and deadlines. Currently, China is implementing a payment rate of about 29% of the total corporate payroll that the employer shall pay, meaning a reasonably large expense for the employer. Endowment insurance generally does not exceed 20% of the total corporate payroll, with medical insurance accounting for 2%, unemployment insurance for about 6%, and work-related injury insurance not exceeding 1% of the total payroll. The Social Insurance Law does not specify the payment rate and calculation basis for such social insurances, giving local governments space to develop policies based on the level of local economic development. In order to save operating costs, some employers refuse to pay social insurance premiums, or pay in part, fail to pay altogether or pay in arrears. This phenomenon happens despite repeated prohibition. According to the Social Insurance Law, an employer that fails to pay social insurance premiums in full in a timely manner will face adverse consequences such as mandatory allocation from the employer's account, and even seizure or foreclosure and auction of the employer's property to an equivalent value, making the social security system

more enforceable. Furthermore, such employers will be subject to an overdue fine at a rate of five per ten thousand, and relevant administrative departments also have the right to impose a penalty from one to three times of the unpaid social insurance premiums. Intensifying penalties and giving relevant administrative departments more powers to impose fines may persuade the employer to comply with social insurance systems.

After the announcement of the Social Insurance Law, the Ministry of Human Resources and Social Security promulgated Several Provisions on Implementing the Social Insurance Law of the People's Republic of China on 29 June 2011 to provide specific operations for the Social Insurance Law, which came into effect on the same day as the Social Insurance Law. The provisions consist of seven chapters with 30 articles, making supplementary and interpretative provisions for basic endowment insurance, basic medical insurance, maternity insurance, work-related injury insurance, unemployment insurance, fund management and handling services so that the Social Insurance Law is more operational.

Overall, the promulgation of China's Social Insurance Law is "significant and far-reaching[175]", but its implementation is far from satisfactory. As social insurance premiums have led to a rise in business costs, many enterprises have decided to cancel their insurance. Shanghai, for example, has come up with three different social insurance mechanisms for different residents within three to five years, leading to a rise in corporate social insurance costs, a fall in the willingness to participate in social insurance and a reduction in demand for labour. In addition, as the Social Insurance Law has included migrant worker groups with lower income into the social insurance system for urban workers with high premiums and high benefits, the current income of such workers has declined since they have to pay premiums. The shortfall in social security funds and insufficient book reserves may lead to social instability when retired migrant workers discover they do not enjoy high security even though they are paying high premiums when they are young. in consideration of the high level of social insurance cancellations in recent years, the Social Insurance Law forbids explicitly the insured from cancelling their insurance, which is bad news for the low-paid.[176]

Social security in an ageing society

In accordance with UN standards, a country is considered to enter an ageing

---

[175] Cui Yukai: "Social Insurance Law: Significant and Far-reaching - Interview with Zheng Gongcheng, Member of the 11th NPC Standing Committee and Professor of Renmin University of China", published on Administration Reform, 2011, 3rd Issue

[176] Dong Baohua, Thinking over Labour Law behind Famous Cases, Law Press, March 2012 edition

society if the population over 65 years old exceeds 7% of the total population. The proportion of the population in China is rising at an accelerated rate; in 2011, the proportion of the elderly population in China reached 13.7%. On 23 October 2012, the Office of China National Committee on Ageing announced that the population aged 60 or older in China would exceed 200m in 2013; China's elderly population will enter a period of rapid growth over the next 20 years, and the elderly population is expected to reach one-third of the country's total population by 2050. As a consequence, China faces a problem of "getting old before getting rich". When China started to become an ageing society, its per capita GDP was only US$800, compared with a typical figure of around US$10,000 for developed countries when they start to become an ageing society.[177] It has become an enormous challenge for the Chinese government to figure out how to use its limited economic resources to feed its expanding elderly population, and there will also be great pressures on its social security system.

One possible way forward will be to transform from a "pay as you go (PAYG)" system to a "combination of social pooling with individual accounts". The PAYG model implemented in China before 1997 is to feed the retired population with social security funds paid for by today's workers, which is feasible if the working population is relatively large. But that will be difficult to afford in China, due to the increasing number of retired people. Therefore, the Chinese government has established employees' individual accounts while preserving the PAYG system for social pooling. Employers pay 20% of the monthly wages of their employees into social pooling, which will be used to pay for the current pensions of retired workers; and 8% of monthly wages of the insured will be deposited into their personal accounts to relieve the pressure of future pensions.

A second way forward is to maximize the scope of people who pay into social security. Over the past decade, the Chinese government has made great efforts to build a social insurance system covering the entire population, and those who pay social security funds have gradually expanded from urban enterprises and their employees to foreign-invested enterprises, private enterprises and other town-based enterprise employees, and even among the rural population and migrant workers, and started a pilot rural pension system in order to solve the problem of ageing in rural areas due to the high outflow of young workers. By the end of 2013, the national endowment insurance coverage reached 79.7%, which is a remarkable achievement, but in terms of the depth of security, the Chinese government is still facing great challenges in enhancing security benefits while improving endowment insurance coverage.

---

[177] See Xiong Jianfeng, China is Entering the Era of Ageing, Phoenix Weekly, Issue 30/379, 2010, published on 25 October

A third way forward is to explore ways to preserve and appreciate the value of social security funds. The Chinese government has commissioned the National Council for Social Security Fund (NCSSF) to look at this issue. Statistics show that the current real yields in personal accounts of basic endowment insurance are less than 2%, while the weighted inflation rate has reached 2.22% since 2005, indicating the pension insurance fund system has failed to keep up with price rises; instead, the value is shrinking. To address this problem, the Chinese government has decided that the balance of social security funds should be used to buy national debt or to deposit at a fixed rate of interest, while setting aside the equivalent of two months for the payment of expenses. However, in the context of high inflation, nearly 90% of social security funds face the risk of highly negative interest rates on deposit. On 20 March 2012, the NCSSF announced that it had made endowment history in China in its attempts to preserve the value of social security funds, having been approved by the State Council, it to invest and operate Guangdong urban basic endowment insurance fund balances totalling Rmb100bn.

Notwithstanding these social security reforms, China is still facing a heavy burden due to its rapidly ageing population. It will be a long and arduous task for the Chinese government to solve social security issues through social security legislation.

Chapter 8

New perspectives on the rule of law: a blueprint for judicial reform at the fourth plenary session of the 18th Central Committee of the Communist Party of China

The Fourth Plenary Session of the 18th Central Committee of the Communist Party of China (CPC) held in October 2014 issued the "Decision of the Central Committee of the CPC on Several Problems Concerning the Thorough Implementation of Rule of Law", and brought forth the overall objective of building a socialist rule-of-law system with Chinese characteristics and a socialist country under the rule of law. While stressing the authority of the Constitution and the position of the CPC as the ruling party recognised by the Constitution, the Decision presented the concept of "rule-of-law system" for the first time, with contents related to rule-of-law reform being mainly about deepening judicial reform. The release of the Decision symbolised that, after the formation of the socialist legal system with Chinese characteristics, the traditional static rule of law by means of legal system is shifting towards the dynamic rule of law by means of the rule-of-law system. Laws written on paper are being carried out in real life, and abstract legal rights are being converted into concrete rights of action. The value of law and justice regained wide attention.

Although China has made significant progress in establishing rule of law, the current judicial system still has many deficiencies. Judicial power belongs to the central authorities and it should be exercised by the court to make rightful judgement; however these characteristics have not been fully achieved. Central administrative power and judging power attributes of judicial power are not fully displayed; internal supervision and restriction mechanism for the operation of judicial power has yet to be formed; the external environment is not optimised; the guarantee mechanism is imperfect; irregular, relaxed, non-transparent and uncivilised judicial practices still exist; and the mechanism for punishing and preventing unfair judicial practice and corruption is defective. All of these problems are detrimental to social fairness and justice as well as legal rights and the interests of people; they have to be solved through establishing a sound legal system. Revolving around several significant problems concerning the rule-of-law reform, such as the judicial management mechanism, the judicial power operating mechanism, judicial supervision and the restriction mechanism and judicial guarantee mechanism, the Decision proposed a series of significant reform measures, which can be interpreted from the following seven aspects:

System improvement: highlighting the central administrative power attribute of judicial power

The judicial system is the foundation of judicial power operation. China's current judicial system was formed in the period of the planned economy. In this system, personnel, finance and property of courts were managed and guaranteed by personnel and financial departments under corresponding administrative divisions, which give rise to a conflict between the central administrative power and local management and guarantee of judicial power. This is incommensurate to the uniform, fair and competitive order of the market economy. The Third Plenary Session of the 18th Central Committee of the CPC decided to promote the uniform management of personnel, finance and property of local courts and procuratorates under provincial level, thus taking a key step towards the reform of the judicial system. A series of concrete measures have been adopted to deepen the reform of judicial system.

i) **The Supreme People's Court has set up circuit courts to hear significant administrative, civil and commercial cases across administrative regions.** After the Third Plenary Session of the 18th Central Committee of the CPC decided to promote the uniform management of personnel, finance and property of local courts and procuratorates under provincial level, people were sceptical about whether trans-provincial civil and commercial cases and influential administrative cases in a province could be judged fairly. Some people suggested jurisdiction by a third party, while others proposed jurisdiction by a superior court. The Fourth Plenary Session of the 18th Central Committee of the CPC determined to set up circuit courts of the Supreme People's Court in a bid to deepen the uniform management of personnel, finance and property of local courts at provincial level. Setting up circuit courts is conducive to ensuring the unification and applicability of laws and maintaining the uniform legal system of our country. It is also convenient for adjudication bodies to solve disputes quickly and for people to lodge lawsuits. Circuit courts are the detached offices and components of the Supreme People's Court rather than independent courts. In terms of working methods, they are also different from traditional circuit trials.

ii) **People's courts are trying to set up cross-administrative divisions to hear trans-regional cases.** There are 3,573 local courts at all levels in China, and their set-ups generally correspond with administrative divisions. Such a judicial system is convenient for clarifying jurisdiction and lodging complaints, and can easily receive strong support from local party and government departments. On the other hand, however, the exertion of judicial power is susceptible to the disturbance of local factors since personnel, finance and property are under the uniform management of provincial courts. The practice of cross-administrative courts hearing trans-regional civil and commercial cases, administrative cases and environmental resource cases can address some problems that are not solved through provincial uniform management, eliminate disturbances to judicial justice caused by local factors, ensure that some cases involving local interests can be judged fairly, and facilitate the uniform and correct enforcement of national laws.

iii) **Promote and implement the pilot system reform that separates judicial power from executive power.** Difficult execution, a kind of judicial phenomenon caused by the imperfect social credit system, has become a stubborn problem that remained unsolved in the three rounds of judicial reforms of people's courts. The Decision suggested the separation of judicial power from executive power within people's courts and the establishment of relatively independent compulsory execution agencies. This will bring into full play the system advantage of executive power taken as administrative power and develop the execution system under uniform leadership and command, and also prevent the simple division of judicial power and executive power from affecting execution efficiency and damaging public trust of the judicial system.

iv) **Reform judicial offices' management system of personnel finance and property, and tentatively implement the separation of administrative power from judicial power in people's courts.** With the continuous deepening of judgement-centred lawsuit system reform and the further segmentation of classified management reform of courts' personnel, the internal administrative affairs management power of people's courts should be isolated from judicial power so as to form a truly judgement-oriented power operation system. In the past, different attributes of various powers in judicial offices were not strictly defined in terms of management, thus leading to a blurred boundary of management and service, and mixed roles of judges and administrative staff. The ultimate result is that, in spite of the large number of judges, only a few of them are really engaged in judicial work, so working efficiency is low. The tentative separation of judicial power from executive power proposed by the Decision can better push ahead the judgement-cantered lawsuit system reform and ensure the independence of trial levels.

v) **Improve administrative proceeding system and reasonably adjust the jurisdiction system of administrative proceeding cases.** Administrative proceedings are one of the three main kinds of lawsuits in China most significantly affected by local factors. In recent years, fewer and fewer cases involving "civilians suing the government" were placed on file for investigation and prosecution, and the number of cases placed on file in 2013 declined by

5% year-on-year, but the rate of appeals was as high as 72.7%. It is common in administrative proceedings that administrative departments adopt various means to intervene in judicial cases for the sake of local and departmental interests. Therefore, it is urgent to reform the set-up of courts, judicial publicity and the filing system so as to further improve the administrative proceeding system, reasonably adjust the jurisdiction system of administrative proceeding cases, eliminate local protectionism and administrative intervention, and solve serious problems of administrative proceedings such as difficulties with filing, hearing and execution at the system level.

Internal judicial mechanism: abide by internal laws of the operation of judicial power

The judicial mechanism is the important element of judicial power and the important factor determining and affecting judicial fairness. It involves all aspects of judicial power, such as case filing, court hearing, judgement and execution, and is closely related to concrete systems such as the judge system, judicial environment and judicial guarantee. Focusing on key operations such as right-of-action protection, trial level system, judgement-centred lawsuit system and judicial duty, the decision strictly clings to inherent laws of judicial power, and further clarifies the thinking on the reform of the operating mechanism of judicial power.

i) **Reform case hearing system and replace file examination with file registration**
The extensiveness and convenience of the right of action are important symbols of judicial civilisation in modern society. If one's rights cannot be defended at court, rights would be unrealisable for the loss of protection, so its value and significance will be discounted. Meanwhile, if social members cannot solve their disputes through lawsuits, they will realise their goals through self-protection or group resistance, thus resulting in social instability. The Decision suggested reforming the case hearing system and replacing file review with file registration, and required people's courts to file and hear all rational lawsuits. This means that people's courts carry out only a formal examination rather than a substantial examination of lawsuit materials submitted by parties when placing a case on file, thus realising the separation of procedure from entity. The tremendous change of the case-filing system provides a guarantee for people to solve disputes through lawsuits, yet it also brings about new challenges to people's courts at all levels. Therefore, its concrete effects remain unclear.

ii) **Improve the trial level system and clarify functional positioning of courts at the four levels.** At present, our country practices a four-level, two-tier trial system. Courts at all levels assume the function of first instance, and intermediate courts and above assume the function of second instance. Courts at all levels are also responsible for retrials. These staggered procedures, overlapping functions and case citations from each other lead to a homogenisation of case properties, adjudication methods, judge quality and functions of local three-level courts, which are unfavourable for the effective allocation of cases and for the scientific construction of national judicial power. Superior courts cannot bring into full play their trial supervision and instruction functions. The Decision proposed improving the trial level system: first instance lays emphasis on fact finding and law application for the first instance court has the advantage in fact collection and analysis; second instance lays emphasis on solving disputes of plaintiffs and defendants over facts and applicable laws affirmed in the first instance so as to make final judgements; retrial lays emphasis on reviewing the legitimacy of final judgements, maintaining the authority and stability of judgements, and realising the finality of judicial judgements. Reasonably positioning the functions of the four-level courts at different trial levels is conducive to improving lawsuit efficiency, cultivating judicial authority and enhancing the judicial credibility of China.

iii) **Push ahead the judgement-centred lawsuit system reform and comprehensively carry out the evidentiary adjudication rule** Taking judgement as the centre is an important symbol of judicial civilisation progress in modern society. The discovery and correction of some significantly misjudged and wrong cases since 2013 have aroused wide concern in society over presumed innocence on doubtful cases, judgement-centred lawsuit system, and evidence-based adjudication. At China's sixth national criminal justice work conference, the Supreme People's Court pointed out that court hearings should be central in case trials, indicating that factual evidence investigation should be carried out in courts, debate over discretion of punishment conducted at courts, and judgement results formed at courts, so as to comprehensively fulfil the principle of direct and oral trial, strictly implement the system of illegal evidence exclusion, and making courts the final stage and key link of confirming a defendants' crime, responsibility and penalty. In civil and administrative proceedings, all proof adduction, confrontation and confirmation should be conducted and completed at courts, and all judgements should be the reasonable results formed after court investigation and debate.

iv) **Improve judicial interpretation and case guidance system, and further urge the Supreme People's Court to unify the standard of law applications.** The trial guidance function of the Supreme People's Court will be reinforced by the deepening of judicial reform. In the light of the spirit of the Decision, the Supreme People's Court will further improve the judicial interpretation system, make procedures of judicial interpretation such as initiation, investigation and deliberation more rigorous, reinforce the pertinence, standardisation, timeliness and effectiveness of judicial interpretation, reform the screening, evaluation, argumentation and release mechanisms of guiding cases, and establish the working mechanism of converting its judgement into guidance.

Judicial independence: comply with the internal logic of judicial justice

Now that judicial power is equal to judging right, the independence of judging subjects is the prerequisite for fair judgments. The Decision will improve the system of ensuring the independent and fair exertion of judicial power and procuratorial power, and take the system as the primary issue concerning judicial justice, which demonstrates the important position of independence in ensuring judicial justice.

i) **Create the record, notification and accountability system of leaders intervening in judicial activities and concrete cases.** Leaders' intervention in the trial of individual cases is a common problem identified by the public. In the light of reform measures that people's courts have implemented, such as the judicial accountability system, judicial publicity and traced supervision, the Decision required establishing the system of extracting, saving, reporting and publicising information concerning leaders' intervention in the trial of individual cases such as telephone records, forwarded materials and verbal instruction, thus creating a favourable external environment for people's courts to exert judicial power independently.

ii) **Improve the system that administrative organs appear in courts to respond to litigation according to laws, support courts to hear administrative cases, and respect and execute judgements made by courts.** The attitude of administrative bodies towards administrative proceedings is an important symbol for measuring the rule of law in a country. Improving the system can make administrative organisations settle conflicts directly with the public, and it also creates an image of law-based administration and lift the whole society's rule-of-law level.

iii) **Improve the system of punishing illegal criminal activities affecting judicial authority such as obstructing judicial justice, refusing to execute judgements and contempt of court.** Justice is the foundation of authority, while authority is the guarantee of justice. The Decision required improving related law systems to incriminate behaviour such as insulting, slandering and threatening judicial workers and seriously disturbing the order of courts, and reinforcing the effort of punishments on those bodies that refuse to execute judgements so as to cultivate and maintain judicial authority.

iv) **Establish and improve the mechanism of protecting judicial workers in the fulfilment of their statutory duties.** Judicial power is equal to judging power, so the correctness of judgements should be based on evidentiary adjudication. The Decision suggested establishing and improving the mechanism of protecting judicial workers in the fulfilment of their statutory duties, discriminating the standard of distinguishing various errors, and ensuring that judges are not subject to investigation for fulfilling their duties according to law. Without a statutory basis and without going through statutory procedures, judges cannot be transferred, dismissed or displaced and demoted.

Democracy: bridge the distance between judicial technicality and affinity to people

To achieve the Chinese judicial system's affinity to people, and realise the unification of judicial specialty, the Decision brought forth several reform measures to guarantee people's participation in judicial practice according to the law.

i) **Ensure people's participation in judicial activities such as judicial conciliation, judicial hearing, and letters and calls involving lawsuits.** Guiding people to participate in dispute resolution concerning their interests such as judicial conciliation, judicial hearing, and letters and calls involving lawsuits is favourable for eliminating confrontation, mitigating conflict, solving disputes, popularising laws, and carrying forward morality, thus making people participate in, trust and defend judicial works.

ii) **Improve the people assessor system and enhance its credibility, and guarantee citizens' assessor rights.** People's assessors come from the grassroots and are familiar with the customs and conditions in society as well as people's daily lives, which can make up any shortcomings in judicial specialty. The reform of the people assessor system is highlighted by the fact that people's assessors will gradually participate not only in fact finding but also in the application of law, thus making best use of their advantages and bypassing their disadvantages, solving the major conflict of the people assessor system, and determining the direction for the next stage of reforms.

iii) **Perfect the social dispute prevention and solving mechanism, and improve the organically linked, mutually coordinated dispute-solving mechanisms such as conciliation, arbitration, administrative adjudication, administrative reconsideration and lawsuits.** The judiciary cannot solve all social conflicts. At present, China's diversified dispute-solving mechanisms do not have full public support, so they are applied only in a small scope. In addition, the dispute-solving teams are of low quality. In the light of the spirit of the Decision, our country will strongly support and develop civil dispute-solving forms such as conciliation and arbitration, diversifying dispute-solving subjects, socialising dispute-solving ways, and professionalising dispute-solving personnel so as to create the necessary conditions to modernise the national governance system and governance capacity.

Publicity: construct the open and transparent sunshine judicial mechanism

Judicial publicity is an important condition for realising judicial justice. In recent years, people's courts have made remarkable achievements in realising judicial justice through judicial publicity. The three platforms of trial procedure publicity, judgement document publicity and execution information publicity, have won high appraisal at home and abroad. The Decision further suggested constructing a "sunshine judicial mechanism" by publicising the judicial basis, procedures, flows, results and valid law documents according to laws, and eliminating black box operations, thus offering concrete guidance for the further expansion of judicial publicity.

i) **Establishing an open, dynamic, transparent, and convenient sunshine judicial mechanism** Being open means that information that has to be made known to the public according to laws should be publicised to the parties involved; being dynamic means that the parties involved can carry out the necessary interactive exchanges with courts through online office platforms; being transparent means that all judgements and execution information that can be disclosed should be available on the internet; being convenient means that the parties involved along with ordinary people can take part in and sit on case hearings, and obtain open information of courts conveniently and quickly.

ii) **Reinforce the system of law interpretation and reasoning in judgement documents** Law interpretation and reasoning in judgement documents is an important condition for the parties involved to accept judgements and stop appeals, and also the necessary requirement of demonstrating judicial civilisation and justice. A reasoning judgement document can objectively contain evidence and reasons held by both parties, comprehensively reflect the basis and wisdom of judges' discretion, and dispel related parties' ideas of appeal and complaint.

iii) **Construct a favourable interactive relationship between courts and the media.** People's courts should consciously accept the supervision of public opinion, and respect news-spreading laws. If possible, courts can arrange special seats for journalists so as to create conditions for the media to conduct supervision and spread judicial information. The media should also respect judicial laws, particularly abide by principles such as the presumption of innocence, the lack of punishment in doubtful cases, and evidentiary adjudication in reporting pending cases, respect the judgements of people's courts, maintain judicial authority, and prevent public opinion from affecting judicial justice.

iv) **Set up the system that courts should be responsible for popularising laws and judges responsible for interpreting laws with cases** Urging all citizens to abide by laws is a fundamental work of ruling the country by laws. People's courts and judges should actively assume the responsibilities of popularising laws and interpreting laws through approaches such as open hearings, judgement document publicity, and typical case release so as to educate the public and urge every citizen to abide by laws.

Demonstrate the national attributes of judicial discretionary power

Now that judicial power is equal to the judging power and discretionary power is made by judicial offices on behalf of the state, it should have the final say after going through legal procedures in legal conditions. The finality of judicial adjudication is a necessary condition for social members to enjoy stability and also a necessary requirement for citizens and legal persons to have reasonable expectation on their own behaviour or those of other people. If the final judgements of people's courts can be overthrown easily, the lives of citizens would be seriously affected, property rights changes caused by market trading would always be in pending status, and it would be impossible to establish a uniform market order of equal competition. Taking the fulfilment of the finality of judicial adjudication as the base point, the Decision brought forth concrete requirements on the reform in a bid to solve problems such as the separation of lawsuit from appeal, difficult execution, etc.

i) **Fulfil the last instance and lawsuit finality system** In China, the court of second instance is the court of final instance. However, affected by the erroneous concept that "people believe in letters and visits instead of laws, and believe in the superior rather than the inferior", cases are often closed but not finalised, and endless appeals are made. Therefore, the final judgement system cannot be effectively fulfilled, thus damaging judicial power and affecting normal social order. At present, on the basis of ensuring the finality and stability of valid judgements, our country should improve the system of second instance being taken as final instance, stress the finality and certainty of retrial adjudication, and fulfil the finality mechanism of letters and calls involving lawsuits so as to demonstrate the national attribute of judicial adjudication.

ii) **Guarantee the appeal right of the parties involved according to laws by reforming the appeal system** Appeals of the parties involved concerning valid judgements and decisions often evolve into unsolvable cases of letters and calls, and sometimes even lead to extreme events. The reasons for such a phenomenon are many, but an important one is that petitioners are deficient in legal knowledge. The Decision suggested establishing the lawyer agent system for appeal cases so as to guide petitioners to express their demands reasonably and legally. Those unable to afford engaging lawyers for economic hardship will receive legal assistance.

iii) **Formulate the compulsory execution law to ensure that winners of lawsuits could realise their rights and interests in time.** If such rights and interests cannot be realised, judgement finality will be meaningless. Therefore, the legislation department should formulate compulsory execution law to make more specific stipulations on execution subject, execution procedure, execution measure, execution adjudication and execution implementation, and quickly set up the legal system to supervise, deter and punish parties subject to enforcement.

Subject and integrity: stick to the internal quality of judges

Corruption is the natural enemy of judicial justice. How to ensure judicial integrity at the level of system and mechanism is a key to judicial reform. In recent years, courts at all levels have carried out extensive education of judges about their professional ethics, actively constructed the judgement execution mechanism under mutual check and mutual supervision, and strictly complied with provisions such as the "five prohibitions". However, corruption cases in power-concentrated fields such as judgement and execution still take place frequently, thus greatly affecting judicial credibility. Focusing on these problems, the Decision pointed out a concrete route for ensuring judicial integrity.

i) **Set up a system of recording inquiries into cases by internal personnel of judicial offices and the accountability system** In recent years, the Supreme People's Court has promulgated stipulations to refrain internal personnel from interfering with cases, and this has achieved a remarkable effect. In the light of requirements of the Decision, people's courts should further segment and fulfil concrete measures, make efforts in "how to record" and "how to investigate", improve cohesive mechanisms, and establish the system of recording internal personnel's inquiries into cases and the accountability system.

ii) **Clarify job responsibilities, job flows and job standards of judges and their assistants, and implement the rigorous case-handling quality accountability system** Establishing a rigorous case-handling quality accountability system is a consistent requirement of all walks of life on judicial officials. The Decision suggested the implementation of a system whereby judges are held accountable for their case-handling quality and for misjudged cases. But there are three preconditions: 1. clarify job responsibilities, whether judges and their assistants fulfil their job responsibilities according to law; 2. clarify job flows, whether judges and their assistants fulfil their responsibilities according to lawsuit procedures and job flows; 3. clarify job standards, whether the discretionary power exerted by judges exceeds the scope specified by law, and whether the behaviour of judicial assistants is reasonable and legitimate. It should be noted that the rigorous case-handling quality accountability system is complementary to the mechanism of protecting judicial officials in their fulfilment of legal duties, and they should be pushed ahead in synchronisation with the reform of the judge punishment and warning system.

iii) **Regulate the contacts and communications between judicial officials and the parties involved, lawyers, special persons concerned, and intermediary organisations** To avoid power-for-money deals and to punish judicial brokers resolutely, the Decision made prohibitive provisions on the following behaviour of judicial officials: strictly prohibit judicial officials from contacting the parties involved and their lawyers in private; strictly prohibit judicial officials from disclosing case details to the parties involved or their lawyers or inquiring about case details for them; strictly prohibit judicial officials from receiving favours or property from the parties involved or their lawyers; and strictly prohibit judicial officials from introducing agent and defence business to lawyers.

iv) **Forbid judicial officials who are dismissed from office and lawyers and notaries who are deprived of certificates for the violation of laws and disciplines to engage in such occupations forever** To ensure the purity of the legal profession, the Decision presented the principle of forbidding judicial officials and legal workers who are dismissed for the violation of laws and disciplines to engage in such occupations forever, which reflected the zero tolerance of corruption and the resolution of eliminating "black sheep" in the judicial field. Judicial officials who are dismissed from office and lawyers and notaries who are deprived of practising certificates for the violation of laws and disciplines are forbidden to enter the legal profession again. If their acts constitute a crime, they will be prosecuted for criminal liabilities.

Judge quality is a precondition and foundation for realising judicial justice. Judges assume multiple functions such as accepting appeals, discovering facts, distinguishing between good and bad, balancing interests and realising justice, which require them to have systematic legal knowledge, broad judicial experience and outstanding professional morality. Based on the professional requirements of the legal profession, the Decision suggested some stipulations on profession admission, orientation training, job security, level-by-level selection and the grassroots service of judges.

i) **Improve the profession admission and orientation training systems** As the subjects of exerting judicial power and discretionary power according to laws, judges assume the important task of distinguishing between right and wrong, and hold the power over people's life and property according to law. Therefore, our country should set up more rigorous professional admission and orientation training systems. The current Judges Law of the People's Republic of China is not strict in terms of stipulations on the qualifications of judges, and lacks a rigorous orientation training system, so it has to be further improved.

ii) **Improve the professional guarantee system, and establish ranking and salary systems for judges** In the light of the Judges Law, judges' salaries and salary standards are stipulated on the basis of features of their judicial works. The Judges Law was promulgated 19 years ago, but our country has not yet worked out an independent salary system for judges, and taken judges as civil servants. The Decision required establishing the special post order and salary system for judges.

iii) **Establish a system that judges are selected level by level and novice judges are recruited by higher people's courts uniformly and have to take up jobs at grassroots courts** The level-by-level selection system is the best way for judges to receive professional knowledge, judicial experience and professional morality, and is in line with the functional positioning of the four levels of courts in China. Judges of superior courts are usually selected among outstanding ones of lower courts, and novice judges are uniformly recruited by higher people's courts. The practice matches up to the uniform management of personnel, finance and property of local courts under the provincial level, and also makes it possible to reasonably adjust the proportion of judges according to changes of caseload in a province. The system that novice judges should take office in grassroots courts can lay a foundation for the level-by-level selection system, and is in harmony with the mode of judge cultivation and growth.

To sum up, the Decision sketched a more perfect, explicit and directional blueprint for the further rule-of-law reform of China, especially for judicial system reform.